The Resistible
Demise of
Michael Jackson

JOHN HUNT PUBLISHING

First published by Zero Books, 2009
Zero Books is an imprint of John Hunt Publishing Ltd., No. 3 East St., Alresford,
Hampshire SO24 9EE, UK
office@jhpbooks.com
www.johnhuntpublishing.com
www.zero-books.net

For distributor details and how to order please visit the 'Ordering' section on our website.

ISBN: 978 1 84694 348 5
978 1 78904 270 2 (ebook)

A CIP catalogue record for this book is available from the British Library.

Design: Stuart Davies

UK: Printed and bound by CPI Group (UK) Ltd, Croydon, CR0 4YY
US: Printed and bound by Thomson-Shore, 7300 West Joy Road, Dexter, MI 48130

We operate a distinctive and ethical publishing philosophy in all
areas of our business, from our global network of authors to
production and worldwide distribution.

The Resistible Demise of Michael Jackson

Edited by Mark Fisher

Winchester, UK
Washington, USA

Also by Mark Fisher:

Capitalist Realism: Is There No Alternative?
Paperback: 9781846943171
ebook: 9781780997346

*Ghosts of My Life: Writings on Depression, Hauntology and Lost
Futures*
Paperback: 9781780992266
ebook: 9781782796244

CONTENTS

Contributors

Ex-child prodigy **Marcello Carlin**'s personal life was demolished when his first wife died abruptly of cancer in August 2001. Looking for a way back into the world, he began to publish his music writing on the blog The Church Of Me which quickly found much acclaim and applause for its innovative approach and unavoidable candor. He has subsequently written extensively about music in numerous publications and on numerous websites, and is an occasional broadcaster on Resonance 104.4 FM. He married the American music blogger Lena Friesen in November 2007 and they live happily together in London.

Robin Carmody is dangerously near thirty, but feels simultaneously older and younger. He tends to feel he has made less of his life so far than he should have, but broadly believes those who tell him these are the nerves of the insecure. His contribution to this book is a microcosm of his many interests, which he hopes will soon come to greater fruition in a full-length book published by Zer0. His current blog, Sea Songs, can be found at in-the-cage.blogspot.com.

Joshua Clover is a professor of poetry and poetics at University of California Davis, with a sideline in Marxist economic theory. Books include the poetry collections *Madonna anno domini* and *The Totality For Kids*; a book on *The Matrix* for the British Film Institute's Film Classics series; and the cultural history, *1989: Bob Dylan Didn't Have This To Sing About*. He sits on the editorial board of Film Quarterly, where he writes a column called "Marx and Coca-Cola". His current work concerns "feelings of financialization" — a phenomenology of "fictitious capital" and life within its regime.

Sam Davies lives in London and writes about music and film for The Wire, Loops and Sight & Sound.

Geeta Dayal is the author of *Another Green World*, a new book on Brian Eno (Continuum, September 2009). She has contributed to numerous publications, including Bookforum, Print, The Wire, Loops, and The Village Voice.

Tom Ewing is a London-based Pop writer. He founded the I Love Music discussion board, and his Freaky Trigger site was one of the first British music blogs. He also writes for Pitchfork Media, and is fascinated by extremely popular culture.

Mark Fisher writes for The Wire, Sight & Sound, frieze and New Statesman. He teaches philosophy at the City Literary Institute in London, and he is a Visiting Fellow at the Centre for Cultural Studies at Goldsmiths, University of London. His book *Capitalist Realism* has just been published by Zer0. His next book, *Ghosts Of My Life: Essays On Melancholia, Hauntology And Lost Futures* will be published by Zer0 in 2010. His weblog is at k-punk.abstractdynamics.org.

Dominic Fox lives in Northampton and works in London as a software developer. He does most of his writing on the train; chiefly for his philosophy/literature blog, Poetix (codepoetics.com/poetix), His book *Cold World: The Aesthetics of Dejection and the Politics of Militant Dysphoria* was published by Zer0 in late 2009.

Jeremy Gilbert teaches Cultural Studies at the University of East London, and has written widely on music, politics and cultural theory. His publications include *Discographies: Dance Music Culture and the Politics of Sound* (Routledge 1999) (with Ewan Pearson) and *Anticapitalism and Culture: Radical Theory and*

Popular Politics (Berg 2008).

Owen Hatherley is a contributor to Building Design, Frieze and New Statesman, and author of *Militant Modernism* (Zer0, 2009). He blogs at nastybrutalistandshort.blogspot.com.

Charles Holland is a director of the London-based architecture practice FAT. He writes about architecture and design for numerous magazines as well as for his blogsite www.fantasticjournal.blogspot.com.

Ken Hollings is a writer based in London. His novel *Destroy All Monsters* was hailed by The Scotsman as "a mighty slab of trippy, cult, out-there fiction, mind-bending reading". He has written and presented critically-acclaimed programs for BBC Radio 3, Radio 4, Resonance FM, NPS in Holland and ABC Australia. His latest book, *Welcome to Mars*, is available from Strange Attractor Press.

Barney Hoskyns co-founded and editorially directs the online music-journalism library Rock's Backpages (www.rocksbackpages.com). He has authored several books including *Across the Great Divide* (1993), *Waiting for the Sun* (1996), *Hotel California* (2006) and the Tom Waits biography *Lowside of the Road* (2009). Formerly US correspondent for MOJO, he currently contributes to Uncut, Observer Music Monthly and other publications. He dwells in southwest London.

Reid Kane is a philosopher and independent researcher based in Baltimore. He regularly publishes on his weblog, *Planomenology* (planomenology.wordpress.com). He is currently working on his first book for Zer0.

Paul Lester was Features Editor of Melody Maker and Deputy

Editor of Uncut before going freelance in January 2007. Since then he has interviewed over 200 actors and musicians, from Neil Sedaka to Richard Hell, Janet Jackson to La Roux. In the last three years he has written articles for The Guardian, The Sunday Times Culture, The Telegraph, The Mail On Sunday, The Daily Express, The Scotsman, Record Collector, Q, The Jewish Chronicle and The Hitsheet, and books on Gang of Four, Wire and Pink. When people ask him who, out of all the people he didn't get to interview in his 20 years as a music critic, he would like to have interviewed, his answer is always the same: Laura Nyro, Randy California, Frank Sinatra... and Michael Jackson.

Suhail Malik teaches in the Department of Art, Goldsmiths, University of London, and is currently working on a philosophy of American power and (with Andrea Phillips) a book on transnational aesthetics.

Ian Penman is a freelance writer. He is working on books about Billie Holiday and Bryan Ferry, both of which will be published by Zer0 in 2010.

Chris Roberts has done a fair bit of music, film and book journalism. His eighth book, *Michael Jackson – The King Of Pop*, was commissioned the morning after Jackson's death and published three weeks later. He releases records under enchanting pseudonyms and his short stories "Crashing" and "The Cake" appeared in L.A.'s Black Clock alongside stories by Don De Lillo, Miranda July and Jonathan Lethem. His poems were once exhibited in an art gallery in Koppang, Norway.

Steven Shaviro is the DeRoy Professor of English at Wayne State University. He is the author of *The Cinematic Body* (1993), *Doom Patrols: A Theoretical Fiction About Postmodernism* (1997), *Connected, Or, What It Means To Live In The Network Society* (2003), and *Without Criteria: Kant, Whitehead, Deleuze, and Aesthetics* (2009). He blogs at The Pinocchio Theory: shaviro.com/Blog.

Mark Sinker writes about music, film, books, politics and technology. He is a contributing editor at Sight and Sound and Freaky Trigger. His monograph on Lindsay Anderson's *if....* was published by the BFI in 2004.

David Stubbs is a journalist and author. He was staff writer at Melody Maker for 12 years and has written for The Guardian, The Sunday Times, The Wire, Uncut and NME among others. His previous books include studies of Jimi Hendrix and Eminem. His latest, *Fear Of Music: Why People Get Rothko But Don't Get Stockhausen* was published by Zer0 Books in 2009. His first introduction to Michael Jackson was "Doctor My Eyes" by The Jackson 5 at the Barwick-in-Elmet Village Hall Discotheque in 1972.

Alex Williams is a writer and theorist based in London, and is the author of the weblog Splintering Bone Ashes. Educated at Christ Church College, Oxford, and Middlesex University, London, he is currently writing an extended work on financial crisis and nihilist political economy for Zer0 Books.

Evan Calder Williams is the author of the cultural and political theory blog *Socialism and/or Barbarism* and a corresponding editor for the Marxist journal *Historical Materialism.* His book on the apocalyptic fantasies of late capitalism, *Combined and Uneven Apocalypse*, will be published by Zer0 in 2010. He currently resides in Santa Cruz, California, where he is a graduate student in literature.

Introduction

MJ, the symptom

"I thought I would make a fine wooden puppet – a really fine one, that can dance ... and turn somersaults in the air. Then, with this puppet, I could travel round the world, and earn my bit of bread and my glass of wine." So says Geppetto in Carlo Collodi's *Pinocchio*. Puppets come up many times in the essays contained in this book – as an image, not only of Jackson's abjection, but also of the seductions and sorcery of his performance. As Barney Hoskyns puts it, "at the very moment when Michael Jackson is seen as a god, when he is lost in voice and dance, he is in fact the most graceful of puppets." The questions that a puppet raises – about the differences between the animate and the inanimate, passivity and agency – were central to Jackson's life and death. Jackson's death seemed to be as inevitable as his success was total. But when, exactly, did Jackson's demise begin, and just how resistible was it?

The Resistible Demise Of Michael Jackson was put together because of a conviction that Jackson's passing should be marked by something other than facile "tributes" or muck-raking biographies. The contributors to the book do not always agree about Jackson's music, but they all agree that Jackson was a symptom that needs to be reckoned with and analyzed. It is clear that his death – which happened just after the disintegration of the economy and the election of Barack Obama to the US presidency – came at the end of an era, an era which he had done as much as anyone else to define.

There has been much discussion recently of another kind of death – the death of music journalism. It is true that many of the old places where good music writing used to happen are now defunct or in decadent collapse. But this book proves that intelligent, expansive and engaged writing on music can still happen. The quality and originality of the essays here shows what can result when writers are liberated from the space constraints and low expectations so often imposed by print media. I'm proud to have played a part in eliciting the writing in this book, and I thank all the writers for their heartfelt and thoughtful contributions.

Mark Fisher
August 2009

1

"And when the groove is dead and gone":
The end of Jacksonism

Mark Fisher

What haunted me in the first day or so after Michael Jackson's death ... as I watched all his videos on constant rerun on the music channels ... as I listened to the chat of people on benches and in cafes, all of us going through the now well-rehearsed routines of mass-mediated death ... what haunted me was the difference between how Jackson looked in the *Off The Wall* videos and how he appeared in the *Thriller* clips. I'm not talking about the surgery, or rather I'm not *only* talking about that. The surgery – at that time, "only" a Disney eye-widening, a Diana Ross nose-narrowing, and a little skin-bleaching, as nothing compared to the collapsing Cronenbergian butchery of later years – is but a symptom of the change that you can see in Jackson's face and body. Something had already disappeared that early, never to return.

The death of this King – "my brother, the Legendary King of Pop", as Jermaine Jackson described him at the press conference announcing his death, as if giving Michael his formal title – recalled not the Diana car crash, but the sad slump of Elvis from catatonic narcosis into the long goodbye. Perhaps it was only Elvis who managed to insinuate himself into practically every living human being's body and dreams to the same degree that Jackson did, at the microphysical level of enjoyment as well as at the macro-level of spectacular memeplex. Michael Jackson: a figure so subsumed and consumed by the videodrome that it's scarcely possible to think of him as an individual human being at all... because he wasn't of course... becoming videoflesh was the price of immortality, and that meant being dead while still alive, and no-one knew that more than Michael...

Greil Marcus's writing on Jackson – or rather "Jacksonism" – is some of his most astute commentary on pop and political economy. Ostensibly a study of how The Sex Pistols were the culmination of a "secret history" of twentieth century avant-gardes, Marcus's *Lipstick Traces* was as much about the covering over of the punk event of "76 – 78" as it was about the event itself, and Marcus very quickly understood the massive role that Jacksonism played in this erasure. A new form of control emerged when shopping malls, VHS videos, charity records and TV commercials became interchangeable aspects of the same commodity-media landscape: consensual sentimentality as videodrome. Well, it was new then, all that, but it's very old now, and scarcely visible to us any more now that we have grown habituated to living inside it. It was capitalist realism in the form of entertainment, and we all bought into it, whether we liked it or not:

> *Thriller* enforced its own reality principle; it was there, part of every commute, a serenade to every errand, a referent to every purchase, a fact of every life. You didn't have to like it, you only had to acknowledge it.
>
> ...By 6 July 1984, when the Jacksons played the first show of their "Victory" tour, in Kansas City, Missouri... Jacksonism had produced a system of commodification so complete that whatever and whoever was admitted to it instantly became a new commodity. People were no longer consuming commodities as such things are conventionally understood (records, videos, posters, books, magazines, key rings, earrings, necklaces, pins, buttons, wigs, voice-altering devices, Pepsi t-shirts, underwear, hats, scarves, gloves,

jackets – and why were there no jeans called Billie Jeans?); they were consuming their own gestures of consumption. That is, they were consuming not a Tayloristic Michael Jackson, or any licensed facsimile, but themselves. Riding a Mobius strip of pure capitalism, that was the transubstantiation.

The fact that the tour was a commercial failure didn't mean anything; it was a template for the kind of supermanaged pseudo-event that has long since become normalized in what we used to call popular culture. Even though, as Steven Shaviro rightly observes in this volume, "The Beatles were every bit as much about marketing as MJ/Thriller was", there was a difference-in-kind between the *Thriller* hypermarketing and any previous promotional initiative. The *Thriller* phenomenon was in fact the first taste of the reality system that has just collapsed. "It was," Marcus wrote, "a version of what Ulrike Meinhof called Konsumterror – the terrorism of consumption, the fear of not being able to get what is on the market, the agony of being last in line: to be part of social life. All over the country, people became afraid of tickets they could not afford to buy, of tickets they might not be able to buy even if they could afford them, of tickets that would seal them as everything or nothing, of tickets that, as the humiliating, exciting process began, were not even on sale." "An economist from the Motown era time-travelling to present-day Detroit would be faced with a puzzle," writes Paul Mason in *Meltdown: The End Of The Age Of Greed*. "If wages have fallen, then who's buying all the burgers, training shoes, six-packs, televisions and hair extensions that keep this army of low-paid people at work on six to nine dollars an hour? Henry Ford said you couldn't have mass consumption without high wages, so where is the money coming from? The answer is credit: credit cards, short-term 'payday' loans, zero-percent car finance, low interest rates and self-certified mortgages."

"The Motown sound," Mason argues in *Meltdown*, "seemed to sum up the deal Henry Ford's system offered the working class: hard work, frenetic leisure and a counter-culture that made everything else look uncool. Above all, it was a world of rising real income. If you work eight hours a day on a production line that does not stop, these three words – 'rising real income' – represent the most important single fact in economics." Up to and including *Off The Wall*, Michael Jackson's music belonged to that old black dream – music as leisure-convalescence, a utopianism confined to time off work (*"gonna leave that 9 to 5 up on the shelf"*), with the fortunate few, like Jackson, elevated into superstardom and then – like he and his brothers in the video for the awesome "Can You Feel It" – sprinkling a little stardust on the hardworking black population below.

Off The Wall is still in the grip of Saturday Night Fever; delirious with all the summer-sweet promise of disco. Here, Quincy Jones and Jackson constructed a song suite that did for late '70s black dance culture what Scott Fitzgerald's novels and stories had done for an earlier, whiter, richer American moment: they shaped the fragile evanescences of youth and dance into beautiful myths, laced with fabulous longings that they could neither contain nor exhaust.

The tracks on *Off The Wall* have an easy disco swagger, which Michael embodies in his dance steps and his grin. The smile may well have been forced, but it doesn't *look* as if it was. Jackson was at least capable of convincingly simulating (en)joy(ment) at this point. *Off The Wall*, accordingly, is his masterpiece, the LP-pinnacle of disco, disco as theology, the songs secular hymns to divine disco itself, the impersonal "force", the inhuman drive, that makes life living but has nothing to do with the vital. Jackson would make better tracks – or *one* better track, of which more shortly – but none of the LPs, including the largely anodyne *Thriller*, get even close to *Off The Wall*. It's a seducer's diary, sung by someone who has himself been ravished, who has given up everything for dance.

"Don't Stop 'Til You Get Enough" practically leads you by the hand to the dance floor, the milky-way swirl of the strings sweeping you up, the deliquescing delight (*"I'm melting"*) of Michael's enraptured falsetto gently undoing any resistant character armor. It's a love song to dance itself, just like "Rock With You", which similarly sees the whole universe in a disco mirrorball. "Rock With You" manages the amazing feat of simultaneously bringing a tear to the eye and a shuffle to your feet. Jackson comes on as benevolent disco-Svengali so he can seduce the listener-girl that the song turns us all into: *"Girl, close your eyes/Let that rhythm get into you/don't try to fight it"* – and who would *want* to fight it? Listen to the way that the synths and strings suggest starlight seen by starstruck lovers' eyes. Is there any record which better captures the cosmic vertigo of falling in love than "Rock With You"? That headlong synesthetic rush in which music, dancing and love feed each other in a reflexive virtuous circle which, even though it seems miraculous, unbelievable, (*"girl, when you dance/there's a magic that must be love"*), at the same time seems like it couldn't possibly end (*"And when the groove is dead and gone/ you know that love survives/and we can rock forever"*) This was soul to sell your soul for. No wonder that Scritti Politti's Green Gartside sacrificed the whole of his avant-garde self in order to sound like *this*. And if you asked me to choose between *Off The Wall* and the entire back catalog of The Sex Pistols and The Beatles, there would be no contest. I *respect* The Beatles and the Pistols, but they had already calcified into newsreel-heritage before I even took heed of them; whereas *Off The Wall* is still vivid, irresistible, sumptuous, teeming with Technicolor detail.

Yes, something disappeared after this. It isn't only that Jackson was still a young black man then – and a sexually alluring young black man, with twinkling desire-drunk eyes – rather than the repellent whitened sepulcher he would become a decade later... Think of the creepy video for "The Way You Make Me Feel", Jackson stalking a woman (who by this point it is impossible to believe he would ever want) down a late-night street, looking both sexually aggressive – his disintegrating face now permanently contorted into that Pierrot grimace-sneer – and sexually neuter, as if the increasingly absurd performance of peacock-posturing intimidation substitutes for any actual sexual desire. It isn't only that he has not yet become deracinated or desexualized, for deracination and desexualization might precisely have been refusals of the compulsory ethnicity and sexuality that have gone alongside the restoration of power and privilege these past thirty years, and Jackson could have been a poster-boy for queer universality... if his dysphoria, his freak-ishness, could have found its way into the music. Instead, it was Gothic Oedipus in his (very public) private life dramas, and consensual sentimentality in the saccharine-bland songs. Only in "Scream" and its video – Michael and Janet in a deserted offworld leisure hive that resembles William Gibson's incest-Xanadu Villa Straylight – did the music and the psychosis ever meet (and for an elaboration of the comparison between the "Scream" video and Gibson, see Joshua Clover's essay in this volume).

But before the *Thriller* phenomenon encased Jackson in the hypercommodity that he was now reduced to being just a little part of – he would soon be only a biotic component going mad in the middle of a vast multimedia megamachine that bore his name – before all that was "Billie Jean". "Billie Jean" is not only one of the best singles ever recorded, it is one of the greatest art works of the twentieth century, a multi-leveled sound sculpture whose slinky, synthetic panther sheen still yields up previously unnoticed details and nuance nearly thirty years on. The only remote parallel I can think of in '80s pop is the sonic architecture that Arif Mardin designed for Chaka Chan on "I Feel For You".

Sometimes, the weariness brought on by hearing it so many

times will make you twitch the dial when "Billie Jean" comes on the radio. But let it play, and you're soon bewitched by its drama, seduced into its sonic fictional space, the mean streets and chilly single-parent single-room apartments that now surround the still-glittering dance floor like conspiring fate. Listening is like stepping onto a conveyor belt. And that's what it sounds like, as the implacable, undulating sinuous cakewalk of the synthetic bass takes over the massive space opened up by the crunching snares Jones and Jackson insouciantly hijacked from hip hop. Check, if you can manage to keep focused as the track crawls up your spine and down to your feet, embodying the very compulsion the lyric warns against... check the way that the first sounds you hear from Jackson are not words, but inhuman, asignifying hiccups and yelps, as if he is gasping for air, or learning to speak English again after some aphasic episode.

Ten years after psychedelic soul, this is cyborg soul, with Jackson as cut-up as Grace Jones ever was – partly by the (James) Brownian motion of his own language-disassembling vocal tics (the mirthless, and indeed emotionally unintelligible, joker-hysterical *hee-hees*, the *ooohs* shotgun-divorced from doo-wop's street corner community to circulate like disembodied wraiths in the survivalist badlands of an inner city ravaged by Reaganomics), partly by the astonishing arrangement. Check the way that the first string-stabs shadow the track like a stalker's footsteps, disappearing into the cold wind like mist and rumor. Feel the tension building in your teeth as the bridge hurtles towards the chorus, begging for a release (*"the smell of sweet perfume/this happened much too soon"*) that you know will only end in regret, recrimination and humiliation, but which you can't help but want any way, desire so intense it threatens to fragment the psyche, or expose the way that the psyche is always-already split into antagonistic agencies: *"just remember to always think twice"*. Does he then sing *"do think twice"* or, in an id-exclamation that echoes like a metallic shout in an alley of the mind, "*don't* think twice"? Everything dissolves into audio-hallucination, the chronology gets confused, the noir string-slivers shiver. Jackson is angry at his accuser (and also at the fans who will trap him into the Image: *Billie Jean* is pop's *Misery*) but also weirdly mournful, hunted, pleading (to the big Other, in kettle logic: I didn't do it, I couldn't help it), the part-objects of his voice circling a psyche without a center. Notice that it's a song about the very things Marcus talks about in *Lipstick Traces*: seduction by Spectacle, about the way in which everyday life is taunted and haunted by the screen (*"she was more like a beauty queen/from a movie scene"*). *Billie Jean* – which was effortlessly modern, a new soul that was devoid of any hint of pastiche – could still dramatize all this; perhaps what you can hear is the very process of subsumption itself, Jackson becoming the brand. After this, there would be few glimmers of any outside.

But what *had* been lost? The Situationist theory that Marcus draws on in *Lipstick Traces* is informed by a crypto-Bergsonism, a sense that reification consists in the encrustation and calcification of the living body. But what if it weren't a case of the organic being subsumed by the inorganic, but one inorganic being replaced by another? Dancing is always about the death drive, about the libidinal disciplining of the body, about forcing the body into unnatural postures and shapes (when Jackson occasionally amazes after "Billie Jean", it is more likely to be because of his dancing than his singing – the impossible-looking anti-gravity of his literalization of the gangster lean in the "Smooth Criminal" video for instance). "Every artist," Nietzsche writes in *Beyond Good And Evil*, "knows how far from the feeling of letting himself go his "most natural" condition is, the free ordering, setting, disposing, shaping in moments of "inspiration" – and how strictly and subtly he obeys at that very moment the thousand-fold laws which make fun of all conceptual formulations precisely because of their hardness and decisiveness (even the firmest idea, by comparison, contains something fluctuating, multiple, ambiguous—)."

Dancing is precisely a question of subordinating the body to what Nietzsche calls "arbitrary laws" – and eventually, after the punishing dedication that Jackson put in, that subordination yields an inspiration that grips and micro-directs the body. A different model of freedom emerges here to the neoliberal one, which centers on the "choice" that Jackson promoted when he turned "Billie Jean" into a commercial for Pepsi. Singing about choice, performing in a dead live show: "a stiff, impersonal, over-rehearsed supper club act blown up with lasers and sonic booms.... [And how many entertainment 'spectaculars' of the last twenty years does that sum up?] Michael Jackson, who began this year as a dancer, turned into a piece of wood" (Marcus). But what if he had stayed a dancer? What if his moves could have been extricated from that supper-club spectacle? What if the young black man in those *Off The Wall* videos had not disappeared?

2

Michael Jackson's twenty greatest hits

Paul Lester

It was never easy to like Michael Jackson. I'm not just talking about the ridicule and scorn that come with openly admitting to being a fan of someone with inclinations both bizarre and indefensible. I'm talking about his music. A lot of it leaves much to be desired. Some of it is superbly produced but lyrically gauche or banal and musically so ordinary and unadventurous it seems to mock all those pundits who have made claims, especially since his death, for his significance as an original and a pioneer.

Musically, the symphonic disco of *Off The Wall* was his peak. We'd never heard anything so lavish, it was like Philly soul magnified and multiplied and given an unholy perfect sheen. But when he was bad – and of course he could be bad well before *Bad* – he was awful. Much of *Thriller* seemed clumsy and clichéd even – especially – when the album was released; any changes it wrought were in the realms of marketing and MTV. Trust me: in 1982, next to ABC's *Lexicon Of Love*, Cabaret Voltaire's *2 x 45*, Associates' *Sulk*, Simple Minds' *New Gold Dream* and Siouxsie & The Banshees' *A Kiss In The Dreamhouse*, a lot of the beats and melodies on *Thriller* sounded trite and old-fashioned, it was mainly sonically dull, and most soul boys and disco kids agreed that it was a disappointing follow-up to *Off The Wall*. In fact, as far as radical mainstream black pop went that year, *Thriller* was no more or less inventive and immaculate than Kid Creole & The Coconuts' *Tropical Gangsters*.

And yet Michael Jackson is probably my favorite pop star of

all time. I don't mean my favorite artist or musician – there are dozens in my personal pantheon who have been better, more creatively inspired, and more often, than him. No, I mean he is my favorite of all those globally notorious ultra-stars, usually dance-based although God knows I prefer him to Bruce Springsteen and Bono, who have achieved world renown through their recordings and fame.

The recordings were patchy, sure, but the fame bit he routinely excelled at. No one did fame as well as Michael Jackson, not even Madonna and Prince in the '80s. There was no one to rival him in the '90s, and really there hasn't been anyone who has come close since. For me, he was the most extraordinary – some might say gruesomely fascinating, and it is easy to mix them up – pop star of our age, of any age. And yet, if Michael was weird, I find it even weirder when observers refuse to admit to having been gripped by him and his numerous transformations – those metamorphoses that made David Bowie seem like a part-time chameleon – over the years. Be honest: didn't that tiny shift back there from black child to androgynous white alien future-creature intrigue you, even just a little?

Then again, maybe those observers are more charitable than me, because all those things that made Michael Jackson my favorite pop star were arguably the things that made life so tortuous for him. Still, I couldn't be held responsible for his anguish and doubt, his mania and mental pain. So I allowed myself to luxuriate, with the comfort of distance afforded the voyeur, in the madness of – I was going to say the King of Pop, but he really wasn't that at all. That really rather suggests that he made the best pop records during his spurious reign, and he hardly did that, and besides, they weren't pop, they were, for the last quarter-century of his career, a curious, generally unsatisfying hybrid of R&B, rock and MOR, unsatisfying because to make the hybrid commercially viable the blandest elements of each had to be squeezed through the studio console.

No, he was the King of Pop Stars. He was also the King of Disco if you want to be picky, up to and including The Jacksons' *Triumph* album in 1980. And in that brief period between the release of "Billie Jean" and "Beat It" he was conceivably the King of the Pop Single. Thereafter, his music saw him increasingly trying to second-guess his public, even if he made no such attempts with regard to his appearance or behavior. That's what I noticed and sort of reveled in. His music after *Off The Wall* frequently sounded compromised, controlled and contained, so he seemed to instead use his face and body, his home and private life, as the spaces to wildly express – expunge, exorcise – all the surplus urges, creative, libidinal or otherwise, that were obviously being suppressed during the making of his music. So while he was busy (actually not that busy – he was never remotely as prolific as Prince) making largely anodyne records, he was also being an amazing character operating at the limits of what is normally expected of a human being, albeit (or do I mean "because he was"?) the most famous human being on the planet.

It seems an odd thing to say about the most successful entertainer since Presley and The Beatles, but there is something about Michael Jackson that screams unfulfilled promise and unrealized ambitions, even if those ambitions were partly those of his audience and partly of people like me – rock critics who harbor crazed dreams on behalf of their subjects. He never really found the right producer after Quincy Jones, and I would have loved to have seen him work with someone who could have channeled those creative or libidinal urges towards the pursuit of something a little more extreme, avant-garde or dazzling than the lachrymose balladry of "Heal The World" or "Earth Song". Beck would have been good. Aphex Twin would have been incredible. Someone of that order might even have coaxed him into making his first ever album about himself.

And yet, despite all of this, Michael Jackson did do noteworthy, even spectacular, things after *Off The Wall* (there were even, in the

'90s, tentative forays in his music towards autobiography and confession). But they weren't always albums or singles. They were moments. Isolated instances when he was left to his own devices and he opened his mouth or moved his body and something astonishing happened. Yes, I worry about liking Michael, I really do, because so many of the things that I like about him are hard to excuse – he wreaked havoc on himself and, if we are to believe all of the scurrile and hearsay, on those around him, and maybe that's what they meant by childlike: he played and partied like an infant, without concern for the consequences.

To like Michael after *Off The Wall* is to like all of the surgical enhancements and oxygen tent/primate-pal National Enquirer lunacy. It was difficult to like him, to know what to make of him, because while he had about him an air of innocence, simultaneous to that there was the taint of deviance, and that's complicated because nobody wants a true innocent for a rock star and no one wants a real deviant, but you wouldn't seriously argue for a fake on either count. Really, though, I long ago dismissed any moral consternation because all the negativity and opprobrium were really just based on speculation and supposition. And anyway, I'm no judge; I'm a fan.

But like I say, it's never been easy being a Michael fan. He has produced far less great work than any other artist, mainstream or minor, that I have ever loved. And yet his peaks eclipse all those doubts, at least while they're being witnessed or experienced. At his best – and I realize that that might mean at his most unhinged – he makes all the other pop superheroes appear shabby and small.

If it's hard to accept that he's dead, it's possibly even harder to believe now that the most popular entertainer on Earth was also the most out-there and outrageous, the total opposite of the mediocre, mediated talents who, like him, are widely consumed and enjoyed by the hypermarket, multiplex masses. I take some pleasure in that.

Michael wasn't one of those merely supremely gifted types who manage to corral their impulses in a clever, sustained way and create good work over the distance. No, he was a genius, and that genius manifested itself in fits and starts, in bright, brilliant bursts throughout his forty-year career, on record, at gigs, in videos, during TV appearances, even photo shoots. Without warning he would rise up and, with an uncanny glow, seize the moment, or create a moment, a moment outside of regular pop time because, let's be frank, Michael Jackson was never really about being first or fast, about arriving in revolutionary quick time ahead of the pack, or any of those things he's been given credit for since 25 June 2009. I'm not even convinced, *pace* the machine pulse of "Billie Jean" and the ludicrous panoply of yelps that apparently so infected Justin Timberlake at such an impressionable age, that he was particularly influential. How could you be influenced by him? You would have to "be like" him. And who is?

No, Michael Jackson was "just" the biggest and, occasionally, the best, and always the best at being the biggest. Still and all, although he may have only done a score or so outstanding things, they are as great, as immortal, as anything any pop star has ever bequeathed to posterity. So let me be your guide as I present, in no particular order, just as a sequence of highs and yet more highs, Michael Jackson's 20 truly essential contributions to popular culture; his Greatest Hits, if you will.

Motown 25: Yesterday, Today, Forever

A consensus has built around such landmark concerts as The Who live at Leeds, Nirvana at Reading or The Sex Pistols at the 100 Club in discussions about what remains the most seismic rock show ever. But any conversation about great "gigs" has to include the five minutes and thirty-two seconds it took for Michael Jackson to moonwalk his way into the history books. On 25 March 1983, during the celebrations to mark Motown's 25th birthday, taped before a live studio audience at the Pasadena Civic Auditorium in California, Michael unveiled the then-new "Billie Jean". It was one of those once-in-a-generation televised events, up there with The Beatles or Presley on Ed Sullivan or the Pistols on *Top of the Pops*. And in terms of electrifying energy and sheer concentrated zeitgeist-altering starpower, what Jackson did that night – not just the way he threw on his trilby or hovered backwards across the stage, or even those mannered hiccups and crotch-grabs, but the way he seemed to realize halfway through that his whole life, hell, the whole history of pop, was leading up to that point – can really only be measured against the fiercest performances by Johnny Rotten or the young Elvis. Oh, and still more flesh than plastic, more black than white, he never looked more beautiful.

"I Want You Back"

The Jackson 5's debut single, released in November 1969, sold six million copies and announced the arrival of the eleven-year-old Michael with breathtaking urgency. Rock's hippie dream may have been ending as the swinging decade climaxed with murder – at Altamont, and over in Hollywood with the Tate-LaBianca killings – as well as with the first high-profile rock star death (Brian Jones) and the breakup of The Beatles, but for soul, funk and black pop in general, the story had only just begun.

"Don't Stop 'Til You Get Enough"

It has long been the job of the pop single to grab the attention of the listener from the off. But this ups the ante somewhat. Indeed, the first thirty seconds of the first single from the fabulous *Off The Wall* album, during which Jackson mutters semi-comprehensibly, although perhaps in thrall to *Star Wars*, about "the force... it's got a lot of power" while the beat gathers momentum beneath his feet before opening the gates, via one iconic explosive "ow!" and a cascade of strings, to disco heaven, comprise possibly the most thrilling intro to any pop single, ever.

"I'll Be There"

Written and produced by Berry Gordy, Hal Davis and Willie Hutch, this was Motown's third biggest-selling single of all time (behind Marvin Gaye's "I Heard It Through The Grapevine" and Diana Ross and Lionel Richie's sickly "Endless Love"); a Jackson 5 ballad that followed their exuberant first three hits ("I Want You Back", "The Love You Save" and "ABC"). It featured Michael's brother Jermaine on counterpoint vocals, but the star, of course, was the eleven-year-old Michael, who soared all over the lustrous melody with the assurance of a boy who would be king.

Jackson meets the Reagans

On 14 May 1984, Michael Jackson visited the White House dressed in classic early-'80s Jacko regalia: blue Sgt Pepper-style military jacket with gold trim, sequined socks, shades, and one sequined white-gloved hand. Was there ever a more surreal meeting of opposites than the one between the world's most eccentric pop star and the deluded ex-actor President? Probably not. "I'm very, very honored. Thank you very much, Mr President and Mrs Reagan," said Michael as Ron and Nancy's faces blanched whiter than Jackson's own. Reagan's misreading of Bruce Springsteen's "Born In The USA" has been held up as a model example of pop subversion from the same period, but really, if you want to see reality upturned and authority unsettled by a strange intervention, check out the photos of Jackson in Washington.

"Ain't No Sunshine"

A slice of tragic angst and a single only in the UK, where it reached Number 8 in August 1972, this was a cover of a Bill Withers song. But whereas Withers's original was gritty down-home soul, on this version the thirteen-year-old Michael transformed it into a haunting elegy and elevated yearning into an art form. As he navigated the dub spaces between the beat and the bass, it was almost like hearing trip-hop two decades early.

HIStory: Past, Present And Future

Jackson didn't have the sort of brain to be able to contemplate a coherent album statement or go for thematic unity – maybe he had ADHD or he preferred the scattershot approach. Whatever, there isn't a *Blood On The Tracks* or a *What's Going On* in his catalog; either an album consistently About Himself or About Something. *HIStory* was as near as he got to making a record that even vaguely resembled a unified concept. It's a double album: the first CD features hits from *Off The Wall* onwards; the second contains a series of songs, plaints really, about the state of the world such as "Earth Song" or the state of HIS world – from sheeny laments such as "Childhood" to ugly tirades like "Tabloid Junkie", "Scream" and "They Don't Care About Us" (with its *"Jew me, sue me/Everybody do me/Kick me, kike me"* line, references to police brutality and rape imagery). So the two CDs as a whole work loosely as a Before and After Fame thing, a story of someone who didn't stop 'til he got enough. And CD2 works as a mini-rant about celebrity injustice, and I say "works" although a lot of people couldn't quite get to grips with the notion of Jackson the cosseted multi-millionaire daring to spend one half of an album complaining about his lot. They could accept – relish, even – the idea of the clownishly peculiar Jacko, but they weren't quite ready for Michael's *In Utero*.

Of course, "weren't quite ready" isn't quite right: *HIStory* sold 20 million copies, making it the biggest-selling double-CD in history. It's funny: detractors, or just plain objective commentators, regularly assert that, commercially, there was some sort of vertiginous decline after *Thriller*. Even reports on Serious News Channels after his death cited statistics re: his album sales post-*Thriller* as cold, hard facts, as co-ordinates on a graph designed to plot his Decline and Fall, as though it was impossible to believe it was anything but a classic narrative with an inevitable downwards trajectory. But the facts are: *Bad* sold thirty million copies, *Dangerous* sold thirty-two million, and even his poorly received last studio album, 2001's *Invincible*, apparently sold twelve million. And that's not even mentioning 1997's *Blood On The Dance Floor*, the biggest-selling remix album ever, with six million sales. And yet still the sense of Jackson as a dismal disappointment after *Thriller* is strong. Either his self-pity was globally contagious, or we had a collective desire to see him suffer penance for his stratospheric success, because somehow the idea of Jackson as a beleaguered artist, operating on the margins, a kind of colossal cult figure, ignored by all but the most devoted, even as he was breaking sales records, is virtually too powerful to deny throughout the '90s and beyond.

So that was his story: hounded by his father for the first half of his life for a failure to achieve even as he was doing exactly that, only to be hounded by us for the second. It seems almost churlish to say at this point that *HIStory* wasn't half-bad – in fact, it was double-good, with that CD of hits and those new tracks, including the rhythmically impressive neo-industrial metal-funk of "They Don't Care About Us" that anticipated the *Blood On The Dance Floor* project and suggested Jackson should maybe have collaborated with Trent Reznor, and the sumptuously sad "Stranger In Moscow", which intimated that, letdown or god, there was no place on earth where Michael Jackson could hide.

"With A Child's Heart"

This makes for distressingly difficult listening in the light of the events of 25 June 2009, and indeed in the light of the events of the last two decades of his life. But it's the obvious moving music to use on the soundtrack of a documentary investigation into his troubled mind, or any morality tale about the corruption of all values requiring a sad-ironic sonic spin. *"With a child's heart, nothing can ever get you down,*" he sang on the 1973 ballad. Well, nothing much, anyway.

"Rock With You"

This might be the most perfect song he ever recorded, but he didn't write it, Rod Temperton did – it's got the Britfunk composer's signature all over it, with a similar polished yet poignant feel to "Posin' Til Closin'", "The Groove Line", "Too Hot To Handle" and all those other wonderful hits the Cleethorpes producer-musician wrote for Heatwave. But Michael was more than just the Sinatra of Disco, interpreting other people's material. He co-produced this exquisite piece of studio boogie with Quincy Jones and he surely had some say in its sound. It was a lovely sound that, like Earth Wind & Fire's *I Am* and Chic's *Risqué*, also from 1979, was presumably achieved by musicians as much as it was the product of the recording console. And yet you can tell from it that the machine soul/black science age is imminent: it sounds too crisp, too clean and pristine – not entirely sequenced but not exactly played either – to come from human hands. As for Michael, without his artillery of exclamations, those Tourette's tics which he'd use as a defense throughout much of his post-*Thriller* career, he puts in a superbly restrained performance, with just enough feeling. He hadn't yet had the soul sucked out of him.

"This Place Hotel"

Originally titled "Heartbreak Hotel", this thumping, orches-trated beat ballad, from The Jacksons' 1980 *Triumph* album, had nothing to do with the Presley song of the same name, but it did confirm what we suspected listening to *Off The Wall* – that Michael was the new Elvis; an Elvis for whose staggeringly wide-ranging audience it didn't matter if he was black or white. Cross-racial demographics aside, song for song ("This Place Hotel", "Can You Feel It", "Walk Right Now" and "Lovely One" were all singles, but there were even better tracks here), *Triumph* was probably an even stronger collection than *Off The Wall*. It was also the last great disco album – "Planet Rock" was coming.

"Billie Jean"

The video, from Steve Barron, the same director who did The Human League's "Don't You Want Me" and A-Ha's award-winning "Take On Me", was striking enough, with its noir-ish detective scenario and images of Michael, Jheri-curled and surgically sculpted, tripping lightly along a path and illuminating the tiles with every magically delicate step. MTV quite liked it too, and before you knew it, black pop was the world's new musical lingua franca. But the song was something else. Kraftwerk may have invented electronica as we know it, but it was Michael Jackson, together with producer Quincy Jones – who originally didn't rate the track and wanted it left off the album – who came up with the idea of a sort of supersonic urban funk, with a machine throb as insistent and relentless as the Krautrockers' motorik beat. But it also had the shine and sparkle of the best disco, with intimations of the aspirational good life. The combination had far-reaching implications. Basically, without "Billie Jean", it could reasonably be argued that Jam & Lewis – and by extension Timbaland, the Neptunes and all the other black producers with avant-garde tendencies of the last 20 years – wouldn't have felt encouraged to take their own magic steps down a path, illuminated by this track, towards a new hi-tech futurist R&B.

"Beat It"

Even if the song itself didn't sound especially incendiary, in the sense of it being a Year Zero act of burning provocation and revolution, at the time, it was never less than tremendously exciting, a memorable meeting of the previously irreconcilable worlds of rock and funk (give or take Sly Stone and George

Clinton), and it did pre-date The Prodigy's not wholly dissimilar "Smack My Bitch Up" by a good decade and a half.

Most of the hyperbolic talk about the *Thriller* album being trailblazing is, of course, courtesy of "Billie Jean", as well as the title track because it was a) so long and b) accompanied by an expensive video directed by John Landis. But much of the blather and its reputation for groundbreaking miscegenation is also down to "Beat It", partly because of the (preposterously overblown) Eddie Van Halen guitar solo, which meant that MTV had one less excuse not to play a video by a black artist. And what a video it was, featuring the subsequently endlessly mimicked – and wide open to parody – routine about the gang of hoods seeking rapprochement through synchronized dance.

But the video also saw the start of Jackson's slide towards protest-too-much displays of macho potency, and in its presentation of the star as street-tough hoodlum, albeit in this instance as a mediator between the rival gangs, you could sense his discomfort at having to pretend to be something he wasn't. And yet as the public probed him for signs of the opposite over the next few years, the more he felt pressured into proclaiming his manly vitality – hence, *Bad* followed by *Dangerous* followed by *Invincible* – when really, he was growing progressively weak.

"Smooth Criminal"

The press said "body dysmorphic", Jackson said "Smooth Criminal". Someone was lying. If Michael didn't convince any more as a fedora-wearing 1930s gangster than he did as the thug Samaritan in "Beat It", he certainly put up a good argument. The seventh single from 1987's *Bad* album was supreme, slick electro-Funk, even though, by the time it was issued in October 1988, it was somewhat underwhelming next to the otherworldly new percussive sounds shimmering out of Detroit and Chicago. It came with a video that cost a cool $8 million, approximately the budget of an independent movie, but then extravagant was

Michael's middle name. (Actually, his middle name was Joseph, after the father who virtually beat him towards pop mega-stardom.) Listening to the bassline, pulsating with male vigor, that propelled "Smooth Criminal" into the charts, you might not think it was worth either the money or the misery, but it did help present Jackson, perhaps for the last time, as a regular boy-rebel archetype, rather than the damaged, even deranged figure of no fixed sex that we came to know him as thereafter.

"Leave Me Alone"

This track, from the 1988 CD issue of *Bad*, was a more realistic representation of Michael Jackson: a whinge about the price of celebrity adulation rather than an assertion of masculine force from the feyest pop star on the planet. Complaints about stardom from over-indulged musicians never go down well with the public, let alone with critics, but this insight into Jackson's fame-addled brain reached Number 2 in the UK, testament to Jackson's melodic and rhythmic savvy. Because unlike your average whiny indie band complaining about the adverse effects of having more than one fan, Jackson didn't use his woes to inflict unlistenable one-chord thrash on his listeners, he allied them to highly addictive, propulsive synth-funk, which, when you think about it, was quite considerate of him.

Meanwhile, the video – including a fast-cut look back at all the shock-horror headlines and front-page stories about cryogenics and Bubbles the chimp and the hyperbaric chamber and the Elephant Man bones – was hilarious, and suddenly you were forced to reconsider every assumption you had ever made about Michael Jackson. Could it be that all those tabloid scandals and outlandish rumors were just a great big joke at our expense, from the greatest myth-maker and surrealist-absurdist hype-monger of the modern era? It's a nice idea, one worth toying with, but it might just have been that he was more self-aware, and more complicit in our merciless scrutiny of him, than we ever imagined.

The "Scream" video

This 1995 track, a Jimmy Jam and Terry Lewis number, was a thoroughly average blast of crashing, careering jackhammer electro-funk, quite crude and lacking in melodic or rhythmic invention. The lyrics, seemingly about the fame that brought Jackson the superstardom he craved yet proved his undoing, could have been rivetingly autobiographical for the mainstream dance-pop milieu, had he bothered to pen something more compelling and insightful than the endlessly repeated line, "*Stop pressurin' me*". But the black and white – or rather, matt chrome and brushed steel – video, was utterly astounding. Directed by Mark Romanek, it bore references to Japanese sci-fi anime and showed Michael and sister Janet, all arty sunken cheekbones and coal-black eyes, going slowly mad in a spaceship. It was a glimpse of an alternate reality where Jackson made like Neil Young and, instead of the middle of the road, veered towards the ditch, signed to Warp Records and worked with Squarepusher and Chris Cunningham.

The *HIStory* statue

Now, many believed the decision in 1995 to float a 30-foot steel and fiberglass statue of Michael Jackson, sculpted in full neo-military glory, down the estuaries of many of Europe's major cities, including London, to promote the *HIStory* album, to have been an act of monumental hubris. And of course they were right. Which is why I was there that day, down by the Thames, frozen in awe at the sight of Jackson as some kind of totalitarian pop dictator.

It is customary, even among enthusiasts of pop, a site familiar with preening narcissists, to deride, even to be offended by, such acts of wanton egomania. But then, I've always had a penchant for paranoiac demigods with a preternaturally inflated sense of their own omnipotence. Because those kinds of people can make magnificently good art, and even when it's magnificently bad art, it's generally more interesting than the norm. The tragedy isn't that Michael was allowed to indulge his whims in this way, but that he wasn't allowed to more often.

Jackson's concert at Sheffield's Don Valley Stadium

"Sinatra, Presley, Jagger, Hendrix – they were all leading up to Michael Jackson", was how my review in monthly music and movie magazine Uncut went after I witnessed Jackson "crash-landing" in Sheffield via a replica space-craft that burst through the Don Valley Stadium stage floor at the start of this concert on his 1997 world tour. As our hero emerged in shiny gold robot gear and a group – a sub-species – of cyber-dancers moved as one, I gasped (I really did) with delight at the terpsichorean, multi-dimensional wonder of it all: "It's a 5D avant-garde circus, a consistent program of vaulting ambition and Cecil De Mille-ian pretension; he moves like Astaire, he thinks like Aphex Twin". Even allowing for an element of talking something up, and the rampant projection of fantasy notions, this sort of reaction is not as common as you might presume among those who write about rock music for a living.

"Butterflies"

The part of my brain that rampantly projects always struggled with Jackson's latter-day output because it was so often so far removed from what I wished he was doing – frequently willed him to do – at that stage in his career. Nevertheless, even if this wasn't evidence that he still had "it" as late as 2001, or offered any proof that he was collaborating with the right people, it was a lovely little track and one of the few standouts from his last studio album. You might even concede that it augurs well for any forthcoming unreleased or nearly-finished music recorded in the last few years of his life. If, that is, you can accept the vast discrepancy between the artist – ravaged, ruined, in immense pain – and his art, or whatever word you choose to use for pleasant, air-brushed pabulum like this.

His death

This isn't a flippant or facetious entry in the pantheon of great Michael Jackson moments. No, his death was "great" – in the sense that it was immense, loaded with historical significance, with the heft and weight of gravitas. He's more than just the superstar with the tarnished reputation now; his death has unlocked the myth of Michael Jackson – the most troubled, yes, but also the most exhilarating performer of the last thirty years, perhaps of all time. Now he can be big again where towards the end of his career he was somehow – like Elvis and Lennon at the end of theirs – shabby and small. If you happen to like Michael Jackson, and believe he was capable of and actually achieved greatness, you might even have allowed yourself a brief moment of relief at his death, because it meant that the haranguing could stop and the hagiography could start. And you could finally, perhaps for the first time in a quarter of a century, breathe out and be a Michael Jackson fan again.

"Man In The Mirror"

Inevitably, no sooner had he died than he was right back where he belonged, at Number 1 in the singles chart with the reissue of this positivist, gospel-tinged message from *Bad*. This, more than any other, was the song that was given a new lease of life through his death, by public demand. Equally inevitably, it was the moment it captured and celebrated rather than the song itself that proved affecting and earns it its position here in the ultimate list of the ultimate artist. It was an odd choice, though, all told, given the lyric. *"I'm gonna make a change/For once in my life/It's gonna feel real good/Gonna make a difference/Gonna make it right..."* That's one way of putting it. Another way of putting it: the man that Michael Jackson saw in the mirror couldn't make enough changes – to his face, to his life, to himself – to make him feel good or make it right.

He was a wounded soul in the guise of a superfreak. He, ever so elegantly and with a voice as quiet as a cartoon mouse, rampaged across the planet and in so doing showed the callous disregard that the rich can have for the poor. At the same time, he taught us about compassion – for the wayward and unusual, creepy and strange – and we should be grateful for that.

He taught us that sexuality was fluid and that people want to cut their flesh for peace of mind. He was otherworldly, he was exotically disfigured, and he was larger – madder – than life. Whether the madness was the fuel that propelled him to stardom, or it was the stardom itself that sent him mad, didn't matter in the end, because in the end he died having achieved more than any other single musician has or ever could. I talked earlier about unfulfilled promise, but that was the pop fantasist in me. In reality, it's unlikely that he would have done any more than he did. Yes, he was deeply troubled and he had tragic flaws, but what did all of that prevent him from doing? Sustaining a mediocre career? Making a bigger-selling album?

He acted out the drama of uncertainty, with us in the role of his dad, providing the perennial chorus of disapproval. Sometimes we cheered and we only made things worse. His could have been a dream of a lifetime but it ended up an American nightmare. But the soundtrack was sublime.

He appeared to move in fast and slow motion.

He cried like a little girl.

To put it mildly, Michael Jackson was a mess. He danced with liquid grace, but he was in many ways a disgrace.

To put it wildly, many of the people who have made records that I love I would probably feel uneasy about allowing them to babysit my children.

And yet, if you knew what he knew and saw what he'd seen, you'd probably scream, too.

To put it abstractly, he was an angel who fell to Earth and he could or he appeared to be able to alter the molecular structure of the air around him.

To put it litigiously: if he was guilty, we are guilty, too, because we still listened to his music long after the court cases and the hideous exposes. And if he wasn't, then we hounded him to death, and we're just going to have to deal with that.

To put it ambiguously, he might have done some terrible things and he might not. He made us trust him. He made us doubt what was right and what was not. And we were so in awe of his peculiar gift, of his gift for the peculiar, that we somehow let it pass. He almost made moral nihilists of us all, because in the end we cared more about Michael Jackson than we did Jordy Chandler, and that was obscene. We cared more about Michael Jackson because he improved the quality of our lives during his life and he will carry on doing so now that he's dead and so the bewilderment continues. He made us swallow the hard truth – and can we be clear about this once and for all? – that you cannot – CAN. NOT. – allow an artist's private life to affect or infect the way you perceive their art. Cannot. Otherwise we might as well throw on the fire right now anything and everything we own by The Beatles, The Rolling Stones, The Who, The Beach Boys, Chuck Berry, James Brown, Lou Reed...

To put it conclusively: we need different words, different ways, to assess Michael Jackson because he was great in such a different way to all the other all-time greats. In a sense his contribution was so slight – a pop record here, a dance maneuver there – and yet in some ways he dominated the scene, he could outshine the sun, with a swivel, a strut, a sashay, across a stage. He didn't so much exert a giant influence as cast a luminous ethereal aura over popular music these past four decades that verges on a ghostly kind of hegemony.

It's never been easy to like Michael Jackson because, apart from anything else, it's almost impossible to explain his appeal, more so even now that he's gone, because there is no bulky body of evidence in terms of work or back catalog, just a few scattered memories of a star who travelled so far from his boyhood self, who found it so hard to grow up and grow old, that he screamed his way in pain to the grave.

3

The boy who would fly:

Michael Jackson

Barney Hoskyns

(Originally published in NME, 17 September 1983)

I've been feeling strange about Michael Jackson since I was eleven-years-old. I remember lying in bed with a transistor radio the size of a large matchbox pressed to my ear, entranced and slightly embarrassed by the choirboy purity of "I'll Be There". I remember thinking, "Gosh, he's only six months older than me; I wonder what he'd be like if he came over, you know, watched TV and played football." Now I can guess.

I loved the Jackson Five records but I never teenybopped to them. I was too busy watching Michael jump around the stage while Jackie and Tito loomed over him like giants, Afros apparently growing by the minute. The cover version of Sly's "Stand" said it all: *"there's a midget standing tall, and the giant beside him about to fall"*. I was green with envy.

It was when I bought "I Want You Back" that the Motown sound first knocked me sideways. Like John Lennon when he first heard the booming organ lead-in to "Stop! In The Name Of Love", I couldn't believe how loud it was. From the piano cascade into the crashing cymbal and guitar, through the bass tearing the bottom out of my speakers, I was literally thrown back from the turntable. Berry Gordy could call it soul bubblegum for all I cared, I hadn't heard such *crazed* music in my life. In the treble register it was anarchy – frantic strings, rippling guitars, hi-hats, tambourines – but through it came this tiny tantrum, a kindergarten whirlwind, belting and swaggering out of swaddling clothes. It had all the power and determination of a miniature James Brown. And it was all I neeeeeed(ed).

Thirteen years on and *still* I wanna be startin' somethin'. Michael Jackson is singing "you're a vegetable", only it sounds like "nashty boy" or "nashty girl". He's charging these words with the bitterest twists, bending and dragging them, winding vowels round his throat, spitting syllables like darts of poison. The drum machine's programmed for eternity; like a piston, it goes on hissing and revolving, turning and driving, too high to get over, too low to get under. You're carried, you can't escape, you're ripped by the voice's current. And it won't stop 'til you've got enough.

How does Michael cut so deep? Why does he do me that way?

*

Sometimes I wonder how great Michael Jackson really is, and how much of his "magic" derives purely from the spell of fame. He is, after all, the biggest star on earth. There's no-one who can command his fee, precious few who can pay it. The promoters of this year's US Festival offered over $1 million. The response was simple: "You're not even close".

His fame fascinates because it is total. Seemingly withdrawn from it, in fact it cocoons him. Like Howard Hughes, he doesn't have a public relationship with fame but abstractly embodies it. So when he starts saying things that sound completely mad, like "if I could, I would sleep onstage", he is simply stating a logical implication.

When one says that Michael lives in fantasy, one is not just referring to the fact that he thought ET was a real living creature, or that his favorite movie is *Captains Courageous* (would you believe one of its characters is a fisherman called *Disko Troop*?), or that he confides more in his pet llama and his mannequin collection than he does in his own family. One is saying that up on the stage, deep in the dark womb of the studio, Michael's voice is a vehicle of fantasy, an instrument ceaselessly running circles round itself, tripping itself up, playing make-believe.

He can take the human voice as far out as Diamanda Galas. On the *Jacksons Live* album, there's an extraordinary half-minute between "I'll Be There" and "Rock With You" which perhaps conveys more of Michael Jackson than anything he's ever done. Breaking free of accompaniment with the playful virtuosity of a saxophonist, he winds up "I'll Be There" with a series of piercingly sustained shrieks, cutting up each cry with a tiny ripple of chuckles. The audience goes predictably ape: reflex gratification. But for Michael, every breath, every laugh, every "hick!" is a link, a phrase, a segment of the flow. So engrossed is he by himself that his own responses to his voice are incorporated into the performance. "BE THEY AAARE! HICK! CAN YER FEEEL EEEEAAART! YIP!" Going up two octaves: "HEEEAH HEE HEE HEE! HEEEAH HEE HEE!" Down again. "AH DEE DADA DADA DADA DUNKA DUNKA DEE DADA DUNKA... I THINK I WANNA ROCK!"

It's a voice which starts into every split spare second, stretching like rubber, filling cracks like water. It's not warm or sensual or "black" but sharp, a squeezing of the throat's aperture, a voice of pure technique. Detaching itself, it gets lost in free flight. Its narcissism is almost not human.

For two months, while preparing in Los Angeles for an interview that never happened, I couldn't hear this voice without feeling that it was all there was to know about Michael Jackson, that in it he released everything which is otherwise denied him, all that must stay quiet. At a point of masturbatory orgasm, it can all but shut out the world. To try to engage it in conversation seemed absurd, dangerous.

*

There was a time when I wrote the Jacksons off. As for Michael, I felt sure that this puckish dynamo, part Frankie Lymon, part James Brown (with something, too, of former 12-year-old genius Little Stevie), would, like all child stars, crack, go mad or end, like Frankie himself, a penniless drug addict. Isn't that how all pop's fairy tales conclude?

But no, Michael fasted, stretched into an unnaturally elongated superfreak, a balletic stick insect, looked into the business, and when the Jacksons left Motown for Columbia in 1975, was lined up to star in a CBS biopic called – you guessed it – *The Life Of Frankie Lymon*.

In all fairness, before 1978 there was little evidence of any production or songwriting talent. Trapped at Tamla for six years, where the hacks of the self-styled "Corporation" became ever more predictable in their selection and treatment of the group's material, they left Gordy's fold in a blaze of controversy, stripped of their name, only to be cosseted for a further two non-albums by the hacks of Gamble and Huff in Philadelphia. Yet one song on *The Jacksons* (1976) bore a second listen. Tucked away at the end of side one, "Blues Away" had a pleasant shape and substance that the rest of the record lacked hopelessly. The credit said Michael Jackson.

After *Goin' Places* (1977), the Jacksons looked beat. The doowoppy strains of "Heaven Knows I Love You, Girl" were quite unsuited to them. Motown had tried them on the Delfonics' 'Ready Or Not (Here I Come)' back in 1970 but, as Nelson George dryly remarked, "no-one ever accused them of being a great close harmony group". From "I Want You Back" through "Mama's Pearl" to "Doctor My Eyes", the Five have always been at their best with bubblegum. Popcorn love, you dig? (New Edition certainly do.) Philly just wasn't their style. As for the orchestral disco funk of "Enjoy Yourself", "Keep On Dancing", et al. – a muted continuation from their last Motown album, *Movin' Violation* – I'd say they were lucky to get hits from this period at all.

When the proof of talent finally came, you wondered why they'd bothered with anyone else, particularly producers as stylistically bankrupt as Gamble and Huff. *Destiny* (1978) wasn't a great album but it had a sprinkling of great moments which one can review now as sketches towards the superb *Triumph* (1980). The ballads, for example, anticipate "Girlfriend" and "Time Waits For No One". "Things I Do For You" points crudely to "Get On The Floor" and "Everybody". Singles-wise, "Blame It On The Boogie" was flatulent pulp but "Shake Your Body" prefigured everything that would so gloriously burst open in "Lovely One", "Don't Stop", and "Walk Right Now". Its wondrous flavour is due to the presence of ex-Wonderlovers Nathan Watts (bass), Mike 'Maniac' Sembello (guitar), and Greg Phillinganes (keyboards), who has featured on Jackson output right up to *Thriller*. These guys do so much more than the half-asleep MFSB of the Philly albums.

On *Destiny*, the best is saved for last. "That's What You Get (For Being Polite)" was the first evidence that the Jacksons – in this case Michael and the (I suspect) very talented Randy – could write a great soul toon. Moreover, it seemed uncannily close to a self-portrait of Michael. The song is about a character called Jack (the "son" castrated?):

Jack still sits alone
He lives in the world that is his own
He's lost in thought of who to be
I wish to God that he would see
Just love, give him love...

The song ends:

Don't you know he often cries about you
He cries about me
He cries about you, about me, about you

Don't you know he's scared?
Don't you know don't you know don't you know?

That's what you get for being Michael Jackson.

*

In *The Wiz* (1978), Michael played the scarecrow who is looking for a brain, an irony not worth laboring here. The film's musical director was none other than Quincy Jones, and a single from the soundtrack, the inoffensive "You Can't Win", was Michael's first solo release since leaving Motown.

Obviously more important was the resulting partnership on *Off The Wall*, a record whose landmark stature need hardly be mentioned. By now it must have been purchased by every pop fan on earth and even as I write is probably being secretly exported to other galaxies. Of course, as an album it's not great, but if the first time you heard "Don't Stop 'Til You Get Enough" doesn't rate as almost the greatest moment of your life, you're obviously some kind of vegetable.

Off The Wall is an oddly mixed bag – Carole Bayer-Sager here, Earth, Wind, & Fire there – yet it's possible to see it both as culmination (in Gavin Martin's words "the final summation of the great disco party") and as the inauguration of a new, softer funk for the '80s. Like EWF's "Boogie Wonderland", "Don't Stop" takes "disco" into the outer cosmos, while the sublime Rod Temperton songs – "Rock With You", "Off The Wall" – look forward to the less frenzied black pop of today. Nothing has topped them. Born out of Heatwave (Temperton-written) and the (Jones-produced) Brothers Johnson, the initial trio of singles took the world completely by storm. Nobody had heard such draped, sweeping choruses before, nor been pummeled by brass like Jerry Hey's Seawind Horns; never had a pop voice stretched so far. *Off The Wall* contains the most intricately timed, fully textured, glossily sensual dance music ever made. It's still a giant thrill.

*

If people hadn't been so busy awaiting *Off The Wall*'s successor, the next Jacksons album, *Triumph* (1980), might be more often lauded as the magnificent record it is. Rivaled in the exalted sphere of superdisco by only Earth Wind & Fire's *I Am* – by which it is more than a little influenced – *Triumph* is genius almost from start to finish: *almost* because as it happens its only weak points are the pompous opener "Can You Feel It" and the closing so-so, Jermaine-ish "Wondering Who". Everything else either melts or stings. The scope of the production, the authority of the arrangements, the sheer strength of sound, all are dazzling.

Above all, it's the supposed "fillers" which really consolidate it as a complete album. 'Your Ways' and 'Give It Up' show how effortlessly The Jacksons can do their own EWF, their own Isleys, even their own Temperton. Of course Michael learnt a great deal from Quincy, but here he goes one step beyond. While nothing beats "Don't Stop" or "Rock With You" (what could?), *Triumph* is finally, simply, a better record than *Off The Wall*.

Check Out This Feeling! "Everybody" is a dramatic reconstruction of "Get On The Floor", "Lovely One" is a radically exciting dance cut, while Randy and Jackie's "Time Waits For No One" is possibly the most affecting ballad Michael's ever been given. Finally, "Billie Jean" Mark One "Heartbreak Hotel" takes Maurice White on at his own game and knocks him out of the ring. Michael's no Phillip Bailey, but Bailey couldn't reach this pain.

Which finally brings me round to *Thriller*. May I ask what all the fuss was about? If Tavares release a duff platter, do people suddenly start preaching about "blandness", "complacency", and all the other cardinal California sins? Gimme a break.

Besides, is *Thriller* a bad record? Hardly, I'll grant you that "Wanna Be Startin'" was a tame successor to "Don't Stop" and yeah, "Baby Be Mine" wasn't such a hot "Rock With You". Oh alright, "Beat It" stank, it was stupid and clumsy and every time the drums came on the radio I prayed it was "Let It Whip". But heavens, *Off The Wall* had "Get On The Floor" and "Falling In Love", and to be honest I never reckoned too much on "Working Day And Night", so what did you expect, perfection?

What did we get? First, anything that brings Eddie Van Halen and "Soul Makossa" under one roof is in my book pretty cool. More seriously, "Billie Jean" was great. I know you all heard it at least 3,482 times, but really, that hissing electro hi-hat, that beat, the bass, Jerry Hey's mad string arrangement. I mean, do we have a fantasmatically supreme record? *Alright!*

Beyond that? Well, there's my own fave, the beautiful Toto creation "Human Nature" – and anyone who knocks Toto in my presence may politely F. off; I suggested they examine "Crush On You" or "I'd Rather Be Gone" from Finis Henderson's album for corroboration of Toto's discrete brilliance. Apropos of which, the group is co-producing the next Jacksons' album, due in the spring (one of the songs is apparently called "The Hurt"). I'm also quite partial to "P.Y.T." due to its extravagantly thick Moog bass. This leaves the only disappointment, which is Rod Temperton, who signally falls to deliver a killer. Even the title cut, despite its "Boogie Nights" riff and blazing brass, is as hacked out as "Turn On The Action" on Quincy's *The Dude*.

This is not, however, enough to stop *Thriller* standing up as one of the strongest albums of the last ten months.

*

Some people seem to think that because he's not big, butch, and badass, Michael Jackson is some kind of saint, a child lost in time. Perhaps it's true. Certainly his peculiar appeal has something to do with his raceless and asexual physique. The epicene translucence of his face is almost otherworldly. It reminds me of only one other black artist, the young Miles Davis.

Michael goes so far as to compare himself to a hemophiliac, betraying an instant paradox; for if he is a hemophiliac, he's one who only feels safe surrounded by sharp edges. In other words, he feels strange around people but not in front of crowds. As Vince Aletti put it, he has "a compulsion to entertain". It is only before crowds that he can "lose himself", touch that innocence where magic reigns.

Sometimes the articulacy of this shy, paranoid, tongue-tied idol is positively unnerving. He hates to describe himself as an actor because "it should be more than that. It should be more like a believer... Sometimes you get to a note, and that note will touch the whole audience. What they're throwing out at you, you're grabbing. You hold it, you touch it, and you whip it back – it's like a Frisbee."

Michael is alone amongst superstars in consistently hinting at misery – at the absence inside. How can he live in himself when he is everywhere outside, when at the age of twelve he was watching *cartoons* of himself on TV? The world is plastered with him, he is a thousand billboards. And the tragic truth seems ancient, that only onstage can he get back inside.

All this is rather wonderfully illuminated by the German author Kleist in his 1810 essay *On The Marionette Theatre*. In the essay, a dancer has become fascinated by marionettes, or puppets. He believes that because they are not conscious, and are thus free of affectation, they are more graceful than we are – they have "a more natural arrangement of the centers of gravity". Scorning the vanity of modern dancers, whose souls often appear to reside on their elbows, he says: "Misconceptions like this are unavoidable, now that we've eaten of the Tree of Knowledge. But Paradise is locked and bolted, and the cherubim stands behind us. We have to go on and make the journey round the world, to see if it is perhaps open at the back."

Hinging on the third chapter of *Genesis*, in which Adam and Eve eat from the Tree and become conscious of their nudity and their difference, the essay makes clear that we cannot simply forget our fall and regain Innocence. If life is the graceless search for grace, knowledge must "go through an infinity" to arrive back at the simplicity and harmony of the marionettes – and, for Michael Jackson, at the innocence of children and animals. They don't wear masks.

Of his mannequins, Michael says, "I guess I want to bring them to life... I think I'm accompanying myself with friends I never had." This is the boy that wants to fly; on a stage he soars into the unreal. "Grace appears most purely in that human which either has no consciousness or an infinite consciousness. That is, in the puppet or in the god."

It is the finest irony that at the very moment when Michael Jackson is seen as a god, when he is lost in voice and dance, he is in fact the most graceful of puppets.

4

He's out of our life:

Michael Jackson, 1958 – 2009

Barney Hoskyns

In September 1979, my friend Davitt Sigerson – then a very good white writer on black music; later the chairman of Island Records in America; still later the author of the fine novel *Faithful* – handed me an advance copy of *Off The Wall* and said it was going to make Michael Jackson a superstar.

The cover didn't promise much: in his tux and Afro, the winsome kid who'd fronted The Jackson 5 looked about as off-the-wall as a student en route to his high school prom. What difference could this album, recorded after several undistinguished years in the post-J5 Jacksons, make to a career that seemed certain to peter out into the semi-anonymity suffered by so many '70s soul performers?

One listen to "Don't Stop 'Til You Get Enough", the album's electrifyingly funky first track, was more than enough to suggest Sigerson was right. An intoxicating mix of stabbing horns, ultra-syncopated Latin percussion, and Jackson's own feverish falsetto yelps, "Don't Stop" propelled '70s black dance music into a new dimension at warp speed. The whole ultra-choreographed X-Factor world we now live in – from Prince and Madonna to Britney and Beyoncé – surely starts here.

Michael had always been the star in The Jackson 5: cute as a button, coyly knowing beyond his years, in total command of the stage. Who at the time knew the abusive regimen that lay behind such expert synchronization and effortless grace? The brothers looked so darned happy. Even when Michael entered puberty and adolescence, his pint-sized frame stretching out into long gangly limbs, he was magnetic.

Jackson was not an innovator. He did not shape the course of African-American pop music in the way James Brown or Stevie Wonder or Sly Stone or Jimi Hendrix or Prince shaped it. What he possessed was a vision of what an African-American entertainer could be, taking Berry Gordy's original conceit of crafting black pop for white teenagers and making it global: a shining crossover star who would dwarf even Elvis Presley.

Teaming up with producer Quincy Jones was the catalytic event Michael required to leave his brothers behind – to pull the various strands of black pop together into one irresistible signature, using the absolute cream of LA studio musicians and technicians to achieve it. Blending the vocal and melodic influences of Motown icons Stevie, Marvin and Smokey with the smooth late-'70s pop-soul sensibility of Heatwave and the Brothers Johnson, Jackson and Jones co-piloted an album that offered something for everyone: the ecstatic propulsion of "Don't Stop", the creamy groove of "Rock With You", the snively abjection of "She's Out of My Life". At the tail end of the '70s disco era, *Off The Wall* set a benchmark for the 1980s.

After the Matterhorn, Everest: Michael had had a taste of superstardom and was compelled to better it. *Thriller* took the template of its predecessor and covered yet more bases. Hiring guitarist Eddie Van Halen to blare all over "Beat It" felt as premeditatedly workshopped as enlisting Paul McCartney to simper alongside Jackson on "The Girl is Mine". But the dizzying energy of "Don't Stop" was picked up by the manic "Wanna Be Startin' Somethin'", and the whole of *Off The Wall* was surely trumped by the extraordinary "Billie Jean", the sinuously funky account of facing a paternity suit by a deranged groupie. The morning after Michael performed the song at Motown's twenty-fifth anniversary show in March 1983, dancing for forty-seven million people with supernatural self-assurance, he was unarguably the biggest star on the planet. The video for the album's title track made him the new icon of MTV.

Then it all started to unravel. For an essentially shy, frightened, immature and (as we later discovered) badly abused 24-year-old to find suddenly that he was the most famous person on earth was bound to do strange things to his fragile mind. Having never known much normality, his pathology began to follow the usual dysfunction of the child star: a gradual retreat from reality, compounded by delusions about his identity. 1987's *Bad* wasn't just bad, it was wholly untrue to his real musical impulses; as fake as his increasingly weird physical appearance and his daft Ruritanian outfits. At a time when Jackson's closest black rival, Prince, was dazzling us with *Parade* and *Sign 'O' The Times* – and when Public Enemy and NWA were turning hip hop into the real cutting edge of black street culture – Michael was... well, a bit *naff*.

Actually, Michael had always been naff but it didn't matter when he was making music as radical as "Billie Jean". With *Bad* and its equally horrible successors *Dangerous* (1991), *HIStory* (1995) and *Invincible* (2001), he seemed to be second-guessing what the public wanted instead of listening to his own instincts. More to the point, he'd lost touch with everything that was organically great about Michael Jackson. When Jarvis Cocker jumped onstage during Jackson's performance of the hideously messianic "Earth Song" at the 1996 BRIT Awards, miming the wafting of a fart in the audience's direction, he was puncturing the balloon of a megalomania that made all but the most myopic fans cringe.

Any credibility Michael still had at that point was now gone, and the desperate auto-coronation of the "King of Pop" – a specious term courtesy of that other chronically damaged child star, Elizabeth Taylor – only made matters worse. The pubescent sleepovers at Neverland came as no great surprise: Peter Pan a pedophile? Tell us something we hadn't guessed long ago.

Ultimately Jackson's tragedy isn't so extraordinary; it was merely played out on a media scale that would have shocked Elvis. No amount of fame and money was going to heal the psychic wounds of the little boy beaten by his ogre-ish father. Classic addiction patterns were evident from the moment the surgeons started chiseling away at Michael's face. Anyone who watched those ghastly Martin Bashir interviews will recall the grotesque scene in which the shopaholic Jackson casually dropped $3.6m on some garish Empire vases. And then, finally, came the miserable predictability of Jackson's addiction to prescription drugs. Well, at least he didn't die on a toilet seat.

Michael Jackson wasn't the first entertainer to be driven mad by fame and he won't be the last: look at the recent experiences of Britney Spears, Amy Winehouse and Eminem. But if there are no lessons learned from the pitiful last years of the "King of Pop"'s life, then surely we are all culpable.

5

Pop utopia:

The promise and disappointment of Michael Jackson

Steven Shaviro

At Michael Jackson's spectacular height, the time of *Off The Wall* (1979) and *Thriller* (1982) and the subsequent television appearances and live tours, there really was nobody like him. He was a vision of ease, grace and energy; as a dancer and as a singer – but also with an undercurrent of sadness that was unusually knowing for one so young, and yet that did not sour into bitterness. Michael Jackson was a supernova; we loved him, we worshipped him, we found his appearances and performances almost godlike – and this "we" was probably one of the widest, most inclusive in the history of the world. I don't see any reason to reject this, or ironically distance ourselves from this, or critique it in any way – although we should be aware of the social and historical contexts of this glory and this amazement.

But of course there was also everything that came after: Michael Jackson's pain and pathology, and the sad spectacle that he made of himself – and that we all made of him as well. We learned about the horrors of his childhood, and uncomfortably glimpsed the more-than-eccentricities of his later years. None of this was unrelated to the genius of his best work; all of it belonged to the same economy of celebrity that formed his essence, and from which also he evidently so grievously suffered. But none of it could have simply been extrapolated from the pain of "Billie Jean" or the splendor of "Don't Stop 'Til

You Get Enough" and "Beat It".

The moment of *Thriller* was an emotionally charged and extremely condensed one. Ronald Reagan was President; it was the dawn of the neoliberal (counter)revolution. We knew that something had ended, or had been lost; but we still had very little sense of what was going to replace it. I could not have imagined – nobody could have imagined – the hypercommodification and hyperfinancialization of the years since then; the reign of universal cynicism and marketing plans. The deep recession of the early 1980s followed the mixed expansions and losses of the 1970s. The 1970s represented the democratization, or generalization (in wealthy countries like the United States at least) of what had been "counter-cultural" about the 1960s; what used to be "us vs. them" had become common to everyone. Later decades' sarcastic dismissals of the excesses and bad fashions of the '70s really testify only to our current utter lack of imagination. In 1982, in any case, we were only at the beginning of understanding how incomplete the projects of the previous decades were fated to remain. Punk had come and gone, an inspiring flash in the pan; and the disco wars had revealed how deeply racially troubled things continued to be – even if the Reagan presidency was the beginning of one of those periodic efforts to deny the existence of these troubles altogether. The period was as we now realize, one of great innovation on the fringes of popular music; but it was also one of consolidation in which white-centric rock 'n' roll (including the music of all those interestingly innovative post-punks) lost its cultural relevance. It is no accident that the triumvirate of 1980s superstars, Michael Jackson, Prince, and Madonna, all focused on dance-oriented musical forms that remained closer to their African-American sources than rock had ever done (I should perhaps also mention the fact that the release of *Thriller* coincides almost exactly with the midway point of my own life to date.).

This is why I find Greil Marcus's comments on Michael

Jackson so utterly insufferable. Marcus is condescending and (at least borderline) racist, as he remarks (after grudgingly conceding that the Jackson phenomenon was "an event in which pop music crosses political, economic, geographic and racial barriers") that, whereas "performers as appealing and disturbing as Elvis Presley, The Beatles or The Sex Pistols" all "raise the possibility of living in a new way", Michael Jackson did not. The Jackson phenomenon, Marcus claims, "was the first pop explosion not to be judged by the subjective quality of the response it provoked, but to be measured by the number of objective commercial exchanges it elicited".

Even under the most charitable interpretation, this is pernicious nonsense. Elvis, The Beatles, and The Sex Pistols were every bit as much about marketing as Michael Jackson was. It was Brian Epstein, The Beatles' manager, who (as far as I am aware) first invented the whole concept of the commodity tie-in for pop music (Beatles lunchboxes, Beatles cartoons, etc.), and who created the feedback loop by means of which the hysteria of Beatles fandom redounded back upon the band itself and amplified its fame and reach (something that had never quite happened in the case of Sinatra fandom, Elvis fandom, etc.). As for The Sex Pistols, how can you ever extricate their rage from Malcolm McLaren's marketing savvy? Greil Marcus makes rather too much of McLaren's Situationist influence, and takes no account whatsoever of the fact that Situationism itself – not in spite of, but precisely on account of, its virulent critique of all forms of commodity culture – became one of the most commercially successful "memes" or "brands" of the late twentieth century.

What it really comes down to, of course, is race. Greil Marcus, as the quintessential white hipster, can only see cultural innovation and subversion when it is performed by white people. Marcus celebrates the ways in which "the pop explosions of Elvis, The Beatles and The Sex Pistols had assaulted or subverted social values", but denounces Michael Jackson's pop explosion as "a version of the official social reality, generated from Washington D.C. as ideology, and from Madison Avenue as language … a glamorization of the new American fact that if you weren't on top, you didn't exist." For Marcus, black people are evidently at best primitive, unconscious creators whose inventions can only take on meaning and become subversive when white people endow them with the critical self-consciousness that Marcus seems to think black people altogether lack. And at worst, black artists and performers are, for Marcus, puppets of the Pentagon and Madison Avenue; reinforcers of the very status quo that countercultural whites are struggling so hard to overthrow.

(A sidenote: we could consider here Marcus's comments on Anita Baker and the Pointer Sisters. At the very least, African-American aspirations to bourgeois respectability, and the way this is often translated musically with a smooth, elegant style, need to be understood in the historical context of American racism and black people's liberation struggles, rather than sneeringly dismissed as Marcus does when he snidely refers to the objectionable fact that The Pointer Sisters "gave concerts with 'Black Tie Recommended' printed on the tickets". It is symptomatic that Marcus singles out black artists as ostensibly representing upper-class privilege. Not to mention that the Pointer Sisters were as much about "*I'm about to lose control and I think I like it*" as they were about smooth elegance.)

All this might seem like raking over old coals; but the intersection between mass popularity and questions of race is still a central one for American culture (note: I am including the reception of British musicians like The Beatles in America as itself very much part of American culture). In the most important respects, The Beatles and Michael Jackson were very much alike, in that they both achieved a mass popularity that exceeded all bounds and crossed over many cultural divides. If we toss out (as we should) Marcus's white mythology, then we might even say that Michael Jackson was the end of something, as much as he was the beginning of something else. Jackson's celebrity, like that of The Beatles before him, and of Elvis before them, was only possible in an age of "mass culture" that no longer exists. In the time of Fordist mass production and mass marketing, cultural products were also mass marketed. This reached a new level of intensity when television replaced the movies and radio as the dominant mass medium. Elvis, The Beatles, and Michael Jackson are all figures of the period between the introduction of broadcast television and the introduction of multi-channel cable television, home video players, and the internet. The latter technologies, together with the general shift from standardized mass production to the regime of just-in-time flexible accumulation, with its endless array of customizable options, mean that no single celebrity figure can ever be as culturally dominant as Elvis, The Beatles, and Michael Jackson were. Recent debates, among music critics and on music blogs, between "rockists" and "popists" are ultimately sterile, because both sides fail to take sufficient account of our current culture of niche marketing, "long tails", customization and "crowdsourcing", not to mention that the advertising and commercial strategies initially deployed on a massive scale by figures like The Beatles and Jackson are now increasingly prevalent on the micro-level. They are no longer just imposed from above; rather, they saturate all our media and all our interactions, oozing up as they do from below. It used to be that you could accuse somebody (as Marcus liked to accuse black artists) of being a bourgeois sellout; but today, everyone without exception is a "bourgeois sellout," because (in the age of "human capital" and self-entrepreneurship) being such is a minimum requirement for mere survival. Today, this is a structural condition of social existence, rather than a matter of personal integrity or choice.

Of course, none of this would matter, really – it would just be another banal self-evidence of our everyday lives, alongside Ikea and Facebook and the iPhone – if it weren't for the beauty and the genius of all of these artists' performances, of their music and their self-presentation to their audiences, and their overall personas. That is to say, of their aesthetic singularities, or of what Bloch or Jameson would call their "utopian" dimension. The modulations of Michael's voice, the sinuous movements of his dancing, the way that his musical arrangements took disco and R&B and gave them both a smoothness and a slightly alien sheen, so subtly that one could say with equal justice that the sharp edges of mournful or joyous black expression had been "mainstreamed," or that the very "mainstream" itself had been alluringly or insidiously carried away, exposed to a strange metamorphosis, allowed to blossom into a new aestheticized state in which pop crassness had itself become a rare, almost Wildean, delicacy.

The point of a successful aesthetic singularity is that it crosses over directly into the form of the universal, without all those mediations that usually come between. Something is so absolutely unique (even when we can trace all the sources from which it arose) and so absolutely, achingly, joyously or heart-wrenchingly *right*, or just itself, that it becomes a kind of universal value (in philosophical terms, this is what Kant was getting at with his insistence upon the universal communicability of an aesthetic judgment devoid of cognitive principles and rules; or what Badiou is getting at when he speaks of an event; or what Deleuze was getting in his account of what he called "counter-actualization"). There was a kind of crack or a rupture, something absolutely inimitable in the way it was inscribed in Michael Jackson's own body, and proliferated throughout that body's performance. But balanced on the edge in this way, always just short of collapse, it was something that resonated with "everybody" (and in Michael Jackson's case, the empirical extent of this "everybody" was larger than it had ever been before, and larger, probably, than it will ever be again, at least in any future continuous with our present).

The utopia of Michael Jackson – the universality of his music, performance, and persona, his appeal to "everybody" – had to do precisely with its challenge to this history of race in America. Jackson was "the first black superstar of the post civil-rights era", Gary Younge writes; he was the first to make a recognizably African-American cultural expression (and this would refer to his body language and his demeanor, as much as to his music) available, in a way that was neither an exotic attraction for white people, nor watered-down (as so much white rock music arguably was) – and this precisely because it was addressed to "everybody" in a way that no previous black music, not even Motown, had been before. In its singularity, Jackson's music constructed a new "universal," one that was very much tied in with hopes for the end of American racism (hopes that were, of course, effectively dashed in subsequent decades, even as "everybody", or at least white people, gave lip service to the idea that they had in fact been fulfilled). So that, as Younge says, "the Jackson I was raised with" was, for him as for so many black people in the English-speaking world, and beyond it, "not just an American pop star but a global icon; not just a individual but part of a family. A black family". Or, as Greg Tate once put it, "black people cherished *Thriller*'s breakthrough as if it were their own battering ram [against] apartheid... It's like *Thriller* was this generation's answer to the Louis-Schmeling fight or something". The cultural significance of this utopian triumph, this newly produced Truth, consisted precisely in the fact that it didn't resonate just for black people, but for what I am calling "everybody" – or, let us say, for all the peoples of the world, except for those white hipsters for whom Greil Marcus speaks, who regarded the whole Jackson phenomenon (or should we say the whole racial liberation movement?) as somehow beneath them, and which they felt entitled to dismiss with contempt.

Everybody aside from Marcus and his band of white hipsters intuitively understood that Michael Jackson "raise[d] the possibility of living in a new way" at least as much as Elvis, The Beatles, or The Sex Pistols ever did.

But of course, no utopia is entirely real, or entirely realizable. There's a forbidden apple in every garden, a worm in every apple. The utopian moment of Michael Jackson's glory was also the prototype for the determinedly non-utopian progression of black figures beloved by white America – Cosby, Oprah, Obama – whose success has provided an alibi for the continuation of what I can only call the "racism of everyday life in America" today. And of course, this was in large part a necessary consequence of the way that Jackson (no less than The Beatles, etc., but also, I would argue, no more) was marketed, commodified, financialized. The intensified commodification of all aspects of life in the last thirty years (to a degree, as I have already noted, that I couldn't have imagined in 1979 or 1982) did indeed start at the moment of Jackson's triumph (though I think that Marcus' implicit association of it with Jackson's blackness is unconscionable). And it did have to do with the fact that utopias are especially marketable in the neoliberal era. Without that flash of greatness and genius, that moment of aesthetic singularity, there would in fact be nothing for the marketers to market (not that such a lack would have stopped them; many successful marketing campaigns have been based on nothing at all). And the way that aesthetic singularity can resonate universally, the way that an entirely novel Truth can become a condition of fidelity, is itself a necessary condition for ubiquitous commodification as well. Michael Jackson both benefited from marketing as no pop celebrity had before him; and became its victim in a manner as gruesome as it was exemplary.

The tension of singularity and universalization, and its simultaneous inextricability from, and irreducibility to, the neoliberal competitive marketization and commodification of everything, was played out by Michael Jackson in the terms both of gender and of race. Let me talk about gender and sexuality first, since this is both what always stares everyone in the face when we think about Jackson's last twenty years, and yet it is extraordinarily difficult to parse. Ernest Hardy insightfully remarks that, even at his height of success and popularity, Jackson "resonated so powerfully precisely because he upended and shimmered beyond gender convention. It seems especially noteworthy that he cemented his solo superstar status during the gender-bending/gender-fucking era of the early '80s, alongside Boy George, Annie Lennox, Prince, a funkily reinvigorated Grace Jones – though he was a seasoned old pro in comparison to all of them."

In his first hits as a pre-adolescent, right on through at least *Off The Wall* (released when he was twenty-one), Jackson somehow seemed knowing beyond his age, affectively in command of the clichés of normative male heterosexuality, without any of the all-too-common signs of over-commitment and anxiety about this. But as he grew older, the normative heterosexual mask became something that seemed, for him, increasingly hollow, and therefore increasingly desperately maintained as an obvious fiction. I am really just translating the common (and accurate) observation that Jackson seemed extraordinarily mature as a child and adolescent, yet seemed to flee more and more into the fiction of a pre-pubertal childhood innocence once he actually was an adult. We speak of narcissism, of Peter Pan syndrome, of the allegations of pedophilia, and so on. But it might be worth remembering, instead, how the other dominating artists of the 1980s (Madonna and Prince) also pushed sexual experimentation in certain non-normative ways; though arguably neither of them went as far as Michael did. I remember the moment (it must have been the late 1980s or early 1990s) when many people began to perceive Jackson as being a little too "weird" sexually, so that they no longer idolized him, no longer wanted to "become" him. Of course, this was all the result of hints and vague suggestions, nothing that Jackson himself ever overtly expressed; wasn't there something here of the "dysphoria" that Dominic Fox has been writing about (although of course this always remains diffuse and diffidently expressed; it never takes the form of "militant dysphoria," there are no signs of the recognition that "personal 'dysfunction' must be understood in the context of this system and its (naturalized) functions", a recognition towards which Fox seeks to move us)? In a certain sense, Michael Jackson's diffuse expression of sexuality, which so many people have found disturbing, because it doesn't fit into any normative paradigm, is the "line of flight" along which he continued to singularize himself, to a point beyond which universalization was no longer possible. It has a sort of negative relation to the deployments of sexuality in American popular culture today, where an evident explicitness and overtness of expression are purchased at the price of an increasingly narrow and normative range within which such expression is permissible, or even thinkable. You can be as raunchy as you want to be, as long as you remain even closer to the pre-established stereotypes of masculinity and femininity than was required in the pre- "sexual liberation" times of the 1950s. Michael Jackson's refusal, or inability, to give more than rote lip service to this requirement, is the aspect of his persona, or expression, that is least understood today, and that desperately needs to be more fully explored.

At the same time, of course, Jackson's "line of flight" played out racially as an endeavor to extirpate his own blackness, and to make himself white. In this volume, Mark Fisher notes how the first plastic surgery in the service of becoming-white had already taken place in between the release of *Off The Wall* and that of *Thriller*. By 1987, at the time of the release of *Bad*, the self-mutilation had already gone so far that Greg Tate could write that "Jackson emerges a casualty of America's ongoing race war –

another Negro gone mad because his mirror reports that his face does not conform to the Nordic ideal". There's a bitter irony to this, when you reflect that, as Tate put it, "back when [Jackson] wore the face he was born with, black folk thought he was the prettiest thing since sliced sushi".

Jackson's self-remaking can only be understood as a kind of Afrofuturist nightmare; a violent (to himself) leap into the posthuman. As Analee Newitz puts it, Jackson "turned his body into a kind of science fiction story. He became an enhanced human, using plastic surgery and pharmaceuticals to change his face and seemingly his race as well. He became whiter than most white people, and his pale bandaged skin became his trademark". Here singularization, or what Deleuze and Guattari call a "line of flight", becomes indistinguishable from hyperbolic normativization. Jackson sought to singularize himself by fleeing any indication of blackness (I mean this culturally, rather than just physiologically; in the sense that the physiology is fully real, but also an index of would-be transformations on all other levels of being as well). Jackson wanted to become generically normative: which is to say, in a white supremacist society he wanted to become white. But in doing so, he only became something even more singular: a kind of grotesque parody of whiteness, a zombified, living-dead simulation of whiteness. He became a figure like those of the first white people: the hideous forms created by the mad scientist Yacub in Nation of Islam legend (as recounted, among other places, in Amiri Baraka's play *A Black Mass*, the musical accompaniment for which was provided by Sun Ra). Of course, the truth behind this sort of transformation is that "whiteness" (like any other normative, hegemonic formation) is a pure imposture and does not really exist; it can *only* be instantiated as a grotesque parody of itself. Only racists actually "believe in" whiteness as being anything more than a marker of privilege and control; and only someone as delirious and demented as Michael Jackson ultimately became, and as wounded by not being able to take its privileges for granted, would ever seek to achieve it in so literalistic a way.

There is an obvious psychological way to account for the misery and self-mutilation of Michael Jackson: it resulted, undoubtedly, from the harshness of his childhood, in which he was driven, by his father and his family, to perform and to become a star so intensively, and from such an early age, that he never got to know any other sort of life. But such an interpretation, even if true, is inadequate to Jackson's genius, to the way he created pleasure and hope and utopian aspirations in the lives of so many, and to the ways that his sufferings and his strangeness are quintessential expressions of American life and society in this neoliberal age.

"...and though you fight to stay alive, your body starts to shiver..."

Marcello Carlin

It is always dangerous to judge anybody on the basis of who they were, what they did and how they behaved in their youth. That is, judge them for the rest of their lives because of the way they started, or were made to start. Especially if from the start they are told in the firmest of tones, and with the harshest of menaces, that they are different from and superior to everybody else.

Nobody told the young Elvis that he was going to be God, and so he was able to maintain that position of Everyman to his people, equal to everybody else and superior to none, the oldest story that his country tells. But Michael was made swiftly aware – and I do not mean to underplay the violence implicit in that word "swiftly" – that he was special and was bound, as in irons, to remain special. No matter that every speckle of special shortened his life by another crucial minute, or hour, or year, as if he had to use up all his donated and inherent energy to maintain the façade of specialness. All to allow his father to experience fame and greatness at second hand, whatever the cost to either.

Damn the misdiagnosed prodigies. For every Shirley Temple Black there has been a Judy Garland, for every Bonnie Langford a Lena Zavaroni, for every Mozart a Mozart. Dying young and inglorious, their lesser energies used up and exhausting the red dye on their balance sheets since all their greater energies had been devoted to making their youth special at the cost of potential adulthood.

I know that of which I speak, since I myself was supposed to be a suspiciously prodigious child, and newspaper clippings of this alleged genius continue to survive. I began talking in a coherent tongue at an absurdly early age, got the hang of elementary reading and writing not long afterwards, and somehow this contrived to make me "special" and "gifted". The fact that I did not start to walk until the age of 18 months should have set off early alarms, but in the sixties such alarms were not yet being manufactured. As it is, I don't really recognize the four-year-old me staring intently at a letter from the National Association for Gifted Children – was I really reading it? And if so, what did I learn? – in the pages of the Scottish Daily Mail. Or the ten-year-old me busily pretending to type on a Smith-Corona typewriter on our kitchen dining table on the cover of the Hamilton Advertiser, the one who was already noted as keeping scrupulous and comprehensive records of the pop charts and was expected to be a published author by the age of thirteen. As it is, my first book is scheduled for publication next autumn, by which time I shall be forty-six. A defiant late starter compensating for the absence of any meaningful early starts?

How was I supposed to know? The first recognized case of Asperger's syndrome was not diagnosed until 1981, too late for my school or my father and nearly too late for me. So I fumbled my way, awkwardly but pretty successfully, through grown-up life for twenty years, and then that life was snatched away from me, and so I had to resort to writing since the person to whom I was accustomed to telling my tales was no longer around and I had to tell *somebody*. And so I got my life back, painfully and messily but it was all there, and the prospect of living longer than my Dad is suddenly a graspable reality.

Michael Jackson, as he was, didn't live much longer than my Dad, who also died not long after his fiftieth birthday of heart failure which I knew from eight painful years of first hand experience to have been the product of a protracted suicide bid. The first automatic thing I uttered after hearing the news on the radio was a mock-resigned (the mock to disguise the shock) "Just like Elvis", but despite Lisa Marie, Michael was never just like Elvis, in any sense of the word "just". True, he hung on for eight more years than Elvis managed, and if it matters (as it does) my Dad's demise owes much more, circumstantially, to Elvis's than Michael's. But did he hang on? He had not issued a significant musical statement in more than eight years. Instead he was lumbered with the wreckage of legend; trials for child abuse which faltered when instincts realized that gifted children will always be children and will always act like children and see the world and other human beings through the eyes of a child, crass crawls to service, or flee from, unimaginable debts. The stupid need to earn a living cemented his approaching passing; were those fifty O_2 concerts always going to be as uncatchable a mirage as Orson Welles' *The Other Side Of The Wind*? Don't we now visualize our imaginations of those concerts as infinitely superior to what any reality would have revealed itself?

But I saw him, at Wembley in 1988, faster, hipper, bolder, lighter than any other entertainer I had ever seen, wearing socks made of angel, and I never thought to look for any strings; the concert was less theatrical – less shiny – than Prince's *Sign "O" The Times* show which I'd caught in Paris a year earlier. But there was never any doubt that he was not equal to the rest of us – either there, or during his demolition of the cozy, shady showbiz facade of *Motown 25*, where he demonstrated to his former employer Berry Gordy how imprudent it was of him to presume to be a second father figure in his life. Look, his feet seemed to smile, what you could have had.

And yet when he emerged from the embryo of the sixties he wanted to be everybody's friend. Listen to that uncomplicated complex simplification of James Brown and "Cloud Nine" that swishes across "I Want You Back" or "ABC" and hear the glow of one who should never need to worry. How he and his brothers allowed the groove to settle, ferment a little, in their Philly years before graduating to "Blame It On The Boogie" and "Shake Your Body (Down To The Ground)", stoking up the fuel and the remembrances, until he finally caught his own chains in 1979 with *Off The Wall*, a pop-up encyclopedia containing everything everyone should reasonably or unreasonably need to know about pop and how to walk it and breathe it; experience his contagious confidence on "Don't Stop 'Til You Get Enough" (with young sister Janet joining in on the percussion, as eventually did the rest of the planet) and feel the ooze of someone who knows that this is his moment.

Off The Wall, aesthetically, was his moment, and there was nowhere for him to go from there except upwards. If the video for "Can You Feel It?" unambiguously pictured him as (a) God, then *Thriller* slowly and subtly confirmed it; sneaking out at the end of 1982, when all thought that New pop had finished, and completely misread for the first few months of its existence (but then "The Girl Is Mine" was perhaps not the best trailer the record could have had), it revealed its hands patiently; "Billie Jean" was already grasping lessons from Martin Fry and Trevor Horn – or Quincy Jones, the Billy Strayhorn to Jackson's Duke Ellington, was there to grasp and advance them – and "Thriller" the song steps up Rod Temperton's warm Britfunk template, chills it and turns it, via the ascending organ chords and Vincent Price's courtly solemnity, into a soulboy equivalent of the ending to Carla Bley's *Escalator Over The Hill*.

Every Michael Jackson album has a deceptively long shelf life, and so *Bad* wasn't as bad as most instantaneously assumed, since Michael and Quincy had listened to Propaganda and they hadn't; also note how the crisscrossing of "P. Machinery" beats and Jimmy Smith's Hammond organ on the title track makes a mockery of the 1987 "argument" between New pop and the faintly ludicrous non-phenomenon of Rare Groove, which valued ancient, unobtainable records and real instruments over living, breathing, machine-friendly musicians. Likewise, *Dangerous* managed to draw lines between swingbeat and The Cocteau Twins. I could go on, but the point is that, as Jackson's stature and godhood grew, his inquisitiveness did not shrink; even in the seemingly unpromising plains of *HIStory* there is ravenous rancor ("Scream" where Jam and Lewis finally get, via Janet, into him), the astonishing Black Power reclamation of "Antmusic" that is "They Don't Care About Us", and oases of unexpected static beauty ("Stranger In Moscow", as profound an example of 1995 melancholy as Blur's "He Thought Of Cars").

And he was expecting to be the new King, and kind of expecting his bigness to be interpreted as holiness – but, as I will never tire of saying, this is the fundamental point and purpose of art; to exceed oneself, to make claims towards God. What was the more egocentric – his 1996 BRIT Awards performance of "Earth Song" or Jarvis Cocker's interruption of it? "Earth Song" plaintively, and then with increasing ferocity, asks questions of the 1967 which spawned it; why haven't we got this golden paradise now? Why, in fact, are we killing everything off, including ourselves? What about Marvin indeed? It's a complex and passionate protest song. Cocker's bum, in contrast, was reductionist, petty, as sarky a tongue stuck out to his better as those which the striking Sheffield miners used to aim at the 21-year-old Cocker attempting to read his Penguin Classics in the local café (and it is significant that Cocker's career began to parachute slowly towards nothingness from this point).

Not that it seemed to bother or stir Michael much, except that after 1995 there wasn't much else; an intermittently interesting but mostly wan remix album, the still (by me) undecided epilogue (as it turned out) *Invincible*. He was gradually compelled to deal with the world, the humbling, humiliating world, the world which baffled him as to why it couldn't simply respect and admire what he could do. If only he could do it again. Maybe those O$_2$ gigs would have formed an astonishing knockout comeback, not to mention the album he had begun to record with Will.i.am of the Black Eyed Peas in the producer's chair. But essentially that half-century of gigs were being performed for the money – or maybe they weren't. Maybe he still felt he had something to prove to his Dad – a father who, like mine, was not averse to violence as a tool for hammering in the assumption of greatness. Perhaps, like my Dad, he had been rehearsing this moment for years, ducking away or bowing out at the last second like the most evanescent of magician's doves.

And of course none of this will, in anyone's end, least of all Michael's, matter. What will matter are his shrieks, gulps and cries of joy (and, occasionally but starkly, sorrow) throughout *Off The Wall*, and especially on its lovely side street of tracks on Side Two – like Stevie Wonder's "I Can't Help It" where he grabs the song and simply swims with it into the sea of swing. The way his socks turned tungsten into pearl. The way he made all of us feel, however feebly we wish to admit it. Particularly when he had to be grown-up, and therefore act human, like the rest of us. We must be careful not to start treating his memory like a child.

The "King" is dead; long live everything else

David Stubbs

The death of Michael Jackson has provoked neither a "Diana moment", nor an Elvis or a Lennon moment. It excited a wild gamut of responses, from psychotic despondency to cruel derision and softer responses in between. Despite the universal fixation on Jackson, it didn't feel like the world stood still, but somehow rushed headlong, at the pace of mobile phone-touting gawpers rushing to the UCLA Medical Center, from one point of speculation to the next.

Many were nauseated at the treacly, mawkish tributes heaped on the superstar, whom they suspected was no more than a common pedophile who had only evaded charges by using his millions to buy off his victims. Others were disgusted at the off-color jokes which spewed in the days following his death, most of which were collated on the website Popbitch. Me, I felt that while Michael Jackson delivered to me the same, incandescent joy as he did millions with "Don't Stop 'Til You Get Enough" and "Billie Jean" *inter alia*, and while being strongly inclined to believe that Michael Jackson was innocent of full-on child abuse and all the sordid penetration that entails, I was glad, from a cultural viewpoint at least, that he was gone. Relieved he is dead. It's hard to have a human response to someone who was never quite human – who was both more than and less than human.

The word "genius" has been bandied about when describing Jackson, while others have described him as the greatest entertainer of all time. Certainly, to watch him glitter and glide and whoop in 1983 as he goes through his robosexual motions at the Motown twenty-fifth anniversary is to be transfixed, in sparkling fits and spurts, in a way that no other pop music has managed. He was mercurial, phenomenal, high wattage indeed. But how much of that is to do with smoke, mirrors, stardust and glitterball, or simply the intensity of the collective gaze, like the rebounding beams of the sun, bouncing back on us, basking in "our" own projection? How much to do with the coy way in which he managed to be ubiquitous and withdrawn at the same time (always on the radio, rarely in the public eye) so that his appearances had the intoxicating, rarefied air of a Second Coming, or transfiguration?

The word "genius" is a nebulous and scientifically useless one in any case but if it's going to be used, it feels more appropriate in the case of a Prince, who was in all aspects his own creation (and indeed, may well be an ex-genius nowadays. Is the condition of genius eternal? Is it a permanent, natural quality or a temporary possession depending on their unique, forceful congruence with the Times they are a Sign Of?). Those reading the tributes to Jackson at his finest 300 years from now might be forgiven for believing that Jackson, too, was the sole author of all his masterworks, that the likes of Quincy Jones and Rod Temperton, born in unsequined Cleethorpes, or even Mick Jackson, the coincidentally named Mancunian composer of "Blame It On The Boogie", had no role to play in his greatest records. They might well believe that Jackson was indeed the inventor of the moonwalk, a myth perpetuated by of all people, Jackson's nemesis Jarvis Cocker on Question Time shortly after his death. In fact, it was debuted by Shalamar's Jeffrey Daniel in 1982 on Top of the Pops. As for variations on that "floating" pedal effect, they can be found on footage dating back to at least World War II, of African-American servicemen dancing to big band jazz, and probably further back than that.

There has been a story doing the rounds of someone spotting a crazed Quincy Jones, doing the recordings of the *Thriller* sessions, kicking around what looked like a crumpled heap of rags on the studio floor which, on closer inspection, turned out to be the prostrate figure of Michael Jackson, screaming "No more squeaks, motherfucker!" In the debatable event that the story's true, it carries with it a nasty, bullying relish, of Jacko the precious, weirdo girl-man getting the bruising to the ribs he deserves, while others would properly argue that much of Jackson's essence lay in those "squeaks", those disingenuously sexual, gratuitous vocal effervescences. However, it does serve as a reminder that Jackson was at his greatest when he ceded creative control to other people. The more he came into his own, the worse he became. It was autonomy, as opposed to his falling apart, that was his undoing. One doesn't have to share the Republican, reptilian sensibilities of P. J. O'Rourke when he dissects the Jackson-penned lyrics of the "We Are The World", the anthem for the Live Aid-connected USA For Africa concerts as performed by a panoply of concerned superstars, in his book of essays *Give War A Chance*, for example.

"We are the world" (solipsism) *"We are the children"* (average age near forty) *"We are the ones to make a brighter day"* (unproven) *"So let's start giving"* (logical inference supplied without argument) *"There's a choice we're making"* (true, as far as it goes) *"We're saving our own lives"* (absurd) *"It's true we'll make a better day"* (See line 2 above) *"Just you and me"* (statistically unlikely)

"That's three palpable untruths, two dubious assertions, nine uses of a first-person pronoun, not a single reference to trouble or anyone in it and no facts," concludes O'Rourke. "The verse contains, literally, neither rhyme nor reason."

"We Are The World" is, by common consent, an early example of "bad" Michael Jackson, which set in like skin rot – well, post-*Bad*, as it happens. "Earth Song" is the other most prominent example. Mourners of MJ were generally swift to bypass these mountainous blemishes and get back to "good" Michael Jackson, the unspoiled pint-sized precocity who fronted The Jackson Five and helped rejuvenate Motown at the end of a war-torn, acid-fried decade. Jackson lovers flocked to YouTube to look up, for example, an orange dungareed young Michael in the spotlight, as his older brothers look on in the background with indiscernible emotions, singing an a cappella version of "I'll Be There" in 1970. It's an awe-inspiring, technically impeccable performance which makes the blood run a little cold. The little boy seems to consist of nothing but frightening talent. He's singing out of his skin – but therein is the problem. Is he already beyond the human pale? It's like contemplating prepubescent muscle-bound boys; the sons of obsessive body builders, pushed beyond any hope of natural development. He's a ten-year-old who has acquired the mannerisms and motions of a performer twenty years his senior, but none of the experience, the interior history, which normally backs up such soulful effusions. He's already strange. On top of everything else, the boy is watching cartoons of himself on television. Richard Williams, the former Melody Maker journalist, reminisced recently about seeing The Jackson Five on an early promotional trip to London, when they were not yet considered that big a commercial deal and journalists had to be induced with beer and treats to come out and see them put through their paces. Williams recalled that the older brothers were co-operative and happy to do interviews. Young Michael, however, sat alone in a corner with a puzzle book, a prisoner behind brown eyes, locked in whatever constituted his self.

(Jackson's reticence in interviews took curious forms. In a justly famous NME piece on Jackson, Danny Baker recalled a press conference in which every question addressed to him by the gathered journalists had to be repeated to him, whispered in his ear, by his younger sister Janet.)

As he entered his very late teens, however, Jackson looked and felt as regular as ever he would. The videos he did with The Jackson Five may look a little spangly and outlandish but no more so than the likes of EWF, Heatwave, etc. in that gloriously crowded, glitterball age. And, with *Off The Wall*, producer and arranger Quincy Jones lent to Jackson an easy, supple, jazzy languor, a loose-limbed swing which courses through the title track, "Get On The Floor", and, of course, the cascading, fountainous, "Don't Stop 'Til You Get Enough", which hits you every time with the same warm splash as it did thirty years ago. Jackson's perfect moment, borne up on a waterspout of falsetto. It's play after work. It's neon and the first drink of the evening. It's urbane joy.

Jackson's little squeaks, testicular whoops and scatty extemporizations were his distinguishing mark, and young women dancing around handbags in late '70s nightclubs would moué them across the dance floor at one another, as if they constituted secret sexual signals. But their provenance, like that of lightning, remains an enigma. Just how was this boy sexual? We'll never really know, would never have known.

The NME described Michael Jackson as "the best singer in the world" around this time but he was still seen as a funk/disco singer, not a breakout artist. He dutifully rejoined The Jacksons for a while prior to 1982's *Thriller*, whose nuclear impact cleaved not just his career but pop and rock before and after. It's a truly remarkable album, though not truly great for all that. It has soft, mawkish lapses, disco filler, "The Girl Is Mine" and, of course, "Beat It", remarkable in that it represents the breaking of the color bar on MTV – it took a slick, noodly Eddie van Halen guitar solo to do that. As it happens, The Isley Brothers had incorporated post-Hendrix guitar into funk almost a decade earlier with their 3+3 album but Jackson is still hailed as a Livingstone in reverse, the first visitor from faraway R&B to shake the hairy white hand of rock.

Of far greater interest than this, Jackson's take on hard rock, is his derivation of soft rock – "Human Nature", co-written by Steve Porcaro of Toto. Bathed in the humid, artificial twilight of the urban west coast, it's a thing of unnatural beauty, with Jackson's vocal shiver arousing an electric frisson across the skin of the song, and the sheen of the '80s production triggering the sort of ecstatic, self-perpetuating, hall of mirrors effect later brought to a high shine on *Scritti Politti's Cupid & Psyche '85*. I may be biased, in that I developed an unaccountable, almost autistic fixation on this particular track when it was released as a single in 1983 during my University days, but it wasn't just me. Miles Davis divined in the song (as well as Cyndi Lauper's "Time After Time") a rich seam of melancholy running fathoms beneath its superficial LA/MOR slickness. It was one of the last songs Davis covered.

However, the moments for which *Thriller* are most commonly remembered are its title track and "Billie Jean". The portents of "Thriller", the monster into which Michael was on the point of morphing, are crude enough, though true enough. In indulging this fantasy and putting it front and center, Jackson is revealed as a creature of absolute soullessness. Great dancing, great vocals, great pumping rhythmic pulse, but it somehow, reveals Jackson in his electric, dead-eyed nothingness – cyber-nought.

"Billie Jean" is a more fascinating case. That taut, ticking bassline reflects the mood of the lyric, seething with controlled fury at an accusation from a fan that he fathered one of her children. There's an intriguing, protests-too-much quality about it, as if the very inference that he is capable, or would partake in, a normal act of human reproduction, insults him to the very glass-fiber of his being. Beyond that, this is the moment at which Jackson loses the languor of *Off The Wall*, begins to seize up, harden and, for the first time, is vulnerable to cracks in the plaster.

Thriller marked huge changes in the interfaces between pop, rock, R&B and MTV. If it marked another of the successive deaths that constitute Michael Jackson's career (as shrewdly lampooned in the satirical US website The Onion's mock-obituary, "Final Piece of Michael Jackson Dies"), then perhaps the album also marks, coincidentally, the death of soul itself. Who, after all, has really made a great, first-hand, stylistically unselfconscious soul record in the last twenty-five years? Has that been possible in the post-*Thriller* climate?

Certainly, Jackson never did. Despite his unnaturally high speaking voice, despite the feminizing as well as bleaching effect of his successive makeovers in the '80s and '90s, Michael Jackson developed a brutally banal fixation on machismo, as if his strongest motion was a repressed and very male humiliation at the spectacle he had made of himself, that his increasingly eccentric actions, once cosseted by millions and a law unto himself, had brought down on him. He was bad, he was dangerous, he was a deeply unconvincing street gangster. He was no longer capable of tender emotions, just stiff motions – a series of impressive but mechanical tricks and tropes. From about hereinafter, it's hard to find images of Jackson performing in which his face isn't screwed up in agonized, masculine contortion. Even when he was doing his "heal the world" shtick, it was raucous, full of *Sturm und Drang* or, on "Earth Song", in the teeth of the imaginary persecution represented by a wind machine. The first half of the video to "Black Or White", meanwhile, morphs all the beautiful peoples and races of the world into one friendly continuum. All this is played out to the new universal/MTV soundtrack of processed and strategically layered guitar, which George Wendt (Norm from *Cheers*) as the stereotype irascible, "doesn't-get-rock'n'roll Dad" finds so annoying when the kid Macaulay Culkin plays it loud in the preamble (and quite rightly, too – ironically, Wendt's own tastes in rock run to the likes of Husker Dü. He actually does get it). The second half of the video, however, in an inexplicable non sequitur, sees Jackson himself morph into a panther and pad out from the studio where the video is being shot onto a deserted, smoky street set that reminds of a cross between something from *The Terminator* and *Singin' In The Rain*. There, he morphs back into himself, then undertakes his entire repertoire of tense, angular robo-moves like they were a set of karate exercises, grabbing constantly at his crotch as if afraid that that's the next part of him that's going to drop off, before smashing a car and nearby window panel to pieces with a crowbar, to a soundtrack of treated growls and grows, half-panther, half-human. Justification for this outburst is offered in the form of some extremely unconvincing pro-KKK graffiti is daubed on the window panel and a swastika on the car windscreen – fascism brings out the primal rage in Michael, we are to understand – but these touches feel for all the world like hasty afterthoughts. The whole sequence comes across like an immaculately set and chore-ographed psychotic episode, conceived and executed at Jackson's behest.

If there's an undercurrent of implacable, inordinate and inappropriate rage inherent in late Michael Jackson, it's certainly inherent in many of his most ardent fans. For a group of people who bandy the word "love" with such frequency, they often appear to be displaying a contrary quality. Like the male fan who, outside the UCLA Medical Center when word of Jackson's condition was taking a while to filter out, exhorted other members of the assembled crowd to smash down the glass front of the building so that they could break in and find out just what "they" were doing to Michael.

In 1988, I reviewed Michael Jackson when he appeared at the old Wembley Stadium. The review noted that as the decade went on, Jackson had taken on a certain corporate plasticity, so to speak, lost forever the easy, natural swagger of the years when he was "merely" a disco star, and now had to negotiate all the deleterious effects of superstardom. However, I concluded, credit to the boy, he'd pulled up his white socks and pulled a great concert out of the fire. I went so far as to say he had been "brilliant". This, however, did not appease one female Jackson fan who called me at Melody Maker shortly after the review appeared. It's over 20 years ago and memory may be playing tricks with me but in essence, the conversation went something like as follows:

ME: Hello?

JACKSON FAN: David Stubbs? Is that David Stubbs? What the fuck are you doing, like slagging off Michael Jackson?

ME: Slag him off? I enjoyed the gig. Did you read the review?

JACKSON FAN: You fucking slagged him, man. What the fuck did you do that for? Who are you, slagging Michael Jackson?

ME: What are you talking about?

JACKSON FAN: Cunt.

ME: I didn't slag him off, I said he was brilliant. That's the last word in the review. "Brilliant". I –

JACKSON: You cunt, you fucking slagged Michael Jackson. Why don't you just fuck off, you fucking cunt? (slams phone down)

This never happened with fans of The Weather Prophets.

There's a long-embedded idea, best put by Fred and Judy Vermorel, that pop fandom, supposedly obsessive and hysterical and fickle and ill-considered, is in fact an authentic wellspring, a trove of secrets and truths undreamt of in the dry musings of ageing music critics. Certainly, to hear the incessant, pealing white wall of noise of teen hysteria, as I did at a Smash Hits awards some years ago, is to be struck by the power of pop fandom as a natural force, as relentless and awesome as the Victoria Falls, and with the same capacity to drown out. If there's any basis for a retort, however, Michael Jackson fans are likely to be at the forefront of those helping provide it. There's a fundamentalism about Jackson fans, way beyond what you'll find in aficionados of Madonna, Britney, Prince, Elvis – an additional, intensely and jealously held conviction that the world is as it patently isn't.

Another charismatic argument, advanced by Nick Cave with regard to Elvis Presley, is that sickness, decline and fall, bloated excess make for a preferable and more interesting spectacle than the rude health and first flush of pop stardom. And so, for Cave, the later, fat rhinestone Elvis, going to Vegas, sweating and forgetting his lines, gorging on giant pizzas as he sat on an exercise bike, tells us more that's more soberly truthful about the (eventual) pop condition than the gyrating young Elvis on the Ed Sullivan Show. Similarly, the argument has been advanced that later Michael Jackson, with his myriad conceits and eccentricities and physical disintegration, tells a more eloquent and tragic story about contemporary superstardom.

Again, maybe so, from some angles, in some respects. However, what's both striking and alarming about Jackson is that all of the monstrous pieties in which he swaddled himself in life and was duly swaddled in death, all the claims he made for himself and which were made on his behalf were in such conspicuous and polar opposition to the truth as to, well, give sickness a bad name.

Take the service following his death, in which we are asked, by a succession of speakers, in particular Al Sharpton, to believe that, frankly, black was white, or in Jackson's case, white was black. Quincy Jones, in an interview with men.style.com, was creditably candid in stating that he never believed Jackson's stories about "chemical peels", describing such talk as "bullshit", and asserting that Michael Jackson clearly did not want to be black ("Look at his kids"). However, at the Staples Center in Los Angeles, there was a clear desire to reclaim Michael Jackson as African-American, despite the avoidance of inconvenient truths and perpetration of preposterous fictions this entailed. And so, Maya Angelou claimed in her poem that Jackson was "sheathed in the love of his family", with a magnificent disregard for the well-documented schism between Jackson and the father at whose hands he suffered years of "discipline". Footage and photos dwelt on the Jackson prior to his pigmentation problems, skating hastily over the last twenty-five years of his fifty-year life. He was portrayed in eulogies as a tireless altruist, the man who "taught us how to love" (Sharpton), a regular family man, a humanitarian whose shining example singlehandedly enabled Barack Obama to come to power. All of these "truths" were held as self-evident. All of which ran counter to the actual details as known of Jackson's life which spoke of a man in the grip of a pantophobic neurosis, addicted to painkillers which would be the envy of any heroin addict, whose many idle hours were spent on whimsical shopping expeditions buying hideous vases for six figure sums, a man who regarded his fellow human beings as toxic as germs. (In Howard Stern's volume, *Miss America*, he recounts visiting Michael Jackson's apartment to meet about an abortive plan for Stern to head up public "Michael is innocent" demonstrations. He recalls Jackson squealing like a smoke alarm when he spotted a domestic underling of whose presence he hadn't been forewarned, washing dishes in his vicinity and having to be ushered from the building by his manager).

Finally, Sharpton assured Michael Jackson's children that their Daddy "wasn't strange". And, once again, it's hard to swat away a crowd of images, leading the charge of which is a man in an oxygen mask dangling a baby out of a hotel window. Really,

8

Michael Jackson at the Restaurant
Vingtième Siècle

Joshua Clover

The Moonwalk in 1981

The first images shown on MTV would also provide its logo
thereafter: public domain footage of the most famous moment in
global television history.

The Documentary in 1985

I'll just come out and say it: Janet's a better dancer. Sure she
borrowed some of his moves. Sure one must also forgive the
whole militaristic *Rhythm Nation* period which was when her
dancing was its most Michaelian anyway. But: "Love Will Never
Do Without You", "You Want This", "The Pleasure Principle".
More athletic acrobatic sinuous. Her fluidity from position to
position has that body portamento we associate not just with
grace but with organic motion. Real time analog humanness. She
can't sing of course. But that turned out to be an occasion for
invention: up against physical limits she figured out a kind of
breathy tussle with the melody leavened with conversational
breaks. I'm not sure Michael had any such limits. When he
chopped words into languageless phonemes he seemed to have
at his disposal some algorithm not yet commercially available.

This is a way of saying that Janet fits the more conventional
metrics. We loved Michael's dancing – after the generic variations first on Motown and then disco choreography but before it
became an icon of itself — but we didn't really have a language

for it. Gertrude Stein's ventriloquized verdict on Picasso: "When you make a thing, it is so complicated making it that it is bound to be ugly, but those that do it after you they don't have to worry about making it and they can make it pretty, and so everyone can like it when the others make it".

Like Picasso and Stein, Michael's influences are none and many. Looming among them is his debt to Gene Kelly's mid-century modern showman; behind that is white Broadway's unspoken debt to black dance traditions. In the essay "Dancin' in the Rain", Carol Clover notes that the 1985 documentary *That's Dancing!* culminates with narrator Kelly celebrating the "Beat It" video. Six years later, as Clover reminds us, Jackson set the notoriously violent coda to the otherwise anodyne "Black Or White" in Kelly's most famous backstreet: "the camera pans and brings into view the telltale lamppost, and when we then see, in close-up, Jackson's feet stamping in puddles on a street that at first seemed dry, we recognize the terrain of Kelly's classic. The connection is sealed when Jackson interrupts his own dance routine to tilt his hat forward, hoofer-mode, and indulge a quick Kelly-style tap sequence." After that – you'll recall – things get weird.

The Umbrella in 1982

But we recognize that hat-tilt from years before. From 1983. It's the opening gesture of Michael's live "Billie Jean" for a global audience. He cants the fedora forward and holds it in its tilt with his one ungloved hand through a brief vamp. Then jettisons it so that things can begin.

We know now that the backslide came down to him from Shalamar's Jeffrey Daniel: there's Daniel on *Top of the Pops* July 1982 popping and locking; some Marcel Marceau and a funny hopping move; and then flowing implausibly backward. In mime gloves. How much of Michael's most famous performance is in this clip in kernel form!

Daniel was a sensation; *Top of the Pops* had him back just a couple weeks later. This time he added props – including a new motivating device for the moonwalk. Umbrella. Strange loop. Viewing the clip at this late juncture it's too good to be true: the magical talisman – the code connector – linking Kelly's title number from *Singin' In The Rain* to Michael's moonwalk. In the British studio Daniel is trying to glide forward into an imaginary wind but it catches his open umbrella and blows him backward into the future – into 1983 – Michael on the stage performing "Billie Jean" at *Motown 25: Yesterday, Today, Forever.*

What then is novel in Michael Jackson's style? Certainly his dancing was less muscular than Kelly's or than Janet's. Daniel is closer: terribly slight, terribly precise. But even Daniel has transitions. Momentum and inertia and centrifugal force. Body portamento. Michael Jackson basically does not.

Jon Pareles gets it half-right in his New York Times obituary: "His dance moves were angular and twitchy, hinting at digital stops and starts rather than analog fluidity except, of course, for his famous moonwalk". He takes the moonwalk for a *misdirection* but it has the digital look too – just differently. In the way of newspapers Pareles lets his incomplete insight fall instantly to the tile and whorl down the drain: a vanishing spiral with the year 1983 at its center.

The Disc in 1983

We loved Michael's dancing but not because it was dancing. It was the new world.

We didn't know it was a new world. We thought we were still analog; that was the context for the dancing's uncanny character. He seemed out of time. Those absolute stops and starts, the frictionless backslide where force and angular momentum seemed to come loose from each other. He patented a stage 'n' shoes gizmo allowing the impossible vertiginous lean forward in the "Smooth Criminal" video: eye-bending at the time but not much longer. Maybe a decade. Once we had all seen the bullet time effect at the movies such effects would lose their interest. Michael's sharp splintering of syllables from words – that seeming of pure sound with edges of impossible fineness – would sound different later when the charts were dominated by songs with phonemes segmented on a hard drive and by the sheer-face bitmaps of Auto-Tune.

But Michael in 1983 was the spectacle of *becoming-digital* in a world that wasn't yet. Sure the transformation had started: a series of background processes haphazard approximations specialty shops. Oddities and fads in a world of oddities and fads – the long Shibuya of capital. From the welter of possibilities he picked out the onrushing digitalization of the world – the world whose endgame is represented in *The Matrix* – and gave it a set of movements. Gave it a body. But to repeat: it wasn't the dancing or music; these were the forms in which an entire way of being become apparent. "Antennae of the race", etc., etc. Periodization made flesh.

Pop music can be divided into three periods: 1) analog acoustic 2) analog electric 3) digital. "Digital" can be divided but its second part is still starting so that can wait. The first era is ruled by the radio and its genius is Bing Crosby (who would be the first major investor in Ampex magnetic tape). The second begins in 1948–9 with the introduction of the 33 and 45rpm vinyl record respectively; its genius is Elvis. The first compact disc is sold in the United States in 1983; *ecce* Michael. These are three of the four most successful singers in history with The Beatles as the fourth. This lends further clarity to Michael's acquisition of The Beatles' catalog and his marriage to Lisa Marie Presley. One must suspect he kept Crosby's skeleton in a storage space somewhere and visited it on Christmas.

The Hive in 1995

Pure products: Axl Rose and Michael Jackson and Kurt Cobain

had consecutive Number One albums (interrupted only by *Achtung Baby*) in a long stretch from 1991–1992.

Already in 1983 "Billie Jean" was about the perils of fame. This would become Michael's main *fixe*. For some reason we were a bit more forgiving of that deal with him than we were with Axl. Kurt died before we could get too aggravated.

Michael had one great song after the '80s, though this required a duet with Janet near the peak of her charms. Behind a (sincere no doubt) mask of anti-racism, "Scream" is a tense and vitriolic plaint about the misery of celebrity and of media scrutiny. It has none of the mordant play with tabloid Jacksoniana contrived in 1989's "Leave Me Alone" – its video set in a spectral double of Neverland Ranch. An amusement park built of two-dimensional rumors from which he eventually breaks free.

By 1995 the scenario of "Scream" is hermetic. Beyond the gravity well. Directed by Mark Romanek for seven million dollars, it's listed as the most expensive video ever made. Michael and Janet flash through a bewildering series of future-interiors where they cavort possessed by a twining of physical delight and hyper-resentment; inevitable given the two leads. The main space is a long cylindrical chamber. Well it's not exactly cylindrical is it? More of a long hexagonal tube – a hollow pencil or an orbital hive – in which the gravity keeps changing such that the siblings are able to leap from wall to wall as if *down* was whichever way they decided moment by moment. The clothes are fantastic, especially the spiky rubber and vinyl ensembles and some faux fur.

Elements designed to recall *2001: A Space Odyssey*, but not only that. Mark Fisher grasps the more pressing context unerringly in describing the setting: "a deserted offworld leisure hive that resembles William Gibson's incest-Xanadu Villa Straylight". He expands on this just briefly to say that only here do Michael's "music and the crumbling mind ever meet".

The reference, as some readers will know, is to the setting for the final section of Gibson's *Neuromancer*: the home of the corporate hyperfamily which is assigned over and over the image of the hive: "The structure of the family is disturbingly analogous to that of an insect hive", etc. As one of its fictional occupants writes: "The semiotics of the Villa bespeak a turning in, a denial of the bright void beyond the hull. Tessier and Ashpool climbed the well of gravity to discover that they loathed space. They built Freeside to tap the wealth of the new islands, grew rich and eccentric, and began the construction of an extended body in Straylight. We have sealed ourselves away behind our money, growing inward, generating a seamless universe of self. The Villa Straylight knows no sky, recorded or otherwise."

The pure products of America go crazy and retreat to fortified strongholds.

The Book in 1984

Acoustic, electric, digital. From this musical progression the larger periodization is clear enough. The earliest era is the transfer of economic and cultural centrality from the UK to the United States. The middle era corresponds to the long postwar boom 1948–73: basically from the introduction of the long-playing record to the breakup of The Beatles plus a few years of after-effect. Like Wings. And then comes the long downturn and the epochal transition to the new economy. The end of industry and the ascent of the service sector. Endless whorls of quantization, digitization, immaterial labor.

There isn't a sentence in *Neuromancer* that isn't about this latter transformation. Every gesture is scored to the collusion and antagonism between on the one hand the industrial, the physical, the analog; and on the other flexible labor, the immaterial, the digital. The assembly line is already cached in the first paragraph as the book lingers over a bartender's prosthetic arm "jerking monotonously as he filled a tray of glasses with draft Kirin": all he needs to do his labor with its single repeated physical motion.

It's there in every pairing the book tosses out. Molly and Case: the bodyguard and the code cowboy. Or Molly and Case when the book begins: the ex-hooker and the ex-hacker. Or Hideo the impossibly skilled ninja vs. Riviera the psychic image projector ("I'm no good with my hands"). The Ashpools and the Tessiers locked away in the Villa Straylight: one committed to the dynastic continuity of the body through a series of clones and incestuous reproduction; the other to preserving the family corporation through an artificial intelligence. Before the climatic battle they gather in the Restaurant Vingtième Siècle. No, really.

The Twentieth Century is just below the Villa Straylight on Freeside: the orbital hive both "brothel and banking nexus". Industry and finance. This is the epochal shift which poses its puzzles for Molly and Case, for Tessier-Ashpool, Société Anonyme, for everyone in the book. For everyone.

The Ranch in 2007

This is why the clip for "Scream" is finally unremarkable despite the effort and expense. The *becoming-digital* had already happened; we were there. *Yes* one thinks *that's something you can do with a computer.* Sic transit dude. Sic transit. The world was digital or post-Fordist or flexiblized or the dozen other catchy names which turn out to be both literal and metaphorical – exactly as befits the specific transition from industry to service economies. From material to information economies. Michael Jackson danced this transformation and sang it too, more intensely and more precisely than anyone else and this is why he is Michael Jackson, and not Jeffrey Daniel or Janet Jackson.

Surely he believed he was the architect of his own destiny just as he was the disastrous architect of his own physiognomy. But "he had never been so much in the grip of inevitable laws, which compelled him, while thinking that he was acting on his own volition, to perform for the hive life – that is to say, for history – whatever had to be performed." Tolstoy's verdict on Napoleon.

The changes clustered here – the changes Michael performed on behalf of the hive – have arrived at their own conclusions and guttered out as historical dynamics must. The economic catastrophe we are currently dating to somewhere around 2007 is the outcome of inevitable laws and compulsions: the increasing distance between the "real economy" and the lately turbid whorls of finance. Or: the outcome of a declining rate of industrial profit. Michael danced that too. He lived it absolutely – peeling off Michael Jackson of smokestacked Gary, Indiana, and of Motown the exemplary industrial city and returning as Michael of Los Angeles and Dubai but more so Michael of *Thriller*. Michael of Everywhere-Nowhere. Michael of Neverland.

It begins in digitization quantization finance. It ends in bad debts credit blow-ups foreclosures across the map. The derelict Victorians of Detroit and mortgages under water in Kissimmee. California as always led the way in sheer volume. Santa Barbara County is a representative case – neither at the top nor the bottom of the crisis curve. In the city of Santa Maria in 2007 Marcos Alvaro fell $8,529 delinquent on his home and was foreclosed on October 12. A fortnight later one Christina Reyes met the same fate for a delinquency of $4,543. Between these two a property in Los Olivos was foreclosed owing $23,212,963 on a loan of $23m. Helicopters hovered over the hive. It was the end of something. This too was a way of embodying the latest transformation – intense exaggerated and awful, though in this case the owner, who was not listed as a resident, was more a part of the mutation than its avant-garde.

decade-and-a-half form, in the popular imagination, a moral counterweight. Defy nature, and your face will fall off! The fable is so compelling that one wonders to what extent Jackson himself may have connived at it, recognizing that the fan's adoration of other-worldly talent requires compensation in the form of lurid displays of all-too-human weakness. There must be something to pity, and defend, in the object of such fantastic projections.

Every angel is frightful, eventually. But Jackson was never an ogre, and resisted media demonization with something of the same slickness that lubricated his dance routines. He could be "wacko", disconnected from reality, but never quite convincingly fitted into the stereotypes of the showbiz tyrant or predatory pervert. The "tyrant" is a monster of insecurity, hysterically self-important because he fears that, without public recognition and acclaim, his self is literally nothing. To say that Jackson's public persona displayed an evident megalomaniac streak is to venture an understatement, but this does not appear to have manifested itself privately in selfish tantrums directed at lackeys; musicians who worked with him speak of him kindly, as well as admiringly, as an otherworldly figure of some gentility. The "pervert" has sick appetites, and a compulsion to satisfy them which overrides the restraining force of social norms: he is an enemy of society, and calls for a disciplinary response. Jackson never appeared to be a creature of appetite, for all his compulsive accumulation of baubles. What did he want from the children he was accused of seducing? He seems to have wanted, above all else, to be a child with them. But what can that possibly have meant to him?

In the video for "Don't Stop 'Til You Get Enough", Jackson is still recognizably the staggeringly-gifted child who commanded incredulous admiration in The Jackson Five, a creature of youth and lightness whose performance defies emotional gravity. His real childhood, a nightmare of physical and emotional abuse, is pushed out of the scene: not because it is repressed, but because the momentary joy of what he is able to do with his voice and his body aboundingly surpasses it. What dominates the performance is not the iron discipline and restraint necessary for its choreographed enactment, but the *sprezzatura* with which it is brought off. Steven Shaviro calls this kind of surpassingly joyful *rightness* an aesthetic "singularity", and suggests that it "becomes a kind of universal value", short-circuiting both "the sources from which it arose" and the mediations through which it is presented. These remain present, effective, exhaustively traceable even; but it is not they that provide the performance with its evanescent signature.

This short-circuiting breaks with the usual contexture of identity, which is a matter of being positioned and formatted in a way that makes the object intelligible to discourses of cultural identification. The aesthetic singularity is just or justly itself, insistently itself, a form of testimony to its own self-being. It may at the very same time be a trick of the light. Jackson's performance does not testify to the existence of anything more substantial than itself; in particular, there is no subterranean racial or sexual essence oozing up through it. Hence its ability to "cross over" culturally, to be a "universal value" for the broadest possible constituency of fans. Among the cultural functions it performs is that of assuaging guilt, rendering temporarily harmless and inconsequential the immense harms and harmful consequences which belong to American culture's history of violence. The ideological *usefulness* of this will not have escaped anyone's attention, and the claim that Jackson's fame and success were the projected results of an immense apparatus of smoke and mirrors is hardly contrarian. A show-child become showman, Jackson was perfectly schooled in exploitation. But that which was so exploited was nevertheless his gift, which was nevertheless dazzling.

In a brief Nietzschean analysis of "dance as a metaphor for thought", Alan Badiou proclaims with typical lyricism that "dance is innocence, because it is a body before the body. It is forgetting, because it is a body that forgets its fetters, its weight...it is also play, of course, because dance frees the body from all social mimicry, from all gravity and conformity." This figure of *innocence* bears examination, because the question concerning Michael Jackson seems to be precisely one of *nuisance* or noxiousness. So much speculation both before and after his death turned on the precise nature and location of the worm in the apple, the proximity of hidden corruption to superficial perfection, so that metaphorically speaking the distress of the surface, its visible attrition, was always referred to an invisible deterioration, fruit of the silent rot beneath the skin. This is not always how we understand fading or damaged beauty, but it is how we moralize about it when we want to see it as a punishment, as the revenge of "gravity and conformity" on that which refuses to age gracefully. According to this gothic stereotype, Jackson's deceased body should have desiccated instantly to grey dust and been swept away by howling winds.

Was he ever innocent? It is possible to see the whole of the Neverland ranch, with its fairground rides and its explicit reference to Peter Pan, as an extravagant protestation of innocence; although Jackson in later life resembled Pan less than a mangled Tinkerbell for whom all but the most devoted audiences had ceased applauding. No doubt someone had told him at some point, "it's never too late to have a happy childhood"; but it was always too late for that debauched child to become "the boy who never grew up". The naivety of those who permitted him access to children on the understanding that he himself was somehow childlike (and therefore harmless) seems wondrous. They were not so much duped, however, as colluding in a fable of innocence regained, virginity restored. We should perhaps understand Jackson's cosmetic surgery as *reconstructive*, as an attempt to materialize an imaginary "body before the body" that his real, increasingly damaged body had somehow replaced or occluded. This is just the kind of fantasy project that a celebrity quasi-deity is well-placed to undertake on behalf of his fans, feeding on their collusive psychological investment in order to provide it with the sublime object it requires. Any analysis of Jackson's dysphoric relationship to his real body (such as is typically framed in terms of racialized self-hatred) needs to take this dynamic of collusion into account.

Jackson's later career seems increasingly built on collusion (and credit, its little plastic friend), a massive extension of the scope of his psychosis. If "Don't Stop 'Til You Get Enough" defied emotional gravity, "Bad" and almost everything that came afterwards *denied* it, initially with panache (as in "Smooth Criminal") but with an increasingly vaudevillian implausibility as time went by. There was occasionally something to celebrate even in that. Certainly one should not treat Jackson as simply "in denial", the hapless prisoner of his own psychic fortifications. He had a talent for vaudeville too.

We might say that the distance from "Thriller" to "Earth Song" is that between sincere playfulness and insincere gravity, the value accorded to sincerity rising in inverse proportion to the ability of the masque to support it. Much of our "light" enter-tainment slides along this scale, from the effervescently camp to the wearyingly sentimental. At the camp pole, emotional seriousness is held in abeyance by invention: lightness, speed and infinitesimally precise timing, Jackson's great virtues as a dancer and musical performer. "Thriller" is crisp, urgent and dramatic; what it has in common with "Don't Stop 'Til You Get Enough" is a certain infectious excitement about itself ("oh wow," it seems to say, "it's that "Thriller" song! I love that one!"). At the sentimental pole, a tremulous force of emotional uplift is mustered against the defeats and sorrows of the world, to which it is never remotely equal. "Earth Song" blusters along with a wholly rhetorical self-importance ("what about *us*?"), posing as a sort of messianic convocation of the forces of peace, love and universal goodwill against a global malevolence that is never quite named. It is insincere precisely in its conjuration of sincerity, its demand that the listener feel sincerely towards it.

The center of moral gravity in "Earth Song" is consciousness of a wrong that has been done to the world, a consciousness that "we" lack but can be rhetorically summoned to raise in ourselves and others. Our sincerity about this task is a sincerity of conscience: a production like "Earth Song" is morally uplifting insofar as it "makes us think" about ecological issues. The song's litany of "what about…?"s reminds us, in no particular order and with no particular sense of relative moral urgency, to be concerned about the destruction of the Amazonian rainforest, the killing of elephants for their tusks, and *war*. The overarching theme is our failure to make time in the present for the future promised to our children: we are renegades with respect to the promise that we ourselves, as members of the human community, have inherited from previous generations. It is Jackson himself, stamping his feet and raging at ecological destruction, who demands *in the name of children everywhere* that this promise be renewed and fulfilled.

This demand is insincere – and cannot be otherwise without absurdity – for two reasons. The first is that "Earth Song" suspends entirely the question of causal responsibility for ecological destruction; it propounds a global *moral* responsibility, but entirely shirks the task of identifying any relationship between, for example, the extravagant expenditure of energy involved in its own creation and distribution, and the conflict and devastation it deplores. The second is that the song's moral demand is articulated from a position of moral innocence, that of a child or child-proxy. When it asks "what have we done to the world?", this "we" is implicitly understood not to include the subject of enunciation: Jackson is ventriloquizing an audience who must be "made to think". The fan who identifies with Jackson himself is not interpellated by the song's rhetoric, but joins with him in addressing it to others.

The video for "Earth Song" closes with ecological destruction running in reverse: elephant tusks re-growing, smoke sucked back into the industrial chimneys from which it belched. The fantasy of innocence regained, of a pure "body before the body" taking the place of the wounded body of the earth, is depicted with an almost comic literalism. The tragedy of Jackson's later career was that he was seduced by the wrong innocence, opting to play out this fantasy of repealing experience rather than concentrating and surpassing it through aesthetic singularization. The latter has its own innocence, its own achieved innocuousness, which does not derive from labored denial and botched attempts at purification – but from the profound simplicity of joy.

10

True enough:
Michael in fifty shards

Chris Roberts

1

As soon as he can walk and talk and sing and dance, Michael is keen to invent the elixir of eternal youth. It's like a calling. In the bedroom he shares with some of his brothers he has a science kit, and whenever they're out he goes to work. He takes a small test-tube and in it mixes honey, emeralds, stardust and the tears of babies. Over the years he tweaks the ingredients, makes small experimental adjustments to the recipe, but finds no success. Wild-eyed, ill-dressed, hair unkempt, he covers blackboards with impenetrable formulae written in chalk. Sometimes he will be at a party and mutter "Excuse me" then distractedly scribble notes and equations on the tablecloth or on a handkerchief. As years turn into decades he keeps on trying, refusing to give up. He grows ever more frustrated. He grows ever more desperate. He grows.

2

Michael emerges from a rocket ship in the summer of 1997, dressed as an astronaut made of gold. "I'm hot," he thinks. He notices he is on stage in a vast stadium and 75,000 hysterical people are screaming and staring at him. "I don't like sweat," he thinks. "It spoils my lines." He stands still. "My crotch is itchy." He stands still longer than he had planned to. Fireworks cascade around his head and shoulders. The people go berserk. "This is strange," he thinks. "I could just stand here, rigid, for ages. They love it." He tests his theory. The longer he just poses there, immobile, the more the people shriek and weep and tear at their hair. Almost two minutes go by. He throws an arm out to the left then snaps it back and freezes again. The people jump, faint, fall over. He never catches anybody's eye if he can help it, but right now he catches the eye of a girl in the front row. She is full of joy, and looks terrified, distressed. "I am so hot," he thinks again. "I'm uncomfortable when I'm this hot." Yet he gets on with the show, as he always has done. He dances. He sings. He hangs from a crane high above the stadium. "I enjoy this," he thinks, "but I'd rather be able to fly. Properly fly." A tank bursts through a stage wall and Michael holds up a palm and it stops. A soldier jumps out of the tank and a little girl gives him a flower and he lays down his weapons. "This is going well," thinks Michael. "This is a good one." More fireworks.

In the wings, Michael gets snappy with his second assistant wardrobe person, who is taking fourteen seconds instead of the allocated twelve to change his boots for him. "Come on," mutters Michael. "Come on, come on." A note of whininess creeps into his voice.

"I'm sorry," says the second assistant wardrobe person, now confused as to whether her priority is to apologize or to hurry up, and thus managing neither to the best of her ability.

"It's OK," whispers Michael, "I love you." Two hours later the second assistant wardrobe person goes home and fucks her boyfriend, a graphic designer she's been seeing for three weeks, and gets on top for the first time. Her boyfriend is pleased and his hands knead the duvet as her cat, Jemima, leaps away. Somewhere else, Michael is by now looking at a bowl of fruit. He contemplates a banana. He picks it up, puts it down again. He takes a few grapes and eats them but finds them less pleasurable than he'd hoped. Jermaine walks over slowly, scratching his cheek, and says, "Brother, you're the King." Michael fiddles with his belt. "Yes," he says. "I am, aren't I? I am the King."

"It's good to be the King," smiles Jermaine.

"Pardon me?" says Michael. But Jermaine has moved away to talk to somebody off the television. Michael surveys all before him. He thought he would be happier than this.

3

Katharine gives birth in 1958. She is not comfortable. She is not comfortable at all. "Sweet Jesus," she gasps between breaths, "Sweet Lord. Oh my." She thinks, "It doesn't get any easier, no matter how many times you do it." Michael is born. A skylark flies overhead. Katharine exhales for what seems to her like the first time in days. Michael cries without guile. Katharine composes herself as best she can, wipes the spit and snot and sweat from her face with the back of her arm, and holds him. "Funny-looking head" she thinks. He has huge brown eyes, long hands. He looks at her. She loves him.

4

Katharine watches Michael in the kitchen. The little boy is dancing to the rhythm of the washing machine. He is dancing like a healthy adult, completely coordinated. Katharine ponders reincarnation. She laughs to herself. "Are you dancing like James Brown, little man?" she says. "Are you? You are, aren't you? Yes, you are, my little baby angel". The doorbell rings. Katharine looks at Michael one more time then goes to answer it. It is a black man, about forty, a stranger, bleeding from the forehead and experiencing stress. "Oh!" exclaims Katharine. "Oh! You must come in, poor man. Come in, sit down." Compassionately, she tends to him in the kitchen. Michael stops dancing and watches. The man says, "I was robbed and beaten. I've knocked on every door in this street and you're the only good person who hasn't shooed me away." Katharine bathes his brow. Michael starts dancing again. "Oh," laughs the man, feeling better, "he's good!"

"Yes," agrees Katharine. "And he sings too." The man asks Michael if he'll sing for him. Michael shakes his head, purses his lips. He wants his brothers, who are at school, to come home now. The man thanks Katharine for her kindness and leaves. Michael bursts into song. Katharine wonders about her boy until the others return from school, when reflection and thought are lost in the hubbub and chaos and activity of their family life. Spoons and forks click and chime against plates and dishes. During the evening meal, Joseph remembers to ask Katharine how her day was. "Quiet," she says. "Michael danced again."

"That's good," mutters Joseph, trying not to talk with food in his mouth. "That's good." He chews his fish. "Number seventeen said there was a beggar in the street," he says, "with dirt all over him and blood in his hair. You know anything about that?" Joseph is himself surprised at how aggressive and accusatory his tone is.

"No," says Katharine softly, "I wouldn't know anything about that. We wouldn't know anything about that, would we, Michael baby?"

Michael understands that he is being addressed but cannot grasp the sense of the words. Although he knows he is not supposed to, he dips his finger into the bowl of mashed potato and points it, potato-swaddled, at his father. Michael laughs but his father does not.

5

Michael and his brother Marlon are staying at Diana Ross's house in 1969. Berry Gordy has put them there. Every day they rehearse, record, are coached, styled and groomed. Diana is often busy but, when available, she mentors the young boys. "Diana?" says Michael one evening, "What is being a famous star really like?"

Diana smiles graciously and composes her answer. "It's wonderful, Michael dear," she coos. "It's magical. It's the greatest feeling on Earth. I am so grateful for the many ways in which I've been blessed. I go out there on that stage, or in that TV studio, and I soak up all the love. I swim in it, I bask in it, I let it caress me all over my lean body. I let it touch me and then I touch it back. I feel it in my heart and in my soul too. It is in many ways sexual, but you will learn about that in due course. It is a flame. It is a glow. Also, many of the more perceptive socio-cultural commentators believe I have accomplished much for the promotion of the Civil Rights movement."

Michael assimilates her response. He loves Diana. She is a goddess to him. "And Diana," he asks, "Is Berry Gordy a god?"

"Oh yes," replies Diana confidently, "he is, and you would be wise beyond your years to always do whatever he tells you to do. And you are wise beyond your years, aren't you, Michael, my love?" Michael blushes.

"Yes Diana," he says. "Yes, if you think I am, I must be."

"Good boy," purrs Diana, her waist as slim as a gentleman's tie, her diamonds as shiny as light itself. "I will take you to Disneyland again tomorrow."

"I love you, Diana," says Michael.

"I love you too, Michael," says Diana. Marlon enters the room, bashfully.

"Miss Diana Ross," he says, "please may I have some water?"

"Shut up!" shouts Diana. "Go back to your room, child, and wait 'til I tell you to come out."

"But... but I only wanted some water..." splutters Marlon.

"I'm not telling you again!" barks Diana Ross. "You're not too big for me to put you over my knee and tan your hide. Can't you see I'm talking to Michael here? Leave this room instantly before my vexation overcomes me!" Marlon hesitates, then turns to leave. "I mean it!" hollers Diana Ross, and at this moment Michael's awe knows no bounds.

Later that night, Marlon wets a bunch of paper towels, creeps over to Michael's bed, then squashes the sopping, dripping towels into Michael's face. "I hate you!" shouts Michael.

"No, I hate you!" shouts Marlon.

"I hate you more!" shouts Michael.

"No, I hate you more!" shouts Marlon. "And Diana is a witch!"

Michael thinks hard. "I...," he begins. He falters. "I...," he tries again, struggles again. "Hmmm." He thinks. He breathes. "I love you, Marlon," he says. Marlon is confused, disarmed. He goes back to his bed and lies down. He lets his thoughts work themselves out in his head. About twenty minutes later he says, "I'm sorry, Michael, my brother. I love you too." But Michael is asleep and doesn't hear him.

Or: Michael is just pretending to be asleep, pretending not to hear.

Or: Michael is dreaming about Diana, and fantasizing about being exactly like her one day.

Or: Michael softly says, "It's OK, Marlon. Love is all around us and love is everywhere and in and of all things."

Or: Marlon says, with increasing urgency, "Did you hear me? Did you hear what I said? You hear me? Michael? Michael?"

6

"Congratulations, boys," says Berry. "Four consecutive number one hits in one year. This is Dream City. We are making a difference." Michael's brothers whoop. His parents whoop. Diana whoops. The adults drink champagne and Michael and Marlon drink cherry soda. Michael's father, on his way to the bathroom, clips Michael around the ear, twice, for no discernible reason. "I know I'm tougher on you than I am on the rest," he explains, "but that's because I believe in you."

One of the adults has a bawling baby in her arms and Michael looks over at it. "What a funny thing that is," he thinks. "Why do people do that? Why would anyone choose to kill the planet by overpopulating it? Is it because they want to leave something behind and can offer nothing else; no talent, no true legacy? Is it just ego? Is everybody stupid?"

One of his brothers comes over. He is sweating. "Hey, Michael," he says. "Great fake-sob on "I'll Be There" the other day. You want some more cherry soda there little brother?"

"Nah," says Michael, "I'm good."

7

Michael and his brothers are on the road, or in the recording studio, or the TV studio. It is tiring but they are young. Michael is very young. He is eleven. Everybody seems pleased with him. People frequently scream in his face, but in a good way. Except his father, who is never satisfied. He makes Michael vomit.

It is 1 a.m. in a hotel in Las Vegas. Michael is sleeping, but then is woken by noises outside the hotel room door. He discerns the voices of a couple of his older brothers and one other, strange, voice. Then, abruptly, the door is pushed open. Michael sits bolt upright in his bed. He is wearing a red t-shirt with yellow sleeves and pajama pants. Three people bundle into the room, turning the light on. "Got a little treat for you, little brother!" says one of his brothers.

"A big treat!" laughs the other.

With them is a groupie. "It's time you became a man," says the first brother. Both brothers laugh a lot. The groupie looks neither bored nor excited. She is just there. Michael feels uneasy as the three move closer to his bed, but he thinks, "If I get out of bed, I'm not safe. I'm probably safer if I stay in bed." His brothers lift him up by his arms, out of the bed. "Do what you gotta do, brother," laughs one. Michael is left standing in the middle of the room facing the groupie, who now looks quizzical. "Hey," she says. Michael has wrapped his arms around himself.

"Hey," he says.

She steps towards him. "You are so cute," she says, smiling.

"I don't want this!" shouts Michael. "I don't like this!" He half-runs to the door and tries to open it, but it's been locked. His brothers are sniggering outside. "Let me out!" he yells. "Let me out, let me out, let me out!" His brothers only laugh some more. Behind Michael the groupie sits on the bed, unsure what to do next. "Let me out," says Michael once more, quietly this time. He hears his brothers walking away down the hall. He turns around and sees the groupie sitting on the bed. "Is it OK if I smoke?" she says. Michael sits on the floor with his back to the door and shrugs. He is a little tearful. She says, "It's OK, it's OK. I'm not gonna hurt you." They stay like this for five minutes or so and then Michael curls up into a ball on the floor. After another few minutes the groupie says, "I guess I'd better go, huh?" Michael stands up and holds out his hand. They shake hands. She chuckles and shakes her head. She goes to the door but it's still locked. "Fuck," she says. "They took the keys, right?" Michael just wants to be alone. "I don't know," he says.

"I'm gonna use the phone, OK?" she says gently. "I'm just gonna use the phone to get out of here and then I'm gone, OK sweetie?"

"OK," says Michael. He stands against the bathroom door chewing his lip while she calls reception and gives them a version of her predicament. It's another five minutes before somebody comes and takes her away. Michael opens a window and gets back into bed but it feels different now so he gets out again and lies down on a coat on the floor and starts humming.

8

"Michael!" says Tatum O'Neal. "I am a child star growing up. You are a child star growing up. We have so much in common that no-one else in the world could fully comprehend. Wanna get it on?"

"My friend," says Michael, "my friend, I love you, but I'm not ready."

9

Sidney Lumet is on the set of *The Wiz,* directing it. Activity and noise whirl around him; extras whistle "Follow The Yellow Brick Road" irritatingly. "This is not working," thinks Sidney. "Damn it to high hell, this is not working. Why is this not working? I have done some truly great stuff. I am a master. And Quincy is quite good at music. Why can we not get a handle on this? Anyhoo, better stick it together with tape and glue as well as I can and hope to fix it in the edit."

In his trailer, not far away, Michael gazes into the mirror. "This will be the making of me," he thinks contentedly. "This film will be what takes me to the next level; from teenage star to celluloid icon and internationally acclaimed solo artist and mature all-round performer. When they look back on my glittering career, this film will, I expect, be the first thing everybody speaks about. It will be the watershed moment. They will say: *The Wiz* launched Michael as the leading screen actor of his generation. They will say: his performance as The Scarecrow was a performance which critics in countless countries described as "heartwarming", while others plumped for "funny and touching". They will say: without *The Wiz,* there would have been no Michael as Peter Pan, Michael as Hamlet, Michael as Batman, Michael as Harvey Milk, Michael as the guy in *There Will Be Blood,* Michael as Willy Wonka, Michael as Dracula, Michael as Jesus, Michael as Gandhi, Michael as the young Obama. *The Wiz* was Michael's defining moment."

10

Quincy Jones is at the desk, watching Michael sing "She's Out Of My Life" in the booth. It is his fifth take. The first four were fantastic but Quincy tells him to do it again because after a tricky start he has established a hierarchy here and he feels they'll get better overall results if Michael ultimately defers to his judgment. On every single take, Michael cries, for real. The fifth is great too. Quincy cannot think of anything he has to gain by saying, "OK, and another one." So he says, "Great, Michael, great, sounding swell, come through and have a listen."

Later that day Michael says, "Quincy, did you think about what we were saying?"

"What's that, Michael?" says Quincy. Michael takes a deep breath. "I really sincerely from the heart with all honesty think we should keep the intro with the cool bass line on "Billie Jean". It makes me want to dance. It'll make other people want to dance."

"Michael," sighs Quincy, "kid. We've discussed this. You want hits. I want hits. No indulgent, boring intros. I'm here because I know this business. I have a wealth of experience, an impressive track record, and I've worked with the best. We cut it straight into the first verse, clean. No nonsense." Michael sulks. Michael sulks for forty days and forty nights, goes on hunger strike for years, wears forks in his hair, gets Bianca Jagger and Lauren Bacall and Ava Gardner and even Mark Lester to leave blank messages on Quincy's phone in the middle of the night, rains locusts down on his house, won't stop hiccupping, drums on the recording console with one of the forks from his hair for eleven hours, cries and hums and stamps his feet, gets his own way. "Oh, all right!" exclaims an exasperated Quincy after a minute or two of this. "I give up. You win. "Billie Jean" can keep the intro with the cool bass line. But it's a bloody foolish error of judgment, you mark my words." There is an awkward silence. "By the way," says Quincy. "Is it true this song is about Paula Abdul?"

"Quincy," says Michael, "Sometimes I think you must be high."

11

"*Off The Wall* was not big enough," Michael protests to Quincy. "I want this one to be bigger."

"Ach," says Quincy. "Come on. Get real. There are limits."

"No," says Michael, "there are not. This will be my biggest thing yet. It will be the biggest thing in the history of the world to date. I am here to save the world and all its children."

"You have to understand the way the industry works," says Quincy.

"I do not," states Michael. "And I simultaneously laugh and cry at this weakness you call "a sense of perspective". This one will be so big it will make cats swim the backstroke and Boccioni and Severini paint gardens in pastels."

"Sheesh," sighs Quincy, "OK, let's see what we can do." He cracks his knuckles and books the string section and powers up the mixing desk but Michael has already started.

Michael is hiring the armies of Persia and Constantinople. He is sweet-talking Helen of Troy and Elizabeth Siddal. He has glued the Taj Mahal and the Petronas Towers, which are not even built yet, to the top of the Great Wall of China. He is lining up forty four monster trucks and a fleet of Panzers. He has a Jumbo Jet on the way and also a Concorde except, look, the Concorde is already there. He has locked down a brass band and the combined intelligence of James Joyce, Louis Pasteur, Charles Darwin and Sigmund Freud. "Freud," declares Michael, "I want you to bring along your genitals, I mean notebooks." Michael has also placed himself in charge of catering. He orders ten thousand cupcakes, five million lollipops, fourteen hundred Viennese steaks and a lorry load of cherry soda. Pepsi call up to ask why he hasn't asked for an ocean of Pepsi, gratis. "I wouldn't touch that muck!" he flounces.

"But we are your sponsors," argue Pepsi.

"This is art," snaps Michael, "Deal with it." He orders mountains and lakes and clouds. He books planets and moons and comets; a constellation or two. Inspired and enthused, he asks for Frank Sinatra and Aretha Franklin and The Great Caruso and Cab Calloway and Michelangelo and Da Vinci, but they can't make it because they have pressing engagements. "How about the bloke from Heatwave?" suggests Quincy.

"OK," says Michael.

The album is a great success and goes on to sell a bigger number of copies than the number of human beings there have ever been, or ever will be, on Earth. Its numbers are bigger than the number of grains of sand or blades of grass or drops in the ocean or molecules or atoms. Its numbers are so big that if you laid them end to end they would cover the length of Reese Witherspoon's chin two times over.

The vast popularity of the album – and a video in which he plays a zombie with a peeling face – messes with Michael's head somewhat. For a period after this, he thinks he is Nero, or Caligula, or Caesar, or Hannibal, or Boudicca. Sometimes, when he believes himself to be out of the public gaze, he can be witnessed juggling panthers while roaring and beating his chest.

12

Percentage chart of the texture of Michael's voice on the song "Human Nature":

Silk 14%; grace 12%; effortlessness 11%; a solitary reed going slowly over Victoria Falls 5%; how nice it feels to him when he touches his own private parts 17%; technique 25%; the fur on the back of a young marsupial 7%; oysters 3%; petals 4%; dewdrops 1%; *droit de seigneur* 1%.

13

Racism is wrong. Racism is upsetting Michael. Having offered a cover story interview to Rolling Stone, only for them to respond by stating that black people on the cover of magazines don't sell, he feels very cross. "I'll show them," he thinks. "Pretty soon their ball will come over the wall into my garden and they'll be begging me to give it back to them. And I'll hold the ball, I'll keep them waiting, and keep them waiting some more. I'll make them wonder if I'm ever going to give them their ball back.

Maybe I'll destroy their ball, with a knife or a pin or something. Maybe I'll give it to my python to play with. Or maybe I'll tell them they can have their ball back intact only if they agree to meet my terms and conditions and display proof that they are willing to modernize, to move with the times. They can maybe have their ball back if there is a seismic shift in the consciousness of popular culture. Yep, that sounds about right." The Reverend Al Sharpton calls up. "Somebody found my record not to their musical taste," says Michael.

"Racists!" screams The Reverend Al Sharpton. "Solely because of the stand you are taking, Michael," states The Reverend Al Sharpton, "a man named Barack Obama will one day be President of The United States of America and Leader Of The Free World."

14

Michael is dazzled by Elizabeth Taylor. Like Diana Ross before her, with whom he has now fallen out, she is the glamorous Hollywood celebrity mother he wishes he'd had. "Marry me, Elizabeth," he pleads. To him, there is nothing freaky about this at all. Michael is delightfully unconventional. "You are my best friend," says Elizabeth, "and I am always here for you. I love you. But I am too old, my precious boy, to be your wife."

Michael thinks, "I must put more hours in on the elixir of eternal youth." They watch a video of *National Velvet*. Then they watch *Suddenly Last Summer*. "Are you sure?" says Michael. "Yes dear," says Elizabeth, sipping gin. "Besides, I feel it is my destiny to one day meet somebody called Larry Fortensky."

"Fair enough," shrugs Michael.

His manager calls. "I really feel you should hang out with Brooke more often," his manager says. "Whatever," says Michael. Elizabeth burps.

15

"Michael," says Brooke Shields, "I was a child star. You were a child star. We have so much in common that no-one else in the world could fully comprehend. Do you find me attractive?"

"Yes!" says Michael, too quickly, too fiercely, and therefore unconvincingly. "Brooke, of course I do!

"You're... you're... beautiful." He wonders if this is enough. He coughs. He thinks, "She is. She is attractive." Behind his back he makes a half-fist and digs his nails into his palm, though he is not conscious of this. Brooke doesn't smile. She appears wistful, faintly sad. Brooke is thinking, "I must be ugly. I must be really ugly. Perhaps as ugly as an old boot that's been left in a muddy ditch in the rain for weeks on end in wintertime and sniffed at by badgers. What is wrong with me?" Brooke summons to mind all the reviews that have referred to her as a provocative sex kitten, or the modern-day Lolita, and tries to allow them to make her feel good about herself, but today they're not working. Indeed lately she has begun to doubt their levels of appropriateness. She tilts her head to one side and her elegant right hand runs through her lustrous hair. She blinks more than is necessary. "Michael?" she says.

"Yes, Brooke?" says Michael.

"Do you think we should kiss?" says Brooke, who feels a need to know, to leap out of limbo. Michael breaks their gaze and looks down at the ground. Long seconds pass. "Brooke," he says. "Darling," he says. "You know I have to look after my voice," he says.

16

Michael's hair catches fire during a pyrotechnic accident as he shoots a big commercial. It hurts like hell. His scalp is burning up. "Ow!" exclaims Michael, and this is entirely reasonable. "Ow! Ow! Ow! Help me!" His head is doused, though not as quickly as it might have been, and he is rushed to hospital, suffering second degree burns. His hair and his appearance and – yeah why not – his psyche are never quite the same again. Have you ever experienced what it feels like to have your head on fire? Physically, not metaphorically? Do not pretend you have. You have not. Unless you are a firefighter, or a soldier, or an innocent civilian caught in the crossfire between two warring factions, and if any of these are the case then you have our respect and sympathy, because that is only proper and right. Or maybe you are a circus act, so yes, you know what it feels like, but somehow you don't elicit as much respect or sympathy because you are doing it voluntarily and we suspect there may be some trickery or smoke and mirrors or sleight of head involved. But the rest of you, you cannot begin to guess what it feels like. You cannot imagine. It changes you. Something shifts inside.

Some have suggested that it is this very moment which ruins everything, which places the worm in the apple, the slithery hissing fork-tongued serpent in Eden. But you have to be very wary when dealing with mythology, because it can be a magnet for unreliable narrators.

17

Unreliable narrators can be frustrating. Examples of unreliable narrators: Nick Carraway in F. Scott Fitzgerald's *The Great Gatsby*, Matthew, Mark, Luke, John, conspiracy theorists, the curators of the rock and roll canon, characters in films who turn out to have been dead all along, the world's media. There are many who believe that Michael's accusers, those who accused him in court and out of court of very bad things, were unreliable narrators. Equally, there are many who believe that Michael's lawyers, who defended him in court against those accusations, were unreliable narrators. There are grey areas. It can get confusing. Sometimes you just don't know what to think or who to believe. It is rumored that the C.I.A. have developed a scentless drug which, if introduced to the global water supply, would cause everybody to tell the truth all the time without exception. This would doubtless result in many benefits to society. It would not benefit you, however, if you were telling Jenny Smith, or Johnny Brown, or whoever, that you did not wish to "date" them any longer because you were "just not in the right place for a relationship at this time". It would compel you instead to say, "Jenny Smith, your hair is like a pile of straw that a horse has taken a piss on." Or "Johnny Brown, your body odor induces a gagging reflex." And these statements, while candid, could cause embarrassment to involved parties. It is also possible that the rumor of the C.I.A. drug was started by an unreliable narrator. If there is such a drug, it was not taken by those friends and confidantes to whom Michael posed the question "So, what do you think of my face?" at any time during the final ten or twelve years of his life. Unreliable narrators can be a whole heap of trouble.

18

Michael is alone in the lab late one night, fiddling with his science kit, still trying to crack this elixir of eternal youth thing. He feels he's getting closer every time, but there is still a sense of deflation when he swallows the latest mixture only to wake the next day and find he is another day older despite his best efforts, extensive research and keen scientific brain. He publishes a maverick thesis in The Lancet which is moderately well received though many remain sceptical. "I'm getting so close!" he confides to a leopard and a frog. "Money is no object. One more big push and I'm there!"

19

John Denver has been campaigning to alleviate hunger in Africa for years, long before it became fashionable, so when he hears that Michael and Lionel are organizing a high profile charity single because they have been impressed by what Irish Bob and his friends have done with Live Aid, he offers his services. He contacts Quincy, but is told he is not required. John, an easy-going guy, watches the whole hoopla on television and cannot help but notice that there are a lot of singers there and that he has, undeniably, been snubbed because he is not, at the time in question, cool. *"We are the world"*, they are singing, *"We are the children."* John turns the sound down and picks up his acoustic guitar. *"You fill up my senses"*, he sings softly to himself, plucking, *"Like a night in the forest..."* Then he tosses the guitar across his living room and says, "Phony-ass bastards." The guitar, its strings brushing against a tall plant, makes a peculiar chord which John has never heard before.

20

The voices in Michael's head are arguing amongst themselves.

Voice 1: "Be modest. Be humble. Share your fortune with those less, um, fortunate."

Voice 2: "Take whatever you want. Taste it. Have it all. Buy another antelope."

Voice 1: "No. Be selfless. Build a railroad. Give."

Voice 2: "Pah! You're only on this Earth once, pal. You rock. Have a ball."

Voice 3: "Guys? Please? Can we not have some decorum? Can we not find some middle ground?"

Voice 4: "You are useless and small and pathetic, Michael."

Voice 1: "I'm sure we can. I do hope so."

Voice 2: "You're such a sap, Voice 1."

21

"I see this as being a gritty, tough, uncompromising video," says director Martin Scorsese, "one which will reposition you and challenge any arrested preconceptions. One which will dissect the notion of the American Dream. One which will chew through to the very heart of the conflicts and pressures within today's multicultural society."

"I want to do synchronized dancing with a lot of camp men in already dated leather and buckles and belts," says Michael.

"Or that," says Martin Scorsese. "That could work."

22

Michael's nose is bad. It detaches itself and goes for a stroll. Passing cloud-covered parking lots and refineries, it makes the bold, impetuous decision to run away. It pops into its apartment, hurriedly fills a hold-all with clothes, toiletries, a couple of books, an iPod and a camera, and dashes to the station. From the station it travels by train to the airport. From the airport it travels by plane to Cephallonia. There it avails itself of the best beaches, bars, restaurants and hotels. It visits nearby islands by ferry and enjoys Greek food. It finds the scenery spectacular and the light enchanting, not to say magical. The nose buys a Greek phrasebook and strives to learn a few key words. "Ne, ne, ne," it repeats, trying to say the Greek for "yes".

"Malista," it mumbles hesitantly, "I am an independent spirit and am relishing my new-found freedom... malista, malista. Ne." The nose is growing tired now, too much sun and alcohol.

The next day it rises early and feels the sun on its bridge. It enters a store and asks for a kilo of oranges. "Parakalo, ena kilo portokalia?" Then it sits on the beach and reads chapter two of the latest Martina Cole novel. Its attention drifts and it cannot prevent itself thinking about Michael. "I don't miss him," it thinks. "I won't allow myself to be that weak. I have come here to prove to myself that I don't need him. I am self-sufficient." The sun beats down and the blue of the sea twinkles and the sky is as still as a brick. The nose is disappointed to realize it is pining for Michael's face. The nose experiences a degree of self-pity, then a degree of self-loathing.

So it goes to Russia, then China, then Niger. Then the Solomon Islands. Yet nothing will shake Michael's face from its memory. It makes a fortune, loses it, makes it again. Over the course of time it is worshipped as a deity by shepherdesses and stoned as a whore by soldiers. It is Candide, it is Rasselas, it is Don Quixote. It marries repeatedly and helps to raise dozens of children, some of whom become trapeze artists and retail workers. Decades later, on its deathbed, with hundreds of thousands of zealous genuflecting supporters praying outside the window, it whispers to one of its wives and two of its cabinet members, "Yes, I have regrets. He loved me."

23

Michael is sitting in his oxygen tent trying to choose a new nickname, one appropriate to his lofty standing in the arts. He does not like Jacko or Wacko. They demean him. He is deliberating. He gets a pencil and makes a list – Mikey Soul? Mickey Rock? The new Peter Pan? He paces across the room, fidgets, comes back, restarts. The Prince of Pop? No... too much like Prince. The Monarch? The Deity? The... oh, how frustrating it is that Elvis Presley had first dibs on The King. The Emperor? The Overlord? Michael's spelling is not terrific: he spent little time at formal school in his youth, what with him being a top entertainer. The Overlord comes out as The Overload. Nevertheless, he persists. The Duke? The Sir... Sir Pop? Sir Music? Sir Music! Yes! No, no, no, come on, fool. The Admiral, The Commander, The Captain, The Major. The Chief? The Lord Of The Dance? The Genius? Maybe The Genius, he thinks. That would fly, wouldn't it? He's not certain, however. He's not feeling it. Is it a tad arrogant? Difficult to gauge these things accurately. He chews the end of his pencil, but when he realizes he is doing this he urgently spits into the solid-gold spittoon at his side and puts the pencil down and wipes his lips with the back of his hand. He decides to go see how his pet chimpanzee is doing and to revisit this project later.

24

Andy writes a letter to The King of Pop, not long before Andy dies. "Dear Mr. King of Pop, It has come to my attention that you are calling yourself The King of Pop. I am sorry to say I must take issue with this, as must my more than decent team of sharp-suited legal experts. I was doing Pop before you were, Sonny, and in the circles within which I move I am often referred to as The King. Sometimes The Queen. And sometimes The Princess. But, generally, The King. Just ask Elizabeth. Although art historians continue to argue over who did Pop first, even Lichtenstein and Johns and Rauschenberg and some of the English have conceded in recent interviews that, like it or not, for better or worse, I am the Big Daddy. I seem to have caught on. Which is fabulous. I still do a lot of Pop – hey, it's what I do! – and I would appreciate it if you would desist from marketing your own ventures under my professional moniker, which I have trade-marked this morning on over three thousand priceless works of art, conceived and executed between 11 a.m. and 11.45 a.m. You used to be such a nice boy. Don't be a bore. I will gladly do your portrait again if you have a minute and a half to spare. I know a little about wigs. Have you ever heard of The Velvet Underground? They were a Pop group and I did lots of Pop with them too, some time ago. So what I'm saying, push comes to shove, is that The King of Pop is my nickname, mine mine mine. Be a love and defer to my legend. Yours, Andy. P.S. Diana says hi. Not that Diana. The other one."

The letter is read aloud to Michael by his own more than decent team of sharp-suited legal experts. "What do you want to do about this, Michael?" they ask, in unison.

"Bin it," he says.

25

Neverland has swings and rides and slides and carousels and big dippers and helter-skelters. It has peacocks and deer and goats and rabbits and elephants and leopards and unicorns and wilde-beest and okapi and fish. It has a Guess-Your-Weight machine and a candy floss dispenser. It has a giraffe. It has a dodo and two pterodactyls and a paddock full of woolly mammoths. It has waltzers. It has a booth where you go for change. It has goblins and pixies and trolls and an enchanting water feature. It has roses, orchids, bluebells, tulips, peonies, stargazers. It is expansive. "I love it here," thinks Michael. "This is my home."

Elizabeth Taylor comes to Neverland, to marry Larry Fortensky, who she has now met. "So this is Larry," says Michael.

"Yes," says Larry, "hi."

"You have a mullet," says Michael, expressionlessly.

Elizabeth interjects. "Will you be our best man?" she asks Michael.

"Sure," says Michael, "Mi casa es su casa".

"It's not a mullet," says Larry.

In the guest quarters that night, a post-coital Larry says, "He can freaking talk."

"Hush dear," says Elizabeth. They watch a video of *National Velvet* followed by *Suddenly Last Summer*.

Michael wanders the grounds of Neverland, faintly sad that Elizabeth is marrying another, but pretty much reconciled to it. He talks to the okapi. "Well, okapi," he says, "Love is a funny old thing, and no mistake."

"In my experience," muses the okapi, "it lifts you up, and then it hurls you down. It spins your head around. It takes you from the gutter to the stars and back. It makes you feel every day is the greatest, then it makes every night a living hell. The rush, then the crash, QED. It's like a drug, in many ways. Did you know that, despite the juicy appeal of the state of delirium so exquis-itely articulated by Keats and Byron and my personal favorite Mrs. Browning, it is fundamentally a chemical reaction, plainly explicable via calm scientific reason?"

"Yeah, yeah, you said," mutters Michael, tying his shoelace.

He strolls over to the caterpillar enclosure. "What's up?" he nods at the nearest caterpillar.

"Raining," observes the caterpillar. Michael concurs. "Got it bad, huh?" asks the caterpillar. "They're not worth it mate. Really not. You're just mugging yourself off."

"You are anachronistically using British street slang from the middle of the first decade of the twenty-first century," says Michael, "How can that be?"

"Dude," says the caterpillar amicably, "you were just discussing poetry with an okapi." Michael concedes the point. He repositions his hat.

"It IS a mullet on the guy though, isn't it?" he says.

"SO a mullet," says the caterpillar, soon to be a beautiful butterfly.

26

Bubbles the chimpanzee is shitting everywhere. On the drapes, on the rugs, on the furniture, on the platinum discs and on the piano. Sometimes he flings his feces across the room, hitting the candelabra, from which it falls minutes later, hitting the marble floor with a dullish "thwuck" sound. Bubbles is grinning and waving, proud of his achievements. He sticks two thumbs up cheerily. "Oh," sighs Michael, his face a picture of woe, "this won't do."

"It's an unanticipated problem," agrees Macaulay Culkin, who has dropped by.

"It simply won't do," reaffirms Michael. He calls one of his management team and asks them to come over. The member of his management team leaves his sleeping wife, dresses, starts the car, and drives for forty five minutes to see Michael at Neverland. "What appears to be the crisis?" he asks.

"Bubbles is making doo-doo everywhere," says Michael, on the verge of tears. "Macaulay left. I don't like it."

"Is he flinging it across the room?" asks his employee.

"Yes."

"With his hand?"

"Yes. Why, what other part of his body would he be flinging it with?"

"I don't know, I was just stalling while I thought of something constructive to say."

"Well, what can we do about it?"

"Seriously? I can only suggest we relocate Bubbles to an outhouse in the grounds."

"But I would miss him!"

"There is that, yes."

"I would really, really miss him! I love him!"

"I understand that, but there is the matter of the feces."

"Do you suppose we could educate him?" asks Michael, optimistically.

"He's a chimpanzee," says the employee, whose name is Joel.

"But Raoul, he's highly intelligent!" exclaims Michael.

"My name is Joel, Michael," says Joel.

"We could potty-train him, perhaps," ventures Michael.

"He's a freaking chimpanzee!" repeats Joel, who is somewhat sleep-deprived and uncharacteristically, unprofessionally irritable.

"You're dismissed," says Michael.

Bubbles gathers a really good handful of feces and pitches a curveball down the hall, narrowly missing the antique Venetian dresser but catching a priceless Rembrandt smack in the chops.

Michael spends two weeks attempting to train Bubbles to use the toilet. He is unsuccessful. The project begins to weary him and he does not enjoy getting chimp feces on his hands. He starts wearing gloves indoors. He is advised that the feces are a health hazard, especially if there are small children in the vicinity. The mansion begins to smell bad. It begins to reek. A month passes. Any more of this and the all-important elixir ingredients stored in the lab could be adversely affected.

"Bubbles could be housed in the former hippos' enclosure," suggests Miranda, a colleague of Joel's, holding a handkerchief to her face and squinting.

"I won't hear of such a thing, Melissa!" shouts Michael. Another month passes.

"Bubbles could be housed in a specially built scenic area around the fourth carousel, the pretty one we don't use much, just half a mile from here," suggests Anja, who has replaced Miranda, who has quit after contracting dysentery.

"Do it," orders Michael. "Make that change."

27

He has done more for charity than any entertainer in the history of the world. This is accepted as fact. He has done more for charity than Eileen Evans, a 62-year-old nurse from Southend, who every morning rises at five thirty then travels on public transport for ninety minutes to feed, bathe and wipe the arses of pensioners with dementia, for twelve hours with a half-hour lunch break. He has done more for charity than Svetlana (second name unconfirmed), a 23-year-old originally from the Ukraine, who is Eileen's boss and who has to notify any surviving relatives when one of the pensioners dies, then listen tight-lipped while they blame Eileen and herself for mortality and accuse the pair of laziness and cold-heartedness. He has done more for charity than Tom Harris, a veteran who has one eye and, in the back room of his local Cancer Research shop, marks prices on second-hand books. He is a volunteer. He does it for something to do. Today he is flicking through a yellowing copy of *Instructions For American Servicemen In Britain 1942*, issued by the War Department, Washington D.C. He reads: "The British are tough. Don't be misled by the British tendency to be soft-spoken and polite. If they need to be, they can be plenty tough. The English language didn't spread across the oceans and over the mountains and jungles and swamps of the world because these people were panty-waists". At the same time as he does this, Eileen Evans is wiping dribble from the face of a 91-year-old man who is yelling abuse at her but does not know he is making a sound. "Bitch!" he shouts. Eileen closes her eyes for a moment. "I'm sorry!" says the man. Then he says, "What? What? What is it?" Michael has done more for charity than any of these people.

28

He is in trouble. He stands accused of terrible things. How has it come to this? How has it been allowed to come to this? Depressed, dreading what's to come, he potters to the lab and tinkers with the vials which now contain his many flawed, obsessive attempts at inventing the elixir of eternal youth. He picks one up, examines it. "Drink Me," says its label. He does. As he'd suspected, nothing happens. He selects another. "Anti-Ageing Solution No. 174 Pour Homme," says its label. He puts it to one side, making a mental note to add an extra sprinkle of peppermint. He picks up another vial. "Jesus Juice," says its label. He appears to be staring vacantly at it for a long time, his thoughts elsewhere.

29

"Hey Mikey," says Lisa-Marie Presley. "I had an unorthodox youth and know all about massive head-stewing fame. You had an unorthodox youth and know all about massive head-stewing fame. We have so much in common. And I don't need your money. Wanna fuck?"

"Goodness," splutters Michael, blushing, "that's kind of... that's sort of..." But Michael is curious now, he's not getting any younger, despite the elixir, plus he has been wondering how he could add ownership of the Elvis catalog to ownership of The Beatles catalog, and so they give it a go. She guides him through it. She says, "Not there. There. That's it." It's not great. "Wanna go again?" asks Lisa-Marie Presley, but she is not asking him, not really. She is telling him. Again, it's not great. "Third time's the charm?"

"Lisa-Marie," says Michael, going down on one knee, "will you marry me?"

"Got any bourbon?" asks Lisa-Marie. Michael, exhausted, sends a couple of the okapi out for bourbon. "So tell me," yawns Lisa-Marie, "what's stirring down in the depths of your soul, my mirror man?"

"Gosh," says Michael, breathing heavily, "I have never known such rare compassion, such piercing insight."

"I guess we could get married," Lisa-Marie thinks out loud. "It'd sure as shit drive a few folks seven shades of pissed." Michael admires her grace, her elegance.

"A merging of dynasties," stage-whispers Michael to himself. "Or rather, I get to shaft the old dead King's legacy. Which, any way you look at it, makes me the undisputed new King."

"Also," chips in an aide, who has been standing bedside with towels and mineral water all along, "it redirects the media spotlight... away from... you know. That. The thing."

"Good point," say Michael and Lisa-Marie in unison.

"On reflection," adds Michael, addressing the aide, "it might have been smarter to send you for the bourbon, as opposed to sending the okapi."

"Why?" asks Lisa-Marie, already sniggering at her own joke, "Are they underage or something?"

"You're a very bad girl," tuts Michael, "and must be properly disciplined. Come here."

"See?" Lisa-Marie asks the aide, "One night and I've made a man of him."

Yet in this case, strangely, and for the first and last time in recorded history, one opening night of hot filthy irrational cathartic mutual lust does not translate into a lifelong transcendent bond of trust, tolerance and simpatico.

30

"Hey Michael!" exclaims British person and former child star Mark Lester. "I was in *Oliver!* at an early age – which means we have so much in common – and because of that strange youthful showbiz experience cannot stop myself placing gratuitous exclamation marks at the end of everything I say! Do you want to borrow some of my sperm?!"

"That's very kind of you," says Michael, "is it good sperm?"

"It's *great* sperm!!" says Mark, adding an extra exclamation mark because he's adamant that, as sperm goes, it's dynamite.

"Sure," says Michael, "why not?"

Arrangements are made. "This Debbie Rowe," says Michael. "She's not a looker."

"Doesn't matter," says an aide. "Irrelevant."

"Has she signed everything?" inquires Michael.

"She's willing to comply with all our terms and she's been thoroughly checked out," says the aide.

"But she's no Liz Taylor, not by any definition," says Michael.

"There are greater issues at stake here," says the aide, steely-eyed and determined.

"I suppose," mutters Michael. "Still and all…"

His better nature overrides his more base instincts. "I shall be like the Pharaoh's daughter," he daydreams, "rescuing Moses in his basket made of bulrushes from the chilly water. And then rescuing Moses' sister. And then Moses' brother."

31

Michael is a dad. Suddenly he can't understand why he ever thought people were nuts to have babies. He showers his kids with affection and costly gifts and blankets and masks. Sometimes he proves his devotion by not dropping them from Berlin hotel balconies. "I love you, my children!" he squeals. "I love you! Love is everything! Love is peace! And harmony. It's harmony too." As soon as they can stand he sets them to work in the lab as his white-coated assistants, feeling some fresh input from the next generation might crack the code. They labor through the night. He feels they almost make a significant break-through when they add caramel, molasses and the steam from a lizard's back to the elixir, but eventually accepts that the kids' evident youthfulness is attributable to their youth. For his part, Michael feels increasingly tired with each day that passes, and experiences odd twinges in his ankles and knees. He reads the Book Of Job, which is a bit of the Bible. "My skin is black upon me," it says, "and my bones are burned with heat".

32

"Why is he doing that?" frets Michael. "What has possessed him? Why is this Joe Cocker person assaulting my stage as I perform my rather marvelous creation "Earth Song" at the prestigious Brit Awards in Britain, which is in Britain, and why is he wiggling his bottom without any natural rhythm? Is he hurting the children? Oh God, he's hurting the children! He must have delusions of grandeur. It's rather tasteless. He must be sick in the head. I find it rather offensive and self-aggrandizing, given the current climate. Certainly his dress sense is poor. Perhaps I can heal him. Do I have the power of healing? Memo to self: get self to ask self if self possesses power of healing. Then report back to self."

33

On stage in front of forty five billion trillion people one night, Michael gets a step wrong for the first time ever. It's over in a flash, the rest of the show is great, nobody else notices the error, but Michael does and it unsettles him, puts a kink in his pride. Hours after the crowd have milled happily away and the main set has been dismantled, Michael can be seen measuring the stage with a wooden ruler, intent on proving to himself that the floor, and not his ageing body, had been in the wrong.

34

Michael is in the bath. He hums a few bars of "The Way You Make Me Feel". He scrubs his toes. Every time he takes a bath he is reminded of media speculation that suggested he was born a hermaphrodite. That was one of his least favorite, of the stories. He thought that one was kind of gross. He dries his hands and places his reading bench across the bathtub and, propping himself up, reads about Dante's *The Divine Comedy*. "The last word in each of the three parts of The Divine Comedy," he reads, "is 'stelle', meaning 'stars'. He gazes into the abyss for a while but it starts to bring him down, so he switches to a book about Neoplasticism. A sign on the wall opposite says: "Now Please Wash Your Hands".

35

Michael is looking at his face in a large mirror. He is reminded of Salvador Dali's melting clocks. By chance the Donna Summer version of the Jim Webb song "MacArthur Park", initially popularized by the late Richard Harris, comes on the radio. Michael hears the line, *"MacArthur Park is melting in the dark, all the sweet green icing, flowing down"*. He turns on the TV and sees footage of vast glaciers melting. He defrosts the fridge. He flips channels and catches a couple of scenes of *Vanilla Sky*. Flips again and gets *The Elephant Man*. But he has seen that a hundred times so he turns the TV off and looks out of the window at the grounds of Neverland. He sees withered trees, tumbleweed and a mangy cat throwing left hooks at a dead bird which is being devoured by maggots.

36

"That's intriguing," he says to himself. "As rocket science so often is. Sergei Korolev's R-7 rocket, which officially went into production in 1953, was not aesthetically pleasing. It had 20 engines, all wantonly burning kerosene and liquid oxygen. It was crude, clumsy – some said "a bludgeon" – and tested unsuccessfully the first six times. It was not by any standards graceful. When I go to the moon, I will not go in one of those. Yet I need to firm up my plans. By what mode of transport shall I venture to the moon? Perhaps Uri Geller can help me with this. There's somebody I'd like to meet. I could meet anybody I wanted to. Anybody. Royalty. Nelson Mandela. The Reagans. Siedah Garrett. Anybody. But Uri Geller has something special."

37

Michael is watching Jermaine on a "reality TV" show. "Michael is so normal," Jermaine is saying to an out-of-work comedian. "He's just like me or you. Very sweet, very caring; he loves to laugh."

Michael changes the channel. He is now watching La Toya on a "reality TV" show. "My brother is so normal," says La Toya. "He's just like any of us. He loves to make jokes and make us laugh; he's very caring, very warm and loving."

"Oh my God, I can't believe I'm in the same house as somebody who grew up with Michael!" shrieks a girl who used to be in *Eastenders*, so loudly that La Toya flinches.

"I so know!" agrees a girl who used to mime and simulate dry-humping in a pop group, "I'm like totally oh my God such an inspiration to me, right?"

"Right!" shouts the first, "you're so right and I feel such a connection with you!"

"Of course," adds La Toya, though the girls are no longer listening, "he has his down moments, just like anyone else." Michael mutes the sound.

His mother rings. "It's the groin-grabbing I don't like," Katharine opines. "It's not nice. Or seemly."

"Totally not in the mood for this right now, Mom," says Michael. He hangs up. He palms a shed-load of gaily colored drugs from the big glass bowl at the side of the sofa and necks them.

38

He goes to visit his favorite comedian, Benny Hill, in England. He plans to go on to London where he will see Lady Godiva and Hadrian's Wall and Snowdonia. Benny makes him tea and runs through a few of his classic side-splitting characters and skits for his celebrated guest. "Oh!" chortles Michael, "that's so funny! You're so funny! I love you!" Benny tells one of his Swedish au pairs to don a police helmet and run around the room in her underwear while waving a truncheon. "Ha ha!" laughs Michael, "that's so great! Please be my friend!" They have some biscuits.

"You know, young Michael," says Benny Hill, "being famous is not always as great as it's cracked up to be. Everyone expects me to make them laugh all day every day, but the truth is I have a growling, seething, hissing darkness in my spirit and frequent bleak spells of utter despair."

"I hear you, buddy," says Michael, adding, "what are these? Jaffa cakes?"

"Sometimes," continues Benny Hill, "I feel trapped in my persona. I am a prophet without honor in my own country. I wish the world perceived me in a different way, for I have the soul of a poet. I am tortured, in the depths of my being, on approximately nine nights in every fourteen." Benny's eyes moisten and his lip trembles, and after an anguished silence of several minutes he says, "Do you feel my pain?"

"Yes," says Michael, "I do, I really do. Now do the one about the milkman again. Please?"

39

He is talking to his okapi again. "Hey, okapi," he says.

"Hey," says the okapi.

"Wish I could fly," says Michael.

"Yeah," says the okapi. "You said."

"Okapi," begins Michael, "what will the twenty-first century be like?"

"It'll be wild," says the okapi. "And by wild, I mean electronic. Digital."

"Cool!" enthuses Michael. "Will we all speed around on self-cleaning hover-jets and will I be able to fly like Peter Pan thus fulfilling my lifelong dream and will there be an outstanding shimmering hologram of me in every home in America and in Europe and in Asia too? And will hurt and suffering be eradicated? And will youth be eternal?"

The okapi sucks thoughtfully on a blade of grass. "I was thinking more: *games*," it says. "Maybe some fun quizzes."

40

Uri Geller is telling him about spirituality. "Bend me a spoon," demands Michael. Uri does this, for the fifty-ninth time that day.

"May I hypnotize you?" asks Uri.

"OK," says Michael, because Uri doesn't have any Jaffa cakes.

"You are in a deep, deep sleep," says Uri.

"Whatever," thinks Michael, "hope this doesn't take too long. Humor the guy."

"Did you ever touch a child in an inappropriate fashion?" asks Uri.

"Of course not!" says Michael. "You total twat! Whose side are you on?"

"I am convinced by your retort," says Uri. "My wife and I are renewing our marriage vows. Will you be my Best Man?"

"OK," says Michael. "If there's Jaffa cakes."

"You're my friend!" says Uri. "How wonderful!" Uri proudly tells his other friends, who are mature enough to veil their resentment. The ceremony begins. Michael arrives hours late, on crutches. "Thank you so much for being my friend, Michael," says Uri.

"Sure," says Michael.

Both Michael and Uri are at this stage unaware that Uri will soon come last on the first series of *I'm A Celebrity Get Me Out Of*

Here. This series, in which Uri comes eighth out of eight in a popularity contest, will be won by Tony Blackburn, with Tara Palmer-Tomkinson as runner up. Darren Day comes sixth and Nigel Benn comes seventh. All of these people would appear to be more popular with the public than Uri Geller. Michael does not attend any of their weddings.

41

At close personal friend Uri Geller's request, Michael is playing on the left wing for Exeter City Football Club. He is nippy and fleet of foot despite his advancing years. Exeter are at home to Torquay United in a vital Carling Cup second round match. Michael receives the ball on the flank, works a neat one-two with Eugene Record of The Chi-Lites then advances into the Torquay penalty area. He tries to go round the much bigger Joe Tex but is unceremoniously brought down. "Penalty!" cry the Exeter supporters as one. The referee, unimpressed, waves play on.

"Aw, c'mon!" protests Michael.

"Get up you cheating cunt," Joe Tex growls into Michael's ear. Michael wheels round to face him.

"Leave it, Michael," advises team-mate Jimmy Ruffin, pulling him away. "He's just letting you know he's there. Let your football do the talking. We've got this one."

"Piece of shit's not worth it," adds Yvonne Elliman.

With the Exeter supporters singing, "Walking in a Wacko Wonderland", the match develops into a tight, goalless, stalemate. Then, in the eighty-fifth minute, with the clock ticking, Michael is sent through the middle by a lovely ball from Millie Jackson (no relation). "Turn and go!" hollers Eddie Kendricks. Michael spins and jinks into the six-yard box. As goalkeeper Patti Labelle, Torquay's best player on the night, comes out bravely to meet him, Michael sends a superb chip over her diving body. The ball heads towards the goal. But what's this? Oh no! The ball has hit the far post. Luckily, Marvin "Big Man" Gaye has been following up and taps the ball into the unguarded net, sending the Exeter fans into unabashed raptures. Marvin, grinning, wheels round and points to Michael, and Michael leaps up into his arms. Their team-mates crowd around them, ruffling each other's hair and winding up as an unseemly mass of bodies on the grass. There's no way back now for Torquay.

Afterwards, Marvin, a lovely man combating his own personal demons, is quick to give Michael the credit for the thrilling victory. "The little man done absolute magic," he tells reporters. "I'm, like, five foot ten!" Michael can be heard shouting from off camera. Eventually Michael emerges from the dressing room, showered and changed, sweaty but glowing. "We're very pleased for the supporters," he says. "Obviously we didn't play our best first half but we stuck at it and got the result and that's obviously what counts end of the day. It's not about me scoring, it's all about the team." The interviewer asks if Michael feels his uncharacteristic exertions of the day will affect his musical career in any way. "Basically I take each day as it comes," replies Michael, "and give 110% every time. It's all about keeping it real."

"Did you at any point consider moonwalking past the defenders?"

"That's a stupid, glib, would-be humorous question and frankly cheap shots like that are beneath you. It would have been inappropriate. I had a job to do."

"Thank you Michael."

"Cheers Garth. All the best mate."

He joins the boys for a few beers then goes for a curry with Uri.

42

Michael is in deep dark trouble again. "Not guilty," he pleads. And pleads and pleads and pleads. It is all the fault of Uri Geller, who introduced TV interviewer Martin Bashir to Michael. "You are dead to me," Michael mouths at photographs of Uri Geller. "You twisted my words, interloper," he hisses at Bashir as, horrified, he watches Bashir's documentary. Outside the courtroom he spontaneously decides to wave at his dozens of loyal fans and dance on top of a car. "I love you!" he shouts.

"We love you! You are innocent!" they reply. After he has clambered onto the top of the car, he realizes it is slippery underfoot.

"Not guilty," he says, giving pots of money to lawyers, as he is compelled to. It is his new mantra. "Not guilty, not guilty, not guilty. I am as white as the driven snow."

43

He is not enjoying the twenty-first century. It hasn't gone for him the way he'd hoped. It doesn't feel like his playground the way the twentieth century did. His reputation is in decline, as is he. He blames the march of time. He blames the ageing process. The failure of the elixir, in which he has placed so much hope for so long. He blames those out to get him. He blames George Bush, Dick Cheney, Tony Blair, Osama Bin Laden, Saddam Hussein and Sony. He blames computers and mobile phones. He tells the okapi a joke. The okapi shrugs, "Heard it."

44

DELETED SCENES:

Michael goes to the Jobcentre. Michael goes to Wal-Mart on his forty-ninth birthday, disguised as Jack White. Michael tries to persuade George Lucas to cast him as Princess Leia. Michael dresses up as Santa Claus and spends Christmas Day alone. Michael finds a first edition of *The Voyeur* by Alain Robbe-Grillet on a stall in Portobello Market. When the guy says it's a quid he has to stop himself involuntarily smirking, do the deal and walk away with the book before he starts shaking. Michael and Janet have a big row when Janet gets famous but make up when Janet, feeling she has proven her point, agrees to adopt a lower profile. Michael attends a Barbra Streisand concert disguised as Mickey Mouse. Barry Gibb recognizes him and bounds over to say hi but Mickey Mouse runs away, ears flapping. Michael tells his people he wants to work with hot new young fresh urban producers who are in touch with the sounds the kids like. "Like Acorn and Eeyore and the one from Black Ice Peas," he urges, enthusiastically. Michael suggests collaborating with Phil Spector but is talked out of it. Michael rings Paul McCartney to apologize for buying the rights to his songs but Heather Mills answers the phone and they talk about legs. Michael designs a stage costume which consists of a codpiece and a crown but is talked out of that too. One sunny day Michael feels briefly happy again, for about an hour, for the first time in too long, and can't explain it or tell you where it came from exactly. Michael writes *Paradise Regained* only to be informed that Milton already wrote it centuries ago. Michael crosses the road. Michael eats an apple.

(SELECT/PLAY ALL).

45

Marlon Brando sits next to Michael in a limo. He is large. "I had 'em all," he brags. "Women. Men. Marilyn. I was a god of love, a bonfire of sex." Michael shivers involuntarily. When Michael is arrested, Marlon is interviewed by LA police about his late night phone conversations with Michael for seven hours. Seven hours! "Don't worry," says Marlon. "I stonewalled. If all else fails, you can come and live with me in Tahiti."

"Thanks for that," says Michael. They go to the soundcheck at Madison Square Garden.

"Michael," says Britney, when they arrive, all but curtseying, "it's such a profound honor to work with you. I can't tell you how privileged I feel to be singing with you here tonight at The Garden. It's a dream come true, it genuinely, sincerely is. You've been my musical hero and inspiration for many years. Without you there would be no me."

"Oh," says Michael, "that's sweet. Thank you."

Michael and Britney perform their duet. It goes fine. Later, Michael's people inform Britney that it will be cut from the TV broadcast that will be watched by countless millions around the world. "Gnash that!" screams Britney. "What the gnash is the deal here? The washed-up mothergnashing pathetic sick wreck can't do this! I'm Britney gnashing Spears! I sold more records last week than that gnashing scarecrow's sold in a decade! Who does he think he is? The King of gnashing Pop? Right, if the year is gnashing 1852! Sort it out, manager, else I'll cut you, bitch."

Britney's manager grimaces patiently, holding his hands up as if to say: What can I do? "It'll be on the DVD," he ventures, sheepishly.

"My sweaty thong it will," says Britney. "He can go gnash himself. And his little boys."

A hush the size of a continent falls over Britney's dressing suite. At this point Kevin Federline, who has been reclining on a velveteen chaise longue, stands up, adjusts his leather pants while brushing taco crumbs from his groin area, and moves over to Britney. Tentatively, he strokes the back of her head. It is warm. He likes it. "Quiet now," he says, "baby girl. I don't believe that's any way to speak about the greatest entertainer of all time."

"Yeah," says Britney, "you're probably right babe."

"Actually Kev," interrupts Justin Timberlake, "I think she's still with me at this point in time? Like, chronologically? And hasn't even met you yet?" There is an awkward moment. "But, you know," shrugs Justin, "go with what feels right. As artists. I'm down with that."

46

Michael is seeking flashes of brilliance. He seeks them here. He seeks them there. He seeks them everywhere. Where are they? Where have you hidden them? He looks in the cupboards. He looks under the bed. He looks in major department stores and independent boutiques. He looks up hillocks and down mines. He attaches a snorkel and looks underwater. He hunts in cities and jungles. He is The Hunter. But he is not the hunter he was. It used to be so easy. He once had more flashes of brilliance in the tiny gaps between his teeth, in his gums, than you have in your entire body. Under his fingernails. In his pores. Flashes of brilliance used to fall out of his arse. But now it's like a mist, a fog, has descended, and cannot be ushered away. It is exhausting for him now to try to summon up flashes of brilliance, whereas once there was no trying involved; they just came. Michael checks in the conservatory one more time. He gets out the stepladder and checks in the attic. No joy. He puts the stepladder away and goes back to bed.

47

The lab is growing dusty. The precious test tubes and vials are only perfunctorily meddled with, nudged around for form's sake, once in a while. The elixir of eternal youth seems to Michael just a beautiful dream now, a dream from which he has been reluctantly waking since the old century gave way to the new. Maybe even before that. "What is happening to me and why won't it stop?" thinks Michael. "First I couldn't fly. And now I find I cannot stay forever young. I am almost fifty. Me, fifty. It's unconscionable. It is like a sick cosmic joke, taunting me. It is a frightening, horrible thing. It happens to everybody. Everybody lives in the shadow of this fear. Yet nobody talks about it. Why is this?" Out of habit, he does take one vial of elixir upstairs to the bedroom, intending to drink it before he goes to sleep. But these days, faith eroded, he sometimes doesn't even bother, and so tonight he just leaves it on the bedside drawer, on and in which several vials rattle around, untouched.

48

"What terrific offers are there today?" Michael asks his remaining people.

"There is *American Idol*," says the loyal Anja. "Guest judge."

"Christ on a bike," sighs Michael. "What else?"

"There is the opening of a major new mall in Boise," says Harry, Anja's assistant.

"Jeez, Louise," says Michael.

"Actually Sir it's Harry," says Harry.

"What about the loyal UK?" demands Michael. "Anything in the loyal UK, which loves me, because it is plenty tough?"

"There is *Friday Night Project* with Justin Lee Collins and Alan Carr," offers Anja, brightly. "You'd get to wear the coat of cash."

"Just strap me down and kill me now," groans Michael, banging his head against the desk. "I need a new promoter."

"This Is It!" announces Michael, who has a new promoter. He is set to turn everything around – his luck, his finances, his reputation – by playing 5,000 nights at London's O_2 Arena, once the site of the historic Millennium Dome, where, famously, Henry The Eighth married Jane Austen. And then everything will be all right. Michael will be the King again. He will "reclaim" his "crown". Tickets sell out quickly. It's like a fairy tale. Michael goes back to bed.

People tell him he must get up and rehearse. He must exercise. He must get back in shape. He asks for more drugs, to help him sleep, to help him stay awake, to keep him slim, to keep him strong, to keep him young. He is drowsy 24/7 now. He doesn't know who half of these people are, these people around him with their beseeching or admonishing faces. He is skeletal. He lies on the bed, feeling the comforting incontinence pad beneath his bottom. "As though of hemlock I had drunk," he mutters. "I crave sleep."

"But you must rehearse and 'reclaim' your 'crown'!" says a face.

"Yes..." murmurs Michael, "yes, it's true, I must 'reclaim' my 'crown'. I... hmmm... just give me a moment here... just...just..." He talks gibberish in his sleep. He says, "Time flies when you're having fun, and also when you're not. Time passes. Listen. Time passes. Time flies but you can't, Michael, you can't."

49

Michael suffers heart failure after an overdose of Demerol. Michael dies because of a dodgy doctor. Michael dies because of the money men. Michael dies to avoid having to go to the London Docklands. Michael dies on the toilet after putting on weight and eating too many king size burgers. Michael is killed in a car accident in a tunnel in Paris while gallivanting with Dodi Al Fayed, and blames the paparazzi. Michael takes a shotgun and blows his head off because Seattle just ain't the same these days. Michael hangs himself in the kitchen in Macclesfield after watching a Werner Herzog film and listening to Iggy Pop's *The Idiot*. Michael is shot by a crazed Salinger-reading stalker called Mark Chapman, as he leaves the Dakota Building with Yoko Ono. Michael dies when his car, driven by singer/girlfriend Gloria Jones, hits a tree in Barnes, South-West London. Michael dies through a bizarre auto-erotic act of self-asphyxiation. Michael takes too many sleeping pills because he's not sure which, if any, of the Kennedys he loves more than Arthur Miller and all the papers have to say is whether he was found in the nude. Michael is killed in a car smash, still young, still handsome, and the other driver's name is Donald Turnupseed. Michael is hit by a tram on the Ramblas, his great cathedral unfinished. Michael fills his pockets with rocks and walks into the river and drowns, declaring that his best work was *Mrs Dalloway*. Michael is shot in the head by Lee Harvey Oswald as he drives through Dallas near a grassy knoll with Jackie, who is wearing a nice hat. Michael is then shot by Jack Ruby. Michael is shot in the chest with a sawn-off shotgun on 25 February 1965 in a Manhattan ballroom after a man yells, "Nigger! Get your hand out of my pocket!" Michael is shot on 4 April 1968 on the second floor balcony of the Lorraine Motel in Memphis Tennessee, aged 39, with Jesse Jackson (no relation) reporting (perhaps with embellishment) that his last words were, "Make sure you play "Take My Hand, Precious Lord" tonight. Play it real pretty." Michael is hacked to ribbons by toga-clad men bearing daggers in the forum on the Ides of March and says, "Et tu, Brutus?" Michael is nailed to a cross alongside some thieves instead of Barabbas and slowly bleeds to death, thus starting a durable religion. Michael is controversially declared dead by Nietzsche, though the statement is frequently misinterpreted. Michael dies of old age or cancer or heartbreak like everyone else. There is ongoing speculation about the nature of Michael's death which may continue for some time. Michael says, "Rosebud. Rosebud."

50

Sometimes it seems as though they will never stop, they will never get enough. Janet says, "Speak up, honey."

Paris addresses the microphone and says, "I love him so much." She is a beautiful kid.

Michael's brain is removed, but it cannot shake off an overpowering sense of ennui sufficiently to engage in solo adventures the way his nose once did. It lacks the necessary vim, the jouissance.

As the detectives trawl through Michael's room, one of them accidentally knocks over a tiny vial of greenish-gold liquid. Unobserved, its contents seep into the rug. After all the criminal investigations are completed, months, maybe years later, most memorabilia is auctioned off but the rug is thrown out by the LAPD because of a clerical error. A young skylark lands on the rug and pecks at it briefly, finding the taste odd. The skylark flies away. Then it lives forever, never ageing, not by one second.

The real abstraction of Michael Jackson

Jeremy Gilbert

The End of History?

London, November 1991... I'd only been living there for a couple of months, but I could have been practically anywhere on the planet, the single most striking feature of the cityscape being – for at least a couple of weeks – the promotional imagery for *Dangerous*. It seemed to be everywhere: on every wall, in every shop window.

It struck me then, that in some very literal sense, Michael Jackson wasn't real. I don't mean that there was a real individual called Michael Jackson of whom these poster images could only convey a false impression: it wasn't the sense that there was an irrevocable split between Michael Jackson and "Michael Jackson" that I was responding to. Even less was it the sense we are all of us, to some extent, fictional constructs without "authentic" selves. Each of these observations are, in their own senses, undoubtedly valid, but what I'm getting at here was something more specific. In some precise way, it seemed to me that the visual over-representation of Michael Jackson had simply removed from him one of the conditions upon which being "real" actually depends.

To put this more simply, I was struck very powerfully by the sense that one of the things that we mean when we say that an object or person is "real" is that there is at least some limit to the number of times we can see its image reproduced on a daily or a local basis; that there are only so many identical life-sized cardboard cut-outs of a person that can appear in public places before that person actually loses the quality of being-real. The actuality of Michael Jackson seemed to have been not merely distorted, but overwhelmed, drowned in the sea of its own images.

Of course, the most obvious philosophical reference to make here would be to Jean Baudrillard and his concept of the "simulacrum". The "simulacrum" is, an "image" or "represen-tation" which has no actual referent in the "real" world. On its own this can be an uncontentious enough concept. Simulacra obviously exist: there is no "real" Dalek, for example, despite there being many ways of representing Daleks. The simulacrum was not a concept invented by Baudrillard, but it was he who popularized a particularly apocalyptic usage of it in the 1980s, with his insistence that, all of contemporary culture was now, at least tendentially, composed of simulacra, as "hyperreality" displaced the old world of the real referent and its various modes of representation. In hyperreality, there were no longer real objects and representations of real objects: there were only simulacra. A friend, who had never heard of Baudrillard, remarked to me around 1990, "When you see a tree in the street, it's not a real tree any more, because of all the trees you've seen on TV". That, in a nutshell, was Baudrillard's hypothesis.

I already knew a little about Baudrillard at the time when this particular sense of Michael Jackson's unreality first struck me, but what also struck me at just that moment was how unper-suasive I found Baudrillard's general thesis, and the fact that somehow Michael Jackson's particular unreality seemed only to illustrate its weakness. Michael Jackson, it occurred to me, had become a simulacrum, but in doing so had only highlighted the fact that the rest of us hadn't.

As the decade wore on, however, the public breakdown in Jackson's ability to simulate "normal" human behavior became ever more visible, making clear that even he had never really been a simulacrum at all, and eventually threatening to offer

glimpses into his potentially dangerous – and as such, terrify-
ingly real – sexuality. It seemed to me then that the material body
of Michael Jackson – both in its potential manifestation of desire
(desire which, it was hinted, refused to submit itself to the glossy
hyperreality of Jackson's public androgyny/asexuality) and in its
visible incapacity to submit to endless modification (as his face
just fell apart in the wake of too-frequent plastic surgery) was
becoming itself symbolic, not of the submersion of the Real, but
of its stubborn and irrevocable return. In fact, even when it
became apparent that the allegations of pedophilia made against
him were almost certainly unfounded, what emerged was
something perhaps even more scary to the contemporary imagination: the fact that Jackson's apparent infantile asexuality
wasn't just an act, but was entirely authentic.

Stepping back again to the early 1990s: somehow – and this
will sound strange, I know – the collapse of Jackson's body and
sanity seemed to me to echo the disastrous deterioration of post-
Soviet society. In the late 1980s, it had been proclaimed that the
end of Communism marked "the end of history", that the velvet
revolutions of Eastern Europe would usher in an age of liberal
democracy and comfortable consumerism for all the peoples of
the world. If any figure represented – globally – the coming
universal culture, then it was the apparently ageless, apparently
immortal, gravity-defying, graceful Michael Jackson of the
Thriller-Bad-Pepsi epoch. Outside history, outside any normal
categories of race, gender or class, Jackson was the everyone and
no-one of unthreatened liberalism; the (dis)embodiment of the
very dream which was promised to the peoples of the former
Soviet Bloc: the individual liberated from all bonds of
community and history, free to move across the surface of the
earth as if gliding over the glass of a great TV screen. The degeneration of their societies into the brutality of gangster capitalism
seemed somehow to match the degeneration of Jackson's public
and actual personae, as the nasty reality of capitalism's

destructive cost hit home in both places. Was it any accident that the titles of Jackson's next album release would be *HIStory*?

Of course, there are other candidates for the job of Symbol of Universalized American Liberal Capitalism: two in particular. Ronald Reagan and Madonna, in their different respective ways, stand alongside Michael Jackson as the iconic figures of this epoch. We can't really make sense of either Michael or his time without taking them into account also. But to raise this point is to raise the question of exactly what that time was, and why it feels so distant from us now.

The Short 1980s

The "1980s" only really lasted for five years. In many parts of the world, the years 1980-3 were characterized by an intensified push on the part of the radical forces which had first emerged in the 1960s – Mitterand's attempt to implement left-Keynesianism in France; the leftist take-over of the British Labour Party; Jesse Jackson's campaign for the Democratic Presidential nomination; the first Sandinista government in Nicaragua; the formation of the Workers' Party in Brazil; the intensification of the anti-Apartheid struggle; etc. – and we certainly hear this in the agitated, anxious utopianism which characterizes so much of the music of the time. 1989 saw the end of cold war, the emergence of Acid House (only a British person of a certain generation could mention these events in the same breath, I know – but I am what I am…), the political paralysis of the Bush presidency, etc., etc.

It was 1984–1988 which really marked the high watermark of Thatcherism, of Reagan's moral authority on the world stage, of MTV in its original format of endless back-to-back music videos, which seemed to be fulfilling all postmodern prophecies with its eschewal of narrative, personality or documentation. This was the greatest period in history for sales of music recordings, and for those artists who could use the media of mass-dissemination to sell them. It was the golden age of "pop", the moment when that term designated something of which somebody might actually aspire to crown themselves "King". This was the world in which Ronald Reagan – his political persona indissociable from his screen role as a cowboy – could claim with a straight face to be setting Americans free from the "burden" of government even while he ran the federal budget into the ground and condemned a generation of the urban poor to life-chances worse than those of their grandparents. This was the world of the *Bad* tour, a world which *Thriller* had helped to usher in just as much as had the first election victories of Thatcher and Reagan.

At the same time, Madonna and Michael Jackson presented to the music industry a vision of its own future which would revolve around the global marketing of individual stars; stars whose visual persona would be at least as important as their music, whose "image" was more important than their sound, whose appeal could be sufficiently universal to measure unit sales in hundreds of millions, whose stage performances, televised to billions, would embody the centuries-old dream of liberal capitalism: the individual stripped bare (often literally), unencumbered by interaction with others. Pop stars would not be in bands. This was the moment of the peak of television's power, when the extensive reach of centralized broadcasting coincided with a residual credulity amongst the global public which made it conceivable to sell products like Pepsi Cola without a trace of humor or irony. Many readers will be too young to remember, but it came as a real shock at the beginning of the 1990s when ads for Coke began to use humor. Up until that point, ad campaigns for global brands like Coca-Cola or Nike had relied on un-ironic displays of youthful grace and vigor and high-energy pop soundtracks to sell the most banal objects to an apparently guileless world market.

This was the world that Baudrillard – a disillusioned and increasingly nihilistic former Marxist – looked on and despaired of. It was a world in which it seemed that cultural theorists must either celebrate the protean liberation from selfhood which Madonna and Michael Jackson enacted, or else turn away in horror and disgust.

The point for us, though, is that it didn't last: none of it. This wasn't the end of history, the apocalypse of meaning, the implosion of the real, but a particular intersection in the complex intertwined histories of global capitalism, communicative technologies and music culture. Young people soon became bored by the MTV format, necessitating a return to much more conventional modes of youth-oriented programming, while electorates became appropriately cynical about the televised sincerity of presidential candidates, largely indifferent to Bill Clinton's lying about his sexual exploits. Michael Jackson, as we know, became a figure first absurd then tragic. Even Madonna would eventually decide to adopt that most concrete and universal of feminine roles, motherhood. On the other side of the same coin – from a historical vantage point we can see that the apparent unreality of that moment was itself illusory. The point about Reagan wasn't just that he deployed the rhetoric of liberalism to undermine its own achievements, but that he had the credibility to pull this off because he really did the thing which most Americans probably wanted him to do: he bankrupted the Soviet Union into oblivion by forcing them into an arms race that they could not win. The point about Madonna and Michael Jackson is that they really were demonstrably extraordinary performers and songwriters: the complete failure of all of their less talented successors to achieve anything like their level of commercial or artistic success is testament to this fact. What made the short 1980s possible, then, was not just the success of a particular kind of capitalism or the short-lived credulity of a global televisual public, but the temporary convergence between these forces and the very real creative power of these remarkable individuals. This is a key point which we will have to come back to: in order to make this global culture possible, corporate America had to make use of the real creativity of these personalities. The question of where that creativity came from, of how we might understand it, of what it might mean, is therefore crucial. But let's leave that to one side for one moment just to concentrate on the differences between our moment and theirs.

The world that we live in now looks much less like that depicted by Baudrillard and much more like that envisaged by that far more serious diagnostician of postmodernity, Jean-François Lyotard. If Baudrillard's postmodern was a world in which all meaning had imploded, Lyotard by contrast predicted a context in which a plurality of meanings would proliferate past the point at which any one view of the world could easily contain them for long. Of course, both of these writers offered some fantastic insights and some absurd generalizations, but the tendency of Anglophone commentators to lump them together and caricature them both as nihilistic celebrators of the end of history does both of them a disservice and mistakenly merges their very different accounts into one. Baudrillard looked at MTV and the LA malls in 1985 and thought that this was the endpoint of history. What Lyotard saw coming over the horizon was the world of MySpace, Amazon, Google and YouTube; a world of endless babble and "little stories", without great unifying narratives, and without global superstars or leaders. This is a world which presents us with terrors and terrible problems of its own, but it is not the hyperreality of Baudrillard's imagination any more than it is a world in which Michael Jackson could have stayed sane and healthy.

More specifically, the music-industry model which Madonna and, above-all, Michael Jackson were thought to have established would turn out not to have been a stable new paradigm at all, but one made possible only by the specific conditions of the short 1980s. Reflect on this. In 1985, everybody thought that this was what the future of the music industry looked like; but in fact, there have been no more Madonnas or Michael Jacksons. The mechanisms for the centralized production and reproduction of mass culture – which reached their peak at that moment, seeming to overwhelm the reality of Michael Jackson with his own over-representation and threatening us all with a similar fate – have not quite developed in the way that many expected. Instead we live in a world of bewildering diversity in which no artist can aspire to such universal appeal as Michael Jackson, and no politician can mobilize a public in the way that Reagan and Thatcher did.

The Music of the Multitude

And still, after a quarter of a century, no album has sold as many units as *Thriller*. Not even *Bad*, for all of the power of MTV and Pepsi-Cola, could touch its sheer popularity. This fact alone tells us something important, something about the disjunction between the power of the TV-capital assemblage – even at this, its most glorious moment – and another kind of power, upon which capital has always relied but which it can never fully control. There are two distinct temporalities to observe here. On the one hand, *Thriller* was the harbinger of the short 1980s, of High Postmodernity, of the brief moment when the implosion of the social into hyperreality seemed like a viable hypothesis. On the other hand, it was also the culmination of something: of the popularization of disco, the universalization of soul, and the assertion of black performers' right to be seen and heard rather than merely ventriloquized by better-paid white imitators. Its characteristic sound sublimated the viscerality of funk into a kind of hyperkinetic force whose effectivity did not depend upon the presence of live artists or a powerful sound system, whose dance-ability could be registered even through the poor reproduction media of walkmans, transistor radios, cheap ghetto-blasters and TV-sets blasting out MTV. In this it enacted at once the universal-ization and the full commercialization of a set of sonic potentials which inhered in most popular African-American music but which had never been so fully actualized on a global plane. This, surely, was the creative matrix which made all Jackson's work possible (most notably the classics, *Off The Wall* and *Thriller*): not just his own individual genius, but the entire complex of interactions which sprawled out across the world (with New York, Detroit, Chicago, London, Lagos and Kingston as their hubs), spanning what Paul Gilroy calls "the Black Atlantic"; the downtown New York milieu which was the experimental crucible of disco; the etheric conversation between rock and soul which had come to define the parameters popular music at that time.

This, of course, is the paradox of Michael Jackson. He was at the same time the most stunning embodiment of all the best that these overlapping worlds could offer, the means by which they would reach their widest publics, and the conduit through which emergent neoliberal capital would take them for all they were worth. Jackson's dancing may have been miraculous, but by 1985 it was the copyrighted property of the Pepsi Cola corporation.

It's not as if we don't hear this in the music. The synthesis of funk, pop-rock, disco and soul that Jackson and Quincy Jones made on those albums was undoubtedly effective and affecting, and realized its purpose; but it's not as if nothing was jettisoned in the process. Let me be brutally frank: from the point of view of pop history, there's no disputing the quality of these records; from a discophile perspective they sound (even, especially, on a decent sound-system) thin, eviscerated, deliberately two-dimensional. The deterritorialization of disco which they enact is thrilling because it carries with it the force of its escape; but it loses the qualities which made the places it has escaped from. Speaking as an occasional DJ: I know it's heresy to admit this, but when playing to a committed disco crowd, those tracks – even "Don't Stop..." and "Beat It", those perfect, perfect radio tunes – are too rhythmically plodding (their urgency contained and controlled, never losing their cool) and too sonically ethereal ever fully to carry the floor. They may come from the dance floor, from the site of collective self-expression and transformation which was the New York disco in its golden moment; but they are heading towards a place in which people listen to music alone, on headphones, insulated from the city, or driving down the freeway like Baudrillard in *America*.

Rather than carry on in such an impressionistic vein, it's worth taking stock of exactly where this sound came from. It didn't spring fully-formed from the mind of Quincy Jones, after all. Specifically, the formula which he worked with was very close to that deployed to such similar effect by The Bee Gees on the *Saturday Night Fever* soundtrack: which had, crucially, been the most-successful-album-of-all-time before *Thriller*. Fusing elements of soft rock and smooth soul with fast funk bass lines and weirdly falsetto vocals, both of these sets of tracks owe an obvious debt to the disco experiments of the previous few years. If you want to home in on one artist and one record from that moment, then try Sylvester's 1977 cut "Down, Down, Down". Let's compare it briefly to, say, "Don't Stop...". It's more frenetic – and in that it may lack some of the eroticism of the Jackson/Jones masterpiece – but it's all-body muscularity and its multi-instrumental depth set off the near-hysteria of the vocals and brass in a way which is clearly made to carry the listener into the crowd rather than away from it. By contrast, "Don't Stop..."'s hypnotic rhythm and smooth spatiality tends to push dancers outwards from the center of the floor and away from each other. This is extraordinary dance music, no question: but it's already starting to sound like music for Michael to dance to, while the rest of the world is watching.

But having reflected on these differences, it's perhaps just as productive to think about what all of the figures just alluded to – Jackson, Sylvester, The Bee Gees and their respective producers – have in common, symbolically as well as sonically. Sylvester was a black gay drag queen whose first single had been a funk cover of Neil Young's "Southern Man". The Bee Gees were failed soft-rockers reinventing themselves as divas through an almost direct imitation of Sylvester's falsetto style. Michael Jackson's obsession with self-transformation was to be written on his face. In all cases, a will to become, to transform, to transcend identity and origin, is made very obvious and very audible. We could bring Madonna back in here as well, and observe that most of her career has been spent mining the post-disco club-scene of queer New York for sounds and ideas, for techniques of self-transformation. Yet at the same time, crucially, none of these artists deploy these becomings in the pursuit of minority or the elaboration of narrow identities: in all cases, their deliberate self-deterritorialization is motivated by a will to-universalization. Jackson didn't just want to be white: he wanted to raceless and all races. Sylvester didn't just want to be a woman: he wanted to be all sexes and none. The Bee Gees didn't pretend to be black or women, but in sonically becoming-black and becoming-woman, they made the most popular album in the world before Michael took the process one stage further in *his* attempt to become-everybody (which is to say, nobody) which led to *him* making the most popular album in the world.

Isn't this the basic answer to the question of these records' popularity? They are all hymns to becoming, and everyone wants to become-something. The power of becoming is the power of desire, which is all the joy there is.

Real abstraction through universalization. Real universalization through abstraction. Abstract universalization through deterritorialization. This, of course, is the logic of Capital itself. It is what makes Capital at once the condition of possibility and the condition of impossibility of everything good that modernity (and postmodernity) has produced.

But the deterritorializing forces which gave rise to these particular vectors of transformation were not only or even primarily capitalist in nature. This is a crucial point to keep in mind. The greatest sonic innovations of the Black Atlantic or the disco "underground" have never derived from the direct pursuit of capital accumulation (and let's be clear: trying to make a buck by selling a few records does not constitute capital accumulation and so does not constitute capitalism, not even the wild "anarcho-capitalism" which some commentators like to attribute to alternative creative scenes). The collective creativity, the pursuit of difference and of new forms of collectivity which drove funk, disco, soul, rock, forward (and back, sometimes) came from just those groups – black people, gay people, women, the poor, the bohemian disenfranchised – who had the most to gain differentiating themselves and others in relation to the normality of mid-twentieth century Fordist capitalism. As Negri has so convincingly argued over the years, it was Capital that needed their collective energy and their sheer ingenuity to drive it into the cybernetic age more than they ever needed capital for anything; even if capital did manage to capture it and turn it back against them eventually.

From this point of view, Michael Jackson more than any other phenomenon might be seen as pivotal in the process by which the great upsurge of radical energy which powered the culture and the politics of the 1960s and 1970s was first harnessed, then captured, then turned back upon its originators, by the ingenious apparatuses of capitalism. This is what we hear on *Off the Wall* and *Thriller*: some of the most intense and potent elements of the funk-soul-disco assemblage being perfected, honed, redesigned, retooled and deployed to devastating effect; but increasingly, the effect is to mobilize the idea of Jackson as the global megastar who represents not Black Music but Everybody... which quickly becomes Nobody... which quickly becomes Pepsi. By the time of *Bad* we already start to hear a caricature, which will descend into the absurd messianic pomposity (the most obvious destiny for all universalist delusions) of Jackson's last years. It's surely no accident that *Thriller* becomes the most successful album of all time at precisely the historical moment when the Left is on the brink of its greatest defeat. Somehow that album and its success constitute both a moment of massive collective desire, and of that desire's full capture by the individualized, commodified logic of post-Fordist consumer capitalism.

And yet, to return to my original theme: this is only one moment in a broader history of change. Just as the short 1980s turned out to be not the end of history, Jackson's career should be a reminder to us not only that capitalism is cunning, deadly, and very, very good at what it does; but also that things can always change. *Thriller* may be the most popular album of all time; but there is no certainty that there will not be another one (just imagine, for a moment... a sort of Chinese Manu Chao, inspired by the Fela Kuti and Thomas Mapfumo CDs her father brought back from his business trips to Africa, inspiring the workers of the Special Economic Zones to organize from her MySpace page... it could happen!). And if nothing else, the final fate of Michael Jackson – decrepit, deranged and broke – stands as a warning to later generations, that even the biggest star the world has ever known cannot withstand the demands of capital alone.

12

The Maharaja of Pop:
Michael Jackson and Bollywood

Geeta Dayal

Michael Jackson had a deep and peculiar relationship with India. India, too, had a deep and peculiar relationship with him. On Jackson's first and only visit to India, during the *HIStory* tour in 1996 – hardly the apex of his creative career – he was met with a maharaja's welcome (the details of the visit are recounted breathlessly in documents released by India's official Michael Jackson fan club). The ravishing Bollywood starlet Sonali Bendre greeted Jackson at the airport in Mumbai, performing the ceremonial "aarti" for Jackson – a special puja, or prayer, normally reserved for deities in Hindu temples. Jackson was then whisked off to the luxurious Oberoi Hotel. Rich foods were prepared according to Jackson's tastes – buttery naans and parathas, butter chicken, sweet white wine, chocolate.

The Indian media whipped itself into a frenzy over Jackson's arrival. Lavish galas were arranged in Jackson's honor, starring the cream of India's glitterati. But Jackson barely attended these parties, emerging only briefly for five-minute cameo appearances. Jackson was in full attendance, though, for a pool party at the Oberoi; at the King of Pop's behest, there was a special pool party for children, most brought in from local orphanages. Jackson also made plans to don a burka to visit Mother Teresa in the Mumbai ghettos, but the plans were never realized.

Before Jackson left India, he left the following mash note on a pillow: "India, all my life I have longed to see your face. I met you and your people and fell in love with you. Now my heart is filled with sorrow and despair for I have to leave, but I promise I shall return to love you and caress you again. Your kindness has overwhelmed me, your spiritual awareness has moved me, and your children have truly touched my heart. They are the face of God. I truly love and adore you India. Forever, continue to love, heal and educate the children, the future shines on them. You are my special love, India. Forever, may God always bless you."

Though the saccharine sweetness of the bedside note (the pillow was summarily auctioned off) seemed a bit forced, Jackson seemed sincere about his "special love" for India. And India, too, had a special love for Jackson. Jackson was the crowning achievement of 1980s globalization, the American pop star that everyone in India knew. "'Beat It' was to our generation in India what 'Video Killed the Radio Star' was to our MTV-watching American cohorts in the 1980s," wrote Vamsee Juluri in a recent article in the Huffington Post. "It was the first music video we ever saw... Michael Jackson was not just a pop star for us; he represented the world beyond India we had only heard about, as well as the possibility of catching up with it." Jackson even looked like he could be Indian; his slow-motion metamorphosis over the years from black to brown to tan to taupe to ash-white made his visage reflect any number of cultures. Every world culture could project themselves onto Jackson, physically, emotionally, and mentally, and India was no exception. Jackson was India's own pop star.

Jackson, for his part, took an active interest in Indian culture and traditions. The Indian new-age guru Deepak Chopra said that, in the final days of his life, he had been reading books by the famed Bengali poet Rabindranath Tagore. Chopra was one of Jackson's closest friends, and his influence rubbed off on Jackson in numerous ways. Jackson had, at various times in his life, immersed himself in meditation, ancient Hindu philosophies, and vegetarianism. These healthful impulses seemed to run counter to his well-documented problems with painkiller abuse, aggressive plastic surgery, and everything in between.

Like the country of India, Michael Jackson was a tangled, sprawling web of contradictions. Recently, a clip of "Bollywood Thriller" – an ungainly video mash-up of "Thriller" and, well, Bollywood – made the rounds on YouTube. But the video didn't emerge out of a vacuum; it was part of a continuum; a tribute not only to Jackson but to a long Bollywood tradition – nearly thirty years of Bollywood ripping off Michael Jackson.

Bollywood cinema stars studied, quite literally, at Michael Jackson's feet. "Thriller", especially, spawned legions of Bollywood imitators. Jackson's elaborately choreographed sequences in exotic locales, with a phalanx of backup dancers, were a natural fit for Bollywood's over-the-top numbers. Bollywood actors who took a special shine to Jackson's moves were called "desi Michael Jacksons". One of the most famous of these "desi Michael Jacksons," the actor Prabhu Deva, told The Times of India: "My first encounter with Jackson's work was when I watched 'Thriller'... I might have been ten or eleven-years- old then and the video had an electrifying effect on me. Passionately inspired to dance like him, I began practicing furiously, and what else can I say but that the inspiration turned to aspiration. As they say, the rest is history. Whatever I am today, as a professional dancer and choreographer, I owe to Jackson. I've seen all his videos; I've followed all his movements..."

The Bollywood actor Govinda was another "desi Michael Jackson", performing a pitch-perfect Bollywood rendition of "Thriller" in a 1986 film called *Ilzaam*. In the hit song from the movie, "Street Dancer", Govinda dons a tight red outfit, following the "Thriller" dance formula step-by-literal-step. Mithun Chakraborty, a Bollywood disco-dancing star in the 1980s, also sported the red "Thriller" outfit in the song "Jeena Bhi Kya Hain Jeena" from the 1984 film *Kasam Paida Karne Wale Ki*, a near-photocopy of "Thriller", right down to the zombie dance

moves and horror-movie schmaltz. The song itself was a fascinating mishmash of Jackson stylistic tropes – at various points, it
cops the bass line from "Thriller," the synths from "Billie Jean,"
the swagger of "Beat It".

Bollywood ably repackaged Michael Jackson for an Indian
audience, amping up the colors and doubling the camp and the
sequins. In one particularly goofy sequence in the 1989 film
Gangaa Jamunaa Saraswati, none other than Amitabh Bachchan –
probably the biggest Bollywood star of all time – rocked a single
silver sequined glove and a black leather outfit, working some
"Bad"-style Jackson moves into a song called "Disco Bhangra".
"I'll show a dance just like Michael Jackson's," says Bachchan in
the movie, to a group of admiring villagers in a lush green field.
"I'll sing to you a tune of love and show you a new dance." Soon
afterwards, the movie erupts into a psychedelic, riotous mess of
traditional bhangra dhol beats, disco synth stabs, and country-
and-western guitar, reaching its peak of utter ludicrousness
when Bachchan does a moonwalk in cowboy boots.

Interestingly, the Bollywood copies of Michael Jackson, no
matter how wonky, somehow felt more rich and sensual than the
real Michael Jackson. For all of Jackson's storied prowess as a
dancer, the crotch-grabbing always seemed strangely asexual,
the cool knife-sharp moves a bit too angular. In "Street Dancer,"
Govinda situates himself in front of a group of pulchritudinous
women — the sort of Amazonian women you'd find on the cover
of a Roxy Music LP. Though the song itself is weak – Govinda
pouts "I am a street dancer!" over and over – there's something
genuinely libidinous at work. Chakraborty's rendition shows
him dancing "Thriller"-style with a beautiful woman – and
unlike Jackson's romantic interest in "Thriller," who seemed
more like a plot accessory than anything else, there was palpable
tension in the air.

Strangely, songs from the later Jackson oeuvre – "Remember
The Time" and so on – had nearly as much impact on Bollywood

as stone-cold '80s classics like "Thriller" and "Billie Jean". V. S. Arunraj, of the blog Bollywood Trends, noted that the later Jackson hit "They Don't Care About Us" directly inspired many Bollywood songs – such as A. R. Rahman's hit song "Maro Maro", from the Telegu movie *Boys*. Small nods by Jackson in India's direction made big waves – take Jackson's appearance at the 1999 Bollywood Awards. To Americans in 1999, Jackson was "Wacko Jacko"; Jackson had divorced his wife, dermatology nurse Debbie Rowe, that year and his finances and future were increasingly in question. But India was steadfast in its affection for the King of Pop; to the Bollywood industry, which had never stopped making references to Jackson in its films, it was perennially as if *Thriller* had just been released. Jackson appeared on stage at the Bollywood Awards wearing a regal black and gold kurta, traditional Indian men's garb, to thunderous applause. In his speech, he spoke about Mahatma Gandhi's impact on his life and implored Indians to do more for children. Bollywood megastar Shah Rukh Khan ascended the stage soon after Jackson left, his voice wavering like a nervous teenage fan. "One second, I'll just kiss this dais because Michael was standing here," said Khan, leaning down to kiss the wooden podium. "Marvelous." A few years later, Shah Rukh Khan paid his respects to Jackson once again, doing the "moonwalk" in the 2001 Bollywood film *One 2 Ka Four*.

Indian culture played a brief role in the music video for Jackson's 1991 train wreck of a song "Black Or White". The song's enormously expensive video pushed the bounds of early '90s digital editing technology to the breaking point. In the video, Jackson dances with everyone, in a message of uber-inclusivity – from tribespeople on a Native American reservation to Russian dancers in the snow – before sauntering brazenly through a wall of fire and somehow landing atop the Statue of Liberty. Then, in the bizarre and transfixing climax, the video suddenly erupts into a free-for-all of digital face-morphing, with every culture gleefully blending into every other one in a series of seamless transitions.

India made its cameo in the video by way of the sudden appearance of an Indian classical dancer in the middle of a busy highway. Jackson grooves with her as cars rush by, mimicking her ancient Odissi dance stylings (in 1991, I wasn't accustomed to seeing Indian people on American television, especially not on MTV – and especially not performing classical Indian dance, which I happened to be studying intensively at the time.).

India's connection with Jackson continues. Several leading lights of Bollywood, including actor Akshay Kumar, are planning Michael Jackson movies. Some influential figures in India are calling for the government to honor Jackson's memory with an official Indian postage stamp. The famed Indian film composer A. R. Rahman is currently working on a special Michael Jackson tribute album. "I told him that India adores Michael Jackson," Rahman said to the Indian television station IBN, after meeting the Maharaja of Pop earlier this year. "Everyone wanted to dance like him, dress like him, BE him," wrote Amitabh Bachchan on his blog. "But no one came anywhere near."

13

In place of strife:

Michael Jackson and the British experience of pop

Robin Carmody

Because for so long nobody was bigger than Michael Jackson, it should hardly be a surprise that no other career better embodies what has happened to the British experience of pop over the 39 years we knew him. He'd never have captured so many hearts beyond his own heartland without the romanticism of pop – the essentially non-consumerist, beyond-control appeal of the tantalizingly new and unfamiliar. And yet it was the scale he reached, the new horizons he conquered, which more than anything else destroyed that very appeal.

In 1970, multiple forces were just beginning to tear apart Britain's post-war settlement. Northern Ireland had rapidly sunk into a state of virtual civil war, and the Prince of Wales's investiture had been fraught with tensions over tactics by Welsh Nationalists working on the same model as the IRA. Barbara Castle's attempts to resolve Britain's endemic industrial problems with the "In Place of Strife" white paper had just fatally failed, and Rupert Murdoch had just acquired The Sun – a descendant of the old-socialist Daily Herald, which for the previous five years had attempted to present idealistically egalitarian ideas in a populist form – and was soon to use his papers to campaign vociferously against the high-mindedness (and thus pop-scepticism) of the post-war state. But this latter development was happening infinitely more quietly than the apparent upheavals and tensions of the 1960s' end, from which the nation was profoundly hung over (and thus all the more likely to not notice Murdoch's arrival and its implications).

In the late '60s, the Campaign for Free Radio was founded by young people of the same ilk – significantly greater in number than those who truly believed in hippie idealism – who would be the future architects of the new Toryism and thus of New Labour: they had been lured in by Harold Wilson's emphasis on technology and modernity, but abandoned him en masse almost overnight, following the banning of offshore radio in 1967. As has happened so often with pop, and especially campaigns associated with it, this movement's rhetoric was fatally unclear and ambivalent in its poise between genuine freedom and the pseudo-freedom that has become institutionalized, along with pop, since the Institute of Economic Affairs asserted its counter-revolution (one of the leading members of the Institute of Economic Affairs, Oliver Smedley, was an offshore radio entre-preneur – he saw his station as the last bastion of freedom against a future Communist government – who shot dead the manager of a rival station.). In the mid-Sixties, the only thing that could be ascertained about the free radio movement's position was its desire to break down the Attlee settlement. Everything else was deeply uncertain – it was aligned with ideologues of the Right, but in love with music whose cultural alignment at that stage seemed to be almost entirely on the Left. After all, during the offshore era of 1964-67, much of the music pushed into the Top 10 by the pirates had come from the sections of American society which were, in practice if not theory, only then attaining anything like full citizenship. And the biggest percentage of that came from Tamla Motown, built on discipline which was sometimes probably necessary – Berry Gordy's pragmatism undoubtedly helped its conquest of white America – but sometimes wholly unnecessary, as with the harsh treatment Joe Jackson meted out to his sons.

The man who exploited Reith's brute force of BBC monopoly to a now almost unthinkably vast audience every single morning – grinning, affable public-schoolboy-gone-mid-Atlantic Tony Blackburn – loved nothing more than that most approachable form of black pop, far more reassuring to him than scarily mixed-prole and sometimes politicized reggae or the sudden creations of prog and metal. And nothing suited that model better than The Jackson 5. "I Want You Back" and "ABC" at the breakfast table must have made life seem that bit more exciting, filled 12-year-olds with a new thrust to get them through their days, whether they were at Morrissey's secondary moderns, Mick Jagger's grammar schools or the daringly egalitarian (and thus, at least at that stage, instinctively more pop-friendly) comprehensives. The Atlantic was wide enough for this pop to be, at once, gloriously empowering and yet enticingly distant. For younger children living in racially mixed urban areas, in particular, it was every-thing they could ever desperately hope to be. And yet it didn't last long – after the first four hits The Jackson 5's UK chart perfor-mance was much more erratic, and Michael's initial solo flowering was brief. When "Anarchy In The UK" hit, the idea that Jackson would ever make a meaningful return must have seemed as distant as the idea of pop romanticism itself, amid a chart littered with MOR and novelties. Even when "Show You The Way TO Go" hit number one in the summer of 1977, it was merely a pleasant piece of disco-lite which had a lot of help from the group's official endorsement by Britain's ultimate establishment. The Jacksons took part in a Royal Variety Performance in Glasgow as part of the Silver Jubilee celebrations – at that time, it was highly unusual for pop to attain such recognition, and in many ways this anticipates Jackson's ultimate cultural undoing.

It was within months of the decisive swing towards neoliber-alism that Jackson, out of nowhere, exploded into life. Commercially, he wasn't supernova yet, especially outside pop's twin heartlands of present and past imperial powers, but *Off The*

Wall was undoubtedly his artistic peak, the one moment where it seemed as though he could make everything work, could square all his – and our – circles. Somehow, it seemed to work alongside the multiple ramifications of post-punk, not (other than to a few already self-parodic hardliners) against them. And still that romanticism of pop was there, creating a tangible sense among those who were inspired by it that anything might just, still, be possible. The new Conservatism could have gone in any direction, could easily have returned to a pre-war social and cultural world with no place for pop. Yet in commercial terms *Off The Wall* would only ever go down in history as a first step, just as 1979/80 was only a first step for neoliberalism. And that was the tragedy.

Excellent as much of it is, the only interesting thing anyone could possibly say about *Thriller* now is the role it played in defining and creating the new capitalism. It is certainly not coincidental that the *Thriller* phenomenon – gathering more strength, gaining more converts and conquering more countries with every week that passed – was precisely concurrent with the decisive cultural defeat of "gentlemanly capitalism". And it may also be for reasons related to the social context of pop that Jackson is most directly comparable to Elvis Presley. The latter's initial appearance coincided almost exactly with the brutal realization that the US simply would not allow Britain to make common cause with France against US interests – an assertion of global dominance, which also decisively pushed France to ally itself with a (West) Germany only tentatively re-entering the international stage and effectively froze Britain out of the nascent EEC. In 1957, the Pelvis seemed to subliminally crush the plans for Anglo-French political union which had been seriously discussed immediately before Suez.

Similarly, the *Thriller* phenomenon completed what the Falklands War had started – it danced on the grave of the hopes for a One Nation Tory (and thus much more European-minded) coup against Thatcher, while also destroying the idea that British pop might take inspiration from the continent (an idea that had been gaining strength with Kraftwerk getting to number one, and the success of Visage, The Associates, one-hit wonders like The Mobiles, a huge pop group like The Human League and even lumpen, point-missing cash-ins like post-Foxx Ultravox, who did at least show just how widespread the whole continental drift of British pop briefly appeared to be). Unlike the impact of the directly comparable *Star Wars* on mainstream American cinema, the influence of *Thriller* on mainstream American music was overwhelmingly positive, blowing away a lot of MOR and country dreck (the Hot 100 in 1982 had been in such a dire state that Crosby, Stills & Nash and America could return to the Top 10) and paving the way for Prince and all who sailed with him. But its impact in Britain was much less overwhelmingly positive, and seemed to merely set the tone for another quarter-century of ever more pathetic chasing of *someone else's* imperial shadows, after a brief period when it seemed – as never at any other point in the last half-century – as though the wrongs of the post-Suez settlement could be, if not wholly geopolitically reversed, at least culturally rebalanced to something more conducive to what Britain should have been.

And yet there were some barriers left standing at the time of *Thriller* – there were still parents who wouldn't let their children watch ITV, and if you confined your radio listening to certain fixed points on Radios 3 and 4 and your TV viewing to certain fixed points on BBC2 you could pretty much remain ignorant of Jackson's existence in a way that is not the case today with pop figures who come nowhere near Jackson's scale. The rest of the decade would be a consistent process of steadily pushing those walls down, to the point where today pop's cultural reach is greater even as its individual stars are smaller – the very process which Jackson pushed to the limit grew beyond his control and rendered him irrelevant. It may well be that the biggest pop stars we have left are those who grew up with it and now have the greatest geopolitical power of all: modern Western leaders are marketed and presented in a manner that first took hold in pop music.

When *Bad* was released at the end of the summer of 1987, neoliberalism had conquered the West and was preparing with each moment for its final push beyond. And this was where Jackson's greatest impact would ultimately lie – not in places like Britain and Australia, which had been primed for something like this for decades, but in a China and an India steadily opening themselves to international trade, an Eastern Europe grasping a new future as the force which had dominated it for so long withered under its own contradictions, and a (continental) Western Europe coming to terms with the economic winds blowing around it. In Eastern Europe especially, Jackson really was precisely what Elvis had been to post-Suez Britain – the decisive force sweeping away the dusty pages of the native culture and the ashes of a dying empire. So much of world-changing political import happened during Jackson's peak years that it was as if Jackson and neoliberalism made each other happen faster – *Bad* was the big push to the end of an empire, *Dangerous* the consolidatory triumph and probably his most successful record in non-Western countries which had not previously been open to pop (the only Jackson show to have been released on DVD is his 1992 performance in Bucharest, in a stadium which at the time of all his previous albums had been a symbol of Ceausescu's power).

Almost everything that can be said has already been said about Jackson's slow decline, and specifically about *that* particular installment of Jarvis Cocker's doomed attempt to assert, on its deathbed, what British pop had once been. It's worth mentioning, though, that the still-huge UK success of *HIStory: Past, Present and Future Book 1* and its singles – by that time, Jackson was more successful almost everywhere outside the US than within it – was actually greater than that of most bands considered Britpop. But it cannot be repeated often enough what Jackson had become at the end – the nightmare that the dream of pop has curdled into, the bitter aftermath of the romanticism which did so much for so many. The fact that he was once such an inspiration makes his end all the harsher, because it sums up precisely why so many of us who would once have defended pop with our lives now feel that we can at best take it or leave it, that it – or rather the system with which it is inextricably intertwined – has become our enemy rather than our friend.

The most interesting postscript to Jackson's life was Momus's suggestion that, now there is not and cannot be one all-embracing "King of Pop", the age of narrowcasting will see a major return to high/low cultural and class divisions and a decisive shift away from cross-class pop dominance. That may well be happening in places where pop was always that bit *more* of an import, in a wholly foreign language and not from a geopolitical partner, where it has not been integrated into the dominant forms of patriotism for as long as it has been here. The rather bathetic, lowered-horizons patriotism which incorporated The Beatles on a sort of "the Americans may have humiliated us, but at least we can still beat them at *one* of their games" level itself now goes back almost half a century, so I cannot see a return to pre-pop cultural conditions happening in England to the same extent (though it may happen to some extent in Scotland should it secede from the Union). But I would suggest that the pop which pre-empted and molded the image of David Cameron as we now know him – the whole axis of middlebrow pseudo-pop which has run from Coldplay to James Blunt, aimed precisely at an audience which has always been suspicious of the twin sources of stimulation, the genuinely highbrow *and* the unashamedly brash and populist, a sort of modern-day equivalent of light classical (if there were riots now, Radio 2 would play "Fix You" like it played Ronald Binge's "The Watermill" while "Ghost Town" was number one) –

may be a British manifestation of such a reassertion of class distinctions. Obviously, it is a wholly negative one, but we couldn't really have expected anything better.

Jackson's legacy, for all that it contains so many moments of unimpeachable inspiration and excitement, now seems far more a lead weight than anything else. There could be no better metaphor for most of what is called pop in English-speaking countries than that. Even in death, he still defines everything. But now, more than ever, it is something we need to get away from. The pre-*Thriller* moment in British pop must, if anything is, be our model. Then and only then can we not stop until we've got enough, and strip those words of their neoliberal connotations.

The only way Jackson's original impact can be even partially recreated is if his precise model is abandoned. Unfortunately, all modern institutional power in the UK – and especially England – is deeply skewed against that. Somewhere, in a universe alongside ours, "I Want You Back" is playing in a Britain where there was a general election in October 1978, where pop's glories were never thus tainted. But parallel universes are only that, false hopes of the other, original kind of romanticism. Michael Jackson went out – as he came in – in line with the world around him. Nothing more could have been expected. Now we must somehow – against all the odds – create another kind of world.

14

"What about death, again":

the dolorous passion of the son of pop

Mark Sinker

The rock was very small now; soon it would be submerged. Pale rays of light tiptoed across the waters; and by and by there was to be heard a sound at once the most musical and the most melancholy in the world: the mermaids calling to the moon. Peter was not quite like other boys; but he was afraid at last. A tremor ran through him, like a shudder passing over the sea; but on the sea one shudder follows another till there are hundreds of them, and Peter felt just the one. Next moment he was standing erect on the rock again, with that smile on his face and a drum beating within him. It was saying, "To die will be an awfully big adventure."

– J. M. Barrie, *Peter And Wendy*, 1911

On 5 April 1960, a respected and successful middle-aged London publisher and family man walked from the bar of the Royal Court Hotel to the nearby underground station, which was Sloane Square, and down the stairs to the platform – where he threw himself under a tube-train, to fatal end. He was 63, and his name was Peter Llewellyn-Davies; fourth to die of the five brothers who had collectively inspired J. M. Barrie's Peter Pan: the character from his play (*Peter Pan: The Boy Who Wouldn't Grow Up*, 1904), and subsequent novel (*Peter and Wendy*, 1911). The fact of this curious, very powerful work of fiction, and the fame of it, its instantly seized-on aura, as thick with unspoken sex as it's frantic with its refusal, had dogged the brothers all their adult lives (two barely reached adulthood). At school, Peter himself was relent-lessly bullied about his links with it; in later life he only referred to it as "that terrible masterpiece"; the memoir (and exorcism) that he spent years assembling from family correspondence, he referred to as "Morgue"; unfinished and set bitterly aside, it contributed to his suicide. Barrie's idea was a spell and a curse, became a too-easy, too-obvious journalist's gag – a metalepsis turned toxic with repetition: that we should somehow be aston-ished not to find the book-character's qualities in the real-life person said to have inspired it: "THE BOY WHO NEVER GREW UP IS DEAD"; "THE TRAGEDY OF PETER PAN", and so on.

*

Like many Britons my age, my first encounter with the reality of Jackson-starlife was Danny Baker's funny and sane feature in the NME in 1981, "The Great Greenland Mystery". The onetime editor of groundbreaking punk fanzine Sniffin' Glue treated the encounter as high comedy, this bright disenchanted working class Londoner traveling all the way in to the baroque absurdity of the Beverly Hills soul industry. It wasn't at all a takedown: Baker loved Jackson's music, even when he thought it was ridiculous. But the basic punk claim of rights, drawn from two and a half decades of rock and pop, from Poly Styrene and Bob Dylan and Little Richard, that our calling as humans is to walk from cowshed to palace to challenge and spar and connect as equals; or perhaps its less prissy flipside, that the breathtaking cathedral you've arrived in is worth exactly as much as your decision to fart in it. The sacred made insolent, the nose-pick made sacred.

Well, actually a lot of the piece is given over to dissecting the unsacred stupidity of the pop press conference: the Jackson brothers doing their bored promo duty, Michael being fey and quirky, shy and spaced. "A cloak of secrecy and protection –

over-protection – seems to surround the heartthrob," wrote Baker. "Whatever lies at its core won't be penetrated in a decade... He strikes me at times as having just a touch of the character that Peter Sellers played in *Being There*". There's a moment of ordinary corporate (or family) paranoia, when the brothers refuse to allow NME's photographer to do his job, insist on supplying official press images; there's a glimpse of recognizable teenage behavior, when they talk about growing up together, squabbling, sharing a bed, and peeing it, while Michael declares that Yellow Mattress would be an excellent LP title. And then the end to their brief time in one room – memorable because very funny (like the rest of the piece) but also because unsettling: Baker's goodbye is a cheerful Londoner's "Mind how you go." Jackson, already tragi-comically distanced from the workings of the commonplace, replies, in blithe seriousness, "Thank you, I will. I will mind how I go."

*

Some time in 2003, Gary Farber posted at his blog Amygdala his "FIRST AND PROBABLY ONLY MICHAEL JACKSON POST EVER", commenting on a forensic scientist's computer simulation of what Michael Jackson would be expected to look at, at 45, assuming, things had turned out, well, what's the word? Normally? This is what Farber says, about the simulation: "Decent-looking, even handsome, guy, right? How sad this fellow instead had himself mutilated, so many times, out of whatever desperate feelings of inadequacy and crazed aesthetic judgment he must have been living with the past few decades, into looking like some drag queen puppet droog imitation of Elizabeth Taylor if she lived in the 47th Chorp Dimension, to the point where anyone who looks at him instantly thinks he must be some sort of lunatic horrorshow monster. What sane person would choose to do that to themself?"

Amygdala is a leftish blog about US politics, and Farber wasn't following the Jackson story as a scholar, let alone as a fan. He's a relatively uninvested bystander making a seemingly commonsense observation about absurdity, and the nasty ugliness of modern American life: Who can't see that something's gone horribly wrong here? When he saw his traffic surge after Jackson's death, he reposted it – which is when I read it. And because I'm not uninvested, and hence unconcerned with commonsense, my immediate response was to turn his query on its head. Why do we assume that only someone very crazy would mutilate himself this way? It made me think back more than ten years, to a documentary I saw about the French performance artist Orlan, whose work involves plastic surgery undertaken on herself. She, too, has had her face multiply reshaped: not to be "decent-looking", let alone beautiful, but to look bizarre, a "drag queen puppet droog", a "lunatic horrorshow monster". And while *The Reincarnation of Saint-Orlan*, which began in 1990, is certainly controversial, even those who attack it, and question Orlan's motives, politics or mental health, have no real problem assigning agency to her. She may be working through symptoms – what artist isn't? – but she's accorded the dignity of self-awareness. She's a professor at the École Nationale Supérieure des Beaux-Arts at Cergy in Paris: she knows what she's at.

I'm not attacking Farber here, or Orlan. I guess I'm asking a question about reception, and how smart people remain susceptible to received wisdom and cliché. Orlan's project is interesting enough – she makes herself look uncanny and repulsive, for real, and we get to think about our response to this. But the context of our response is actually fairly carefully precontrolled: her work comes surrounded by her own explanations of it: terms like nomadism, hybridity and difference, function as the equivalent of the laugh-track on an iffy sitcom. All these careful little signals to render the encounter safe: to ensure we don't react Farber-

vegetable/You're just a buffet, you're a vegetable/They eat off of you, you're a vegetable". Then he cites the video for "Smooth Criminal", the song from 1987's *Bad*: how it first strikes you: – "a fairly absurd cast-of-hundreds production number, full of playfulness and spectacle and a bizarre séance type thing" – and the strange disconnect with the words suddenly coming out of Jackson's mouth: *"He came into your apartment/He left bloodstains on your carpet"*.

Kogan continues: "Since his dancing, costumes, and singing (even on radio and record) neither augment nor neutralize nor express nor define the lyrics, "bloodstains on your carpet" (should anyone notice it) takes on a weird integrity. Like, huh? Who ordered that? I didn't know it was on the menu!" And indeed not just in the words: "in his videos a bit, too, which are often about 'pursuit'; maybe a little in his voice the way he "overdoes" various "owwws" and "eeeeeeooooo" and sexy sobs and gasps, and in his dance the way he turns so sharp."

Kogan's term for this not-on-the-menu mini-adventure is the "Free Lunch", and he's at pains to distinguish it from other moves, which fancy critics can chase if they want: not a shock effect and not necessarily something that stands out from the context, but rather something that happens in addition to what is "officially going on"... nothing to do with "suppressed matter" (e.g. "that which is suppressed in the dominant discourse"), which is work and I'll let puritans waste their time on it... a free lunch can be intended and heavily remarked upon (though it often isn't) as long as it's generally seen as either extraneous or (if it unexpectedly becomes central) unanticipated.

There's a lot going on here. First, to bring us up to date: Jackson as a perverted Gothic malefactor, abroad to hurt, is no kind of a Free Lunch any more, not at all: the unmoored throwaways became the central story; Kogan actually starts his discussion with a joke about Steve Albini's band Rapeman, that if Jackson rather than Albini had named a project Rapeman, it really wouldn't come across as tired punk shtick, not in the '80s. All turnabout since then: today the "matter suppressed in the dominant discourse" long ago stopped being "work" – these days you have to work for an idea like "Rapeman" not to be what's "officially going on", for it not to be the stuff you first respond to. In 1989, you could (correctly) note that Jackson seemed to be playing prowler and target, "doing 'Midnight Rambler' again and again", his dance round Jagger's dance of performer as stalker-killer, and round himself (in "Billie Jean", for example) as stalked, as the vegetable this "they" feeds off – and for some reason almost no one was attuned to notice, or to take you up on the conversation. Take the briefest walk down Jackson's lyrics today, and you find your hard-won disenchanted critical eye staring bleakly back at you out of what he was singing about twenty years ago: "*I am the damned/I am the dead/I am the agony inside a dying head*" (from "Who Is It" on 1991's *Dangerous*). He was the distracted Cassandra of himself for more than half his life: all this prophecy and really no one picked it up, in or out of the "dominant discourse".

Second: the distinction I think should still be maintained, between the kind of psychological reading of songs from *Thriller* onwards, as cries for help – or acts of disruptive resistance against some consensus or other – and where the idea of Free Lunch takes us. The Free Lunch argument is that, in anything we find it worth paying attention to, there's a cluster of stuff going on: some shaped by primary intention, some unconsciously, some by conventions or tabloids or uninvested half-attentive observers with semi-related agendas, all there to be picked at by the kind of critic who enjoys reading against the grain – but Free Lunch says there can be more than this. The elements that aren't Free Lunch are mainly tangled up in agency: some make it the center (art as the artist's will projected); some put it in doubt (art as a package of symptoms). There's a particular relationship of expectation, what we're officially supposed to be getting out of authored art:

an established reception area of expectation that – as a result – can miss some of the stuff that's going on. Orlan the professor at the École Nationale Supérieure des Beaux-Arts at Cergy in Paris knows the language and has the contacts to set up a context of appreciation which straitens every element of content into a direct engagement, of delivery of service (or not), between client and business.

Immeasurably more powerful – or so you'd think – the True King of Rock, Pop and Soul (as he was crowned in 1989) doesn't get to be the author of all of himself, or even all his work. But right there – in dozens of songs and videos – is material that any unprepared ear or eye can pick up and use, about blood, terror and dread: about mutual cannibalization: that's the Free Lunch, not there because you're after edgy art; not the results of a hunt for pathologies but there anyway; unconstrained (at least until it's pointed out). There's no sense that that these elements aren't totally public: Jackson put some of them on the biggest-selling LP of all time; he's never been some garret-housed avant-garde crank refusing to square his work with the mainstream; nor was he, for some forty-five years, in any way overlooked or under-exposed.

Jackson's work is Gothic as all get-out, and yet to treat it all as one long chaotic pained cry for help is as wrong-headed as the idea that the whole of his story is one seamless conceptual stunt. Watch him dance: actually watch him – dance being a notorious blind spot for a lot of intellectuals – and what do you see? You see a lifetime's ruthless discipline, which should put you in mind of the instrumentalized childhoods of East European gymnasts, or a master-acrobat like Jackie Chan: bruised infancies stiff with real terror. And you see, with this, and out of it, a strange, private, mastered pleasure: the world of someone who has no one they can ever quite share the good or the bad with, so that both become a kind of overheard hummed soliloquy of play-joy, play-fear, play-communication. You won the prize of prizes, and there's no one can really even know what that means for you. Because all your partners are only ever paid-for twitching zombie extras, doing your conscious bidding, "behaving" as you direct. All condensed in one more-or-less anorexic elfin body, Jackson was left to enact, for himself, all the deep roles of his life, including the random, serendipitous walks-ons; he has to supply his own surprises.

*

Citing Pan and Barrie isn't so hard for a writer; it arrives as writing: you cut and paste. The lineage that's harder to trace exactly is the one Jackson brought himself from: his work rather than his fantasy. Compared with Jackson's casts of thousands and vast Hollywood credits-lists of co-creators, James Brown fashioned African-American music's predecessor Leviathan from a tight, manageable crew: rarely as big even as the major jazz big bands, which were always half in his mind. He too garnered quasi-political titles – Prime Minister of Super Heavy Funk – but the one everyone remembers is "Godfather of Soul".

Which is an odd and a contradictory term in itself: and not – I assume – inadvertently. "Godfather" of course references the novel (1969) and the film (1972): that glamorized study of Italian-American thug-life so sharply distinct from the more elevated churchly connotations of the word 'soul'; the complex cultural-nationalist journey from penniless peasant immigrancy to political respect, cultural pride, control over your heritage and your social niche, as a needle-thread walk between the godly and the criminal.

Brown didn't dub himself the "Black Godfather": his response to the black cultural nationalist project was a song called "Soul Power". In 1971, it was natural to take this as a canny showman's oblique, even sugarcoated declaration of allegiance with Black Power as an organized movement. But Brown's self-image and sense of civic responsibility were bigger than this (he took phone calls from presidents about matters of public order – and told them things they didn't want to hear): he saw it the other way round. You can nitpick the details of his analysis – just like Don Corleone, Brown had long ago made a pact with undiluted capitalism, trusting his ability to wrest value out of that more than almost anything else – but you can't really deny that, in his superbly, implacably ambiguous way, he turned the outflanking maneuvers and postures of the radical identity politics of the late '60s from a rallied, brittle certainty into a blunt, open question. Respect, pride, control: what do we lose when we achieve all these?

The word "soul" is the heart of this question, as roomy as it's precise, a hard meaning to parse but not at all a vague one. It arrives, after all, out of Christian theology – and of all people, Brown, a master of rigor and economy, of private system transformed into public ritual, is not using it merely as a hand-wave towards cultural solidarity or the superior ethics and attitude of bloodline. Of course – like all his music – "Soul Power" is also about sexual joy, racial pride, the specifics of a heritage, the matter of memory (food, look, the way a people speak, the way they move through the street). But also this: *"I want to get under your skin/If I get there, I've got to win/You need some soul, come on get some/and then you'll know, where I'm comin' from..."*

So not in-born, not racial: rather a sensibility that can be shared, passed on. The metaphor's sexual – of course – and runs direct at the fear of connection: at identity politics as a sanctioned cultural apartheid; at the psychic shelter of merely sticking with your own, as a political shibboleth.

Well, it's pretty easy to lose your way when you're sketching the unspoken: to project when you should be listening or observing, to glimpse the reflections of your own desires and interests and stubborn habits in things that move you; that call to you. Guesswork is perilous; and Brown (as with many pre-rock musicians) preferred the toughened ambivalence of the refusal to verbalize his projects by the rules of the mainstream press conference, as a way to shoulder-bully himself all possible moving (dancing) room. His own life story left him to trust the unspoken, the Jackson family absolutely his successors here. The room he fought for, politically, and won, is the room that Jackson lived his life out in, its geometry a nervous given, its freedoms and its dangers more or less unchanged.

I said "Leviathan" above, and I should probably unpack that a bit: the idea of an entire social body, the dispersed, dyspraxic monster of the community, as manifested and controlled and enabled healthily to cohere, in the body of the prince, the decider, the artist-of-state, the menu-setter. This is a central element of Brown's soul politics: he inherits and self-consciously elaborates and innovates within, a tradition of music-as-collective-polylogue. Gospel as one ancestor, well known as Brown's first love: its call-and-response, its partial stated duty to a higher force (as some believe) than the market, its role in the institutions that structure the black community within and against American history (no black church, no Civil Rights), this is one version of collectivity. Jazz is another – Brown more than once noted that blues, this extensive African-American language of exile, flight, anguished solitude within the dancing crowd, was never really his prime personal sustenance. But jazz was important to him: the multi-tongued music of improvised social adaptation in the moment. Two distinct ways, already, to fashion a Soul Leviathan – though you'd only here get to the meaning of Brown's project by juxtaposition and contrast; just as you do, one step on, with Jackson's out of Brown's.

And there's more to the politics of soul than the shared practice of generations of black American musicians, key though this clearly is. The soul is the atom of Christian morality: the indivisible unit. It's that part of us that makes us equal before God. And it's this beneath-the-skin equality, before and after whatever differences of birth or education, body or mind, may accrue or occur during our lifetimes, that root one very powerful reading of American democracy. The American political project, at peace with itself or in turmoil, starts with the axiom of equality: "We hold these truths to be self-evident, that all men are created equal, that they are endowed by their Creator with certain unalienable Rights, that among these are Life, Liberty and the pursuit of Happiness".

And the course of the first hundred-odd years of the Republic was a war, sometimes cold, sometimes murderously hot, to establish (along with all acceptable meanings of Happiness, Liberty and Right) who gets to fall in this category "all men", and who – for example – is just an animal and a chattel and a commodity. Who gets – since the Republic was set up by farmers, businessmen and lawyers – to trade what: and who ends up being traded.

*

All this, but both sides of it. Agonizingly and immediately. Soul power is about joy and pride and togetherness, lovely and necessary things – but also about terror and a terrifying, almost contradictory intensity of individualism. Created equal before God; created equal before the market. If all the LPs are the same shape and size, it's the sound they make that will matter. (At a certain moment, Furtwängler conducting Beethoven for *Deutsche Grammophon* is exactly interchangeable with *Blood On The Dance Floor: HIStory In The Mix*. This is a leveling as frightening as it's thrilling, sat quietly mute at the heart of the pop world. No surprise so many want to start from here...).

Soul is a counterstrike against the fact of slavery – but those who know what it was to have been slaves have the experience to be careful to work through pragmatics towards absolutes. All musicians, all artists operating within the market, must

175

commodify their gifts, their talents, their perceptions and visions and insights. If I had more space to explore the politics of Brown's music, I'd look to showing that – not the first, perhaps, but by seizing his times one of the foremost – he combined a commodification of himself, the salesmanship of the idea of everything he was, physically and spiritually, with an establishment of his own self-ownership. His unalienable right to commodify what he did and who he was.

Hence, maybe, the puzzlement we sometimes feel when we explore agency in all this. Who made Brown's music (he was not everyone's favorite boss)? How much is he the master of his own destiny, how much the puppet – how much is the whole of the soul project the mapping of this question? It's not as if legalistic IP rulings are going to solve the mystery of who did what, how, in the conflicted collectiveness of his music: you could almost say that everything Brown did was a project to render such solutions unreachable; to ensure the matrix of creative input remains unreadable. Though obviously that's not a common-sense way to introduce the meaning and purpose of funk. Still, anyone who knows – via family folktale, via community heritage – what it is to exist as nothing but a commodity will likely have plenty of justification for distrusting the wiles of reason and the snares of law.

Once there was a word people set against the idea of agency: "passion" – lost now to years too much over-eager press-release deployment. The sense is still there, buried in distant but related parts of speech: active versus passive. Active and agency come from the Latin verb *ago, agere, actum,* to drive, to lead; passive and passion (and patient) from *patior, pati, passum sum,* to endure. It's fully present there in the (archaic?) religious sense, the Passion of Our Lord, passion meaning suffering as intervention; it's still there psychologically. Suffering as intervention in its collective form: a group music, a menu-setting micro-Leviathan taking the social polylogues of gospel and jazz, and brought to them a radical democracy of self-presentation, which – to this day – remains as undigested, a problem for all the music that came after it, as Kogan wrote in 2000 in his essay "Death Rock 2000": "Funk at its invention was really extreme; everything became rhythm, foreground became background and vice versa, nothing simply supported a "lead" instrument or singer. The vocals were drumbeats, the drums punctuated and completed the vocals. The horns were staccato percussion. The beats were not evenly spaced: instead, even more than in the rest of rhythm and blues, everything was in complementary note clusters, no instrumental part replicating another, each tumbling over the others in a perpetual-motion machine."

Funk is not usually the name given to the music Michael Jackson made (though James Brown's is a name Jackson revered; a work Jackson knew inside out). And Brown's Leviathan-troupe was tiny, its project both imaginable and manageable. By contrast the sheer world-striding vastness of Jackson's extended Passion Play, his attempts to sculpt a undigested collectivity, out of music-constituents (all the scattered languages of pop, including movies) unable ever to exist together in the same time and place, and within a music arena subject to far more forces, was far less controllable than anything Brown faced – for all that Jackson seemed, by inheritance and personal achievement, to have escaped and cushioned himself from the kind of suffering he knew as a child, and would have faced all the more if his family had never escaped Gary, Indiana.

Still, when it comes to matters of self-ownership, Brown – brought up by a loving aunt in a whorehouse – learnt a lot about the limits and dignities of self-ownership that Jackson never got to find out. The vegetable in the buffet, the naked lunch on the end of the fork – Michael was just five when it began, and the person writing out the menu was his own father.

*

I never found the several very long Vanity Fair exposés of Jackson's sex life especially convincing. Maureen Orth knew what she believed, and mustered dozens of anecdotes to bolster it. And the compromised and the *partis pris* supplied them; no one offering anything that wasn't wholly towards an obvious end, that you ended none the wiser. The distorting filter of interests was far too powerful.

And front and center of every episode of the story – which made me trust them all the less – was an element no one was facing or addressing. Not the issue of child-adult sexual relations, inappropriate and abusive because equality is impossible, physically and psychologically: everyone was of course all over the jargon of these inequalities, moralizing or rationalizing or touting for business. The inequalities no one was really talking about were economic and cultural. How does any multi-millionaire avoid exploiting – and damaging – those hugely less well-off? How can a celebrity's interactions with the rest of humanity not be inappropriate, not be abusive? Would you let any member of your low-income family – child or adult – anywhere near a superstar? How is this not going to end badly? How is it not always already a titanic damage? – How is Jackson's music not a plain-as-you like, conscious, willed map of just this damage?

The judgments of the poor are – of course – distorted by their need for the wealthy to behave well towards them. Even a rich man born dirt-poor can't easily recalibrate his responses to this fact – if he even chooses so to calibrate, and plenty don't bother. And it's not just about money: celebrities live in a world where their way of seeing shapes that of others. They are hard to say no to: not just because they can hire and fire, rewarding the yes-men far above their pay grade, but because you don't get to be a celebrity without a heightened skill in charm and persuasiveness. It's your gift; it's your job; it's your power.

Peter Pan in Neverland; the Emperor Tiberius on Capri: Jackson deft-stepped from his heritage into a pop world and a pop culture where near-children had garnered unprecedented power; where sex was declared something only teens knew or understood; where adolescence was idealized as untainted: a space before corrupted decisions and social separation; where to be grown-up was somehow to simultaneously to have sold yourself to the machine and to have re-entered the state of spinsterish virginity. The ability to realize dreams risks the absolute loss of the ability to process things that aren't dreams: wisdom, reality, history. Topsy-turvy anti-mundane energy of this – in both its leveling and its empowering effects – was intoxicating; hugely alluring, hugely disorientating. Brown had cast himself, pleading and driving, as work-boss of a people brought together in his music, through the eyes and ears of a long-beleaguered, battling community. Jackson – Leviathan of every kind of music, from a family that had internalized so much of society's violence – aimed far higher. He would make himself both healing meal for all of pop's tribes – zombies too! and kiddies! – and the monster that drove us to the meal. To step away from the bitter everyday inequalities we know in our daily lives – and this is something we sometimes absolutely have to do – is to risk calling up inequalities we don't yet have the antennae to recognize; or to process; or to counter.

*

I look at the face on the cover of 2001's *Invincible* – cropped close; grayed out; one pert eyebrow dissolving into pixels; knowing image of the media clown-soul beneath the skin – this slyly appropriate set-up to a rigorously confident record that's all splintered shifts of register and machine-collisions of perspective; all beats made of grunts and electronic growls. Final track on this final (non-compilation, non-remix, full-length) release is "Threatened": the Reincarnation of St. Wacko in the last of its song-form spasms. Rod Serling, himself twenty-six years dead, is reanimated for the voiceover, describing what's to come as "somewhat unique", and thus needing a "different kind of introduction". Nineteen years before, "Thriller" – with its epic film-fed lead-in and Vincent Price cameo – seemed so simple in its pop pulp feel that "bloodstains on your carpet" could come still across later as unrequested and unexpected and even out of character. What about the declaration, in "Threatened", of Jackson as the beast we should be beware: *"You should be watching me, you should feel threatened… A nightmare, that's the case/Never Neverland, that's the place…"* Even conceived as retread and self-homage, this song could hardly be more aware of how squirmy people will be feeling about all the implications of repetition.

Jackson had entered into dispute at this time, with label and then-manager; the latter denounced as a racist, the former for failing to promote *Invincible* properly. Unavoidably this puts me in mind of Prince in 1993, in dispute with Warners, changing his name to an unsayable symbol (because Warners had ownership of the one he was born with), and performing with the word "slave" Sharpied onto his cheek.

The menu for general commodities and the menu for culture would seem to be at odds. Industrialization is geared to strip out surprises, and surpriselessness is something we want from our vendors: so we can trust what we're getting: no annoying little variations in our cereal taste or our bra size, the pleasure or the comfort or the usefulness we know we can reliably anticipate, plus at minimized cost! And uniformity in LP size and recording speed was pretty convenient too: plus a super-neat way – as noted above – to turn the quest for quality and value into an exciting competition: everyone's off from the same blocks…

But who wants in on culture without surprises – on music or movies or books which give you nothing you didn't know you were going to get? In a world where the internet has hugely expanded the chatter of potential response and exploration, the word "spoiler" is a genuine accusation: we don't want to know what we're getting. Free Lunch, you say? Don't give the end away! It's the only one we've got!

In the first version of this essay, in a hurry to tie things up, I tried to spin the notion of down-the-rabbit-hole unexpectedness into an act or a symbol of resistance, to the prison regimes of obligatory fun and professional rebellion, of what the rest of the crowd paid for and what the critical discourse thinks matters, to the bounds and bars of deadlines and release dates and focus-grouped endings, and who your label and your manager tell you are, and what you agreed to sell yourself as. The leisure industry is a disenchanting treadmill even if you didn't drag yourself all the way up from where Brown or Jackson began, a punishing physical grind set about with clichés and inattention and mischief, the torrent of your own imagination coming back at you in near-random cut-up form, no longer yours to control or determine.

But this is wrong: surprise is an element in art that commerce needs, maybe more than any other. When the record company says "We need another *Thriller*", they mean, "We need something that captures as big an audience as perfectly freshly," not "We need an unremarkable retread" (however handy a retread is for their promo routines). We get retreads a lot, and – to avoid being caught out and disappointed? – have taught ourselves to expect them; to see and hear them when they aren't there. Commodities – even the non-cultural ones – are never uncomplicated, however variously complicit we are in stating otherwise. They're hugely complex sedimentations of desire, craft, of known and hidden social relations. For all kinds of competing ends, needs and agendas, consumers and vendors fight to underplay this – as do critics, those hang-dog bad-conscience go-betweens. We all have reasons to identify the simplified or the streamlined: to agree that we agree that here it is, even when it isn't. To settle for the repetition we anticipated, denying ourselves the right to walk up to whatever it is we actually got, and spar with it.

And maybe this actually is where the real trap comes, for the willful imagination: my attempt to freeze an idea of openness; switching the horror of boredom and letdown for the horror – if you like – of being locked forever in the moment where adventure and invention and imagination are all still unfettered; where the realization of the future isn't swathed in loss.

*

The ruins we live among are far harder to see – and pass judgment on – than the ruins that clogged earlier times: Google "Peter Pan" today, perhaps alongside its discarded (and stupefyingly unexpected) first-draft title, "The Great White Father", and you'll find plenty of clever young internet folk giving J. M. Barrie a kicking. Here was a successful and admired Edwardian male, the best-selling playwright of his day: on easy terms with the high and mighty, able to pass anywhere in the metropole of a vast decaying empire, and so yes, of course its many absurd bigotries infested his dreams. There is arguably no period in British history more easily lampooned and critico-politically harpooned – not to say patronized – than the Edwardian era; Barrie belonged to it, and takes his lumps as a consequence.

He was also an exceptionally odd, unhappy, heartbroken man: a man of the serious mainstream theatre who suddenly wrote a play based round this peculiar idea, that of a 12-year-old boy who could not grow old, and the kingdom he would rule: Neverland, an island battlescape of pirates and redskins, plus the Lost Boys, the gang of runaways Peter distractedly leads, misleads, ignores, betrays, leads again. This child-god at the story's center – named for Pan the avatar of untamed animal urges, trapped before adulthood had clamped down – is the beguiling inspiration of all who meet him, but heartless, self-absorbed, self-centered, cruel in his indifference. Barrie knew the idea was potent: he also knew it was peculiar, problematic, a vastly alluring emotional catastrophe, deeply embedded not just in his own wounded psyche, but in that of his entire epoch, eternal youth as a death drive.

(Third last song on *Invincible*: "The Lost Children", a pretty Disney-sweet hymn to those without family, *"wishing them well"* – that smoothes into closing infant-chatter: "So quiet in the forest!" "All the lovely flowers!" Then a pause. These chirrups and rustling aren't quite so calming. Are those eyes gleaming in the darkness? "It's getting dark. I think we'd better go home now." What kind of joke is this, two songs before "Threatened"?)

In Barrie's circle was one Scott, a naval officer, who briefly romanced the actress who first played Peter Pan on-stage. Famously, of course, on the eve of a war of total cultural collapse, Scott failed to reach the South Pole first, dying with four of his men on the return journey. From his final camp, he wrote Barrie a letter, and Barrie made this letter the centerpiece of an address he gave in 1922, after the war, to the students of St Andrews University. Even without the letter it would be a haunted talk, evocative yet elliptical, distractedly melancholic, sometimes avuncular and chatty, sometimes determinedly cryptic, attempting to rescue the ideals of nobility and honor and heroism from the crash of the war; hoping – but it seems doubting – that the young will ever again be able to trust their elders, and doubting also that they had reason: "My own theme is Courage, as you should use it in the great fight that seems to me to be coming between youth and their betters; by youth meaning, of course, you, and by your betters us... Learn as a beginning how world-shaking situations arise and how they may be countered. Doubt all your betters who would deny you that right of partnership."

It quotes Scott's letter, to give a flavor of the language of measured fortitude in the face of death, but immediately slips away towards a very different language, as he imagines Scott and companions still lying frozen and youthful a decade on, and retells a once-famous (and apparently true) tale from the High Gothic era of Alpine scrambling: A climber fell into a crevasse on a glacier. His companion, a scientist, went sadly home and calculated when the torn body would emerge at the glacier's foot: forty years later, the climber's friends, all now old men, gathered to greet the preserved remains as they duly arrived.

This seems an almost pathologically odd way to mourn the dead, polar dead or war dead: though Barrie was absolutely in the grip of mourning – the Llewellyn-Davies boy he'd always been closest to, Michael, had died by drowning the year before, not yet 21, perhaps in a gay suicide pact. All the things this Michael had never had, Barrie no longer wanted or trusted, even as he battles with himself to find facts and wisdom to hand on to the students. And maybe this is what mourning always is, a kind of frozen snapshot of the whole of something at the moment a particular force or possibility is gone out of it. As began at some moment in the '90s to overwhelm Jackson also, playwright as he was to his own anti-adult character: and the sense now of everything we couldn't see or say being suddenly visible and speakable.

*

The weekend of his death I overheard this exchange, as I left a Hackney newsagents behind two black schoolgirls.

Girl one: "[something something] but I can't do it about Michael Jackson."

Girl two: "Why not? Oh yes, we're doing him in history, aren't we?"

I have to confess this made me grin a bit. Partly because, yes, it seems bizarre and even silly that my own project – understanding pop and its discontents – is overlapping with stuff that's being taught in Hackney schools (I'm half-delighted, half-appalled). But partly because I'm looking forward to being around to hear the language needed to get all the above in; to hear his HIStory decanted, undiluted, into everyschoolday prose. There's a dread that it'll be mulched down and predigested: that he'll be granted a too-safe kind of avant-garde agency; that he'll be turned into merely a sequence of symptoms, his own and those of the age. And there's a naughty hope he really can't be.

Orlan's a funny-looking French lady who wants us to think about the price of ideals of beauty; Gary Farber wants to reaffirm comfortable normality, to gather Jackson back into an ideal of sweet-faced childhood and its unfraught outcomes. These are perfectly decent, citizenly goals – and so they miss the ludicrous, breath-taking, sovereign scale of Jackson's drive. He wanted – in the skip of his feet and the unearthly body of his voice, and in the many soundlands and sightlands he backdropped himself with – to represent and command, and unite and heal, all the shattered, crashing forces of the world. Dressed up as a kid's notion of a general, lugging a vast statue of himself along on the HIStory Tour, Great White Father to all the lost nations of the world.

More and more these forces are on maneuver as half-borrowed fragments: "HIStory" itself (from *HIStory: Past Present and Future, Book 1*) less a song than an extended montage of overlapping sound-clips: national anthems, martial music, selected radio announcements at totemic moments, the speeches of the great, Edison testing the first phonograph, Neil Armstrong about to moonwalk, a chorus that's a rewrite of "Blowin' In The Wind". As artist's signature, a clip of a child's voice: "Whatever I sing, that's what I really mean. I don't sing it if I don't mean it."

Does he mean it? *"All nations sing/Let's harmonize all around the world"* ("History", 1995) Does he mean it? *"Demerol, Demerol/oh god he's taking Demerol/hee hee hee"* (from "Morphine", *Blood On The Dance Floor: HIStory In The Mix*, 1997). Most of "Morphine" could soundtrack *The Matrix* (industrial hyper-crunch with better singing and beats): maybe that's a clue to his idea of his reality of his meaning it? When he sings about Demerol, it's pretty and ballad-gentle and lyrical, his giggle more like a caress.

In James Brown's music, the controlled enforcement of the irresolvable and the undigested – the problem, the tension the music presents and enacts – needed the unity single of one stage at one, and all the conflicted forces hard up against each other, to manifest: the players walked here into encounter and challenge to battle it out; as audience we're caught up in this conflict; must process it, or acknowledge it, or subject ourselves to it.

By contrast, the tensions Jackson's music presents and enacts have till now often seemed too dispersed: merely a matter scattered and modes and styles and genres, like zones in a theme park, tidily adjunct: a child's play of montage, like a kid getting to play pirate and redskin and spaceman one after the other. With Jackson you couldn't always see it or feel what was in front of you, because of the scale of it; because of the intensity of his self-discipline and internalization. Where Brown knew how to make the hardest work look and sound and feel like hardest work, Jackson's ruthless auto-bondage disguises every effort as a kind of tiny private daydream. Until now, when all the moments are frozen in mid-crash.

So let's highlight one more fragment. "Earth Song" is his unfeigned shrieked outrage at the sliced-up face of the entire planet: how can anyone gaze on such mutilation and not see some sort of lunatic horror show? And its final line may be the strangest, funniest, cheekiest Cassandra-lyric Jackson ever wrote: *"What about death, again?"* How to even start tidying down where this is from or what it means: Whose death? Death as what? As willed act? As suffered Passion? As planet's play? The serendipity of yet another carpet-pulling Peter Pan gag: death of everything as Awfully Big Adventure? His own death as our Free Lunch: our happy healing meal? The gag point of encounter we all finally walk to and find ourselves at last equal, to spar and challenge: the center of the yellow mattress, the sacred fart?

What came first to my own mind, the morning of the 26th: "the hauntology of zombie Jacko is I suspect going to be ferocious." And my friend Cis picked me up and said, "Isn't hauntology when you're spooked by reminders of the road not taken? How can someone so central to pop have a hauntology?" But his entire life was roads not taken – hinted at, played with, open for you to take and leave – and now he's dead so there's even more road not to take. The hellhounds are out of his head now, poor wizened little fellow, along with the twitches and the pranks, but how many of the billion heads that watched all this unfold did they get into? And what will be done with all of that?

15

"You're just another part of me":

Captain EO and the metaphysics of the NGO

Evan Calder Williams

Can't you see?
You're just another part of me.
Woo! Another part of me.
– "We Are Here to Change the World", from *Captain EO*

What makes *Captain EO*, the 1986 "3-D musical motion picture space adventure", starring Jackson, directed by Francis Ford Coppola, and produced by George Lucas for Disney theme parks, so pivotal and symptomatic? Something of the tone and look of it, to be sure, but more that it represents a consolidation of the kind of MJ already visible in his involvement with Pepsi and "We Are the World". It is part of the long moment when Michael stops making music to dance to and starts making music to convince us – or perhaps himself – to "heal the world". *Captain EO* is so important because it makes clear the parallel between this message and the metaphysics, cultural presence and the structure of the NGO (non-governmental organization).

In this period, a new imperialism was taking shape, in which those being colonized were no longer designated as enemies. Instead of being classified as conflicts between sovereign powers, wars became clashes between "humanitarian interventions" and the insurgents who refused to accept the "restructuring" of their state according to neoliberal conventions of international access to markets and resources. And with that came the false universality of an inclusion of those enemies who you don't dare call as such: *you are on our side, you just don't know it yet.* NGOs, whose mission ran from hunger relief to debt "relief", functioned as the humanizing face of these imperial projects, both laying a groundwork for larger organizations (such as states themselves) to get involved in these "troubled" areas and acting as a public relations band-aid on those areas already invaded or damaged from a century of exclusion from the global circuits of capital. In other words, beneath the "good intentions" of NGOs and the surface appearance of an under-funded group of "one world" humanitarians, ran a massive flow of money and military might largely responsible for the very problems addressed by the NGOs. They became, wittingly or not, an advanced tactic in the broader neoliberal program of privatization and new imperialism.

Captain EO is a child's primer – and a childlike mask – for the discourses and tendencies of this neoliberal imperialism, anticipating the Washington Consensus era of humanitarian interventions and economic prescriptions in all its self-congratulatory anxiety. Like a time capsule containing blundering aliens, musical lasers, and choreographed group dance numbers, *Captain EO* is a shimmering promise of the barbarisms of the near future. Of course, its near futurity is cast in the swirling milky garb of a distant galaxy. The narration begins: "The cosmos. A universe of good and evil where a small group struggles to bring freedom to the countless worlds of despair."

It is no great stretch to hear the echo in this of so much of neoliberal discourse about freedom and the world order. Even the cosmological scale is not out of place, the battle couched in terms of incompatible modes of universality (capital, God, democracy, in increasingly odd combinations and oppositions). What steps into this deadlock here is the "small group", a "ragtag band led by the infamous Captain EO": a scrappy under-funded heterogeneous crew united by a true belief in their ability to change the world and a willingness to circumvent the normal channels and procedures. But *Captain EO* was itself by no means under-funded or "ragtag": at the time of its release, it was the most expensive film (per minute) ever made. Like Jackson's own NGO/charitable organization, the Heal the World Foundation, founded in 1992, it needs to make a killing on the world market to be able to throw time and money back at the bloody problems which that market causes.

And how is Michael (as Captain EO) different from other revolutionaries or mercenaries? What distinguishes the fantasy of Captain EO/Michael isn't so much the soft tone of his speech or the emphasis on love and beauty (because, as the film shows us, one can speak softly and still carry a big stick, as long as that stick is a song of universal love). It is the resolute ahistoricity of the mission he has been assigned, the fantasy of the band of misfits fighting the good fight against a time that has no place for them. They have the double task of convincing history that the era of war is over *and* of declaring their enemies to have been allies all along.

The obvious reference throughout *Captain EO* is the *Star Wars* trilogy. *EO* is explicitly a *Star Wars* reloaded, from its special effects to its "quirky" side characters (the utterly insufferable farting elephant Hooter). The cultural seepage of Lucas's trilogy is taken as a given for watchers of *EO*: Jackson's Lucas-film exists only in the minimal differences it draws out between itself and its source material. But it's when we approach the crew's destination, the planet of the "Supreme Leader", that we really start to see the messianic imperial clarity of *Star Wars* warp in Jackson's peculiar lens.

From afar, this is Death Star 2.0, with a space-fighter chase through its channels pulled directly from *Star Wars*. Then we get closer... and the planet turns out to be a world of scrap, a refashioned landfill, cobbled and salvaged into something livable. And what all this gives is a sense that this is precisely *not* an empire, or at least not the manufactured consequence of an all-powerful, financialized empire familiar from *Star Wars*. Instead, we see what looks like just the opposite: the survivors of what look like imperial aggression staking a claim on a landscape that is not built from scratch, but inherited.

(This declaring of the "inherited landscape" as the site of the enemy may itself be the moment of Jackson's biggest "betrayal". For in the early '80s, he was the one dancing on and working through a music industry landscape that a TIME article described as "the ruins of punk and the chic regions of synthesizer pop": stepping into the wasteland and making it his own, becoming the Empire, becoming that Death Star of immense gravity and unsteady orbit, an artificial world disconnected from, yet still, affecting this world.)

With the first hissing words of the "Supreme Leader" to Jackson and his companions, EO's "enemies" acquire historical specificity: "Silence! Infidel! You infect my world with your presence!"

From the designation of "Supreme Leader" to the specificity of *infidel* as epithet, she is coded explicitly as the figure of Ayatollah Ruhollah Musavi Khomeini, albeit in H. R. Giger electric cable bondage-wear: a female cyber-Islam Giger-Khomeini. Two years before the end of the Iran-Iraq War, the supposed threat of Khomeini's Shi'a Pan-Islamism was apparently palpable enough to worm its way into the smiles and dance wars of Jackson's Epcot vision.

This figuring of the Supreme Leader also brings to the surface the politics that would come to swallow Jackson and his music, the universalizing one-cosmos justification of the invading saviors (EO himself states that they have come "uninvited and unannounced") versus the singularity of a world, that fact that each of these "countless worlds of despair" is actually already someone's world.

It is this singularity that is lost in Jackson's music and the central reason I draw this parallel between his music and the global vision of the neoliberal NGO. What is lost is any sense that not all things are equivalent and translatable. The insistence in Jackson's music that people are, and always have been, part of the system of equivalence is at once brutally realist – for who can stand outside the totality of the world system? – and cynical in its supposed loving embrace. What EO and his crew bring is a revelation about the inner beauty of the Supreme Leader, which just needs a key to unlock it. "To bring a gift to someone as beautiful as you...", as EO puts it. Or as it is more commonly phrased in our times of the planned decimation of peoples and local economies: *to bring market relations to someone as democratic as you...*

And so begins the central set-piece of the film, "We Are Here To Change The World", the song that sets the template for the terrible, sentimental, hollow, derivative, unhinged pseudo-political output that came to dominate all Jackson's post-*Bad* output and cultural position. It has the sounds we'd expect: wobbly yet insistent funkish basslines, tight hi-hat clicks, clean choral backing, Michael's occasionally soaring vocals. Lyrics slipping between Christian eschatology (*"We're on a mission in the everlasting light that shines/A revelation of the truth and chapters of our minds"*) and the creepy inclusivity that erases all real differences (*"Can't you see?/You're just another part of me"*). And so they dance and fight with choreography and lasers; and the trashmen, transformed into jumpsuited back-up dancers, join Michael in defeating their former leader.

That final transformation of the Supreme Leader gives the ultimate neoliberal *coup de grâce*. Your enemies are no longer *enemies*, no longer granted their own story, but folded back into your narrative, forced to accept the cultural terms of occupation and be thankful. Here, this jubilatory Stockholm Syndrome takes the form of the transformation of the Supreme Leader into Angelica Huston in a headscarf. She now constitutes the "acceptable" kind of Arabness: Princess Jasmine in a Hellenic temple of exotic yet non-threatening delights. Like the later video for "Black or White," native cultures are celebrated only insofar as they can be folded into the One World of the Pepsi Generation. And in doing so, ground from which the colonized can resist is removed. For the imperialists can endlessly respond: *but there is just one world, we're just trying to heal it.* Undermining even the right to the wastelands of industry, and posing that obscene non-question at the end of a gun: *we're doing this to help you, this war is for your sake, don't you want to be modern and democratic? Why are you still resisting?*

16

"Stalin's tomb won't let me be":
Michael Jackson as despot

Owen Hatherley

"Why have you come from the West? Confess! To steal the great achievements of the people, the accomplishments of the workers."
– "KGB interrogator" sampled in Michael Jackson's "Stranger in Moscow" (1995)

Beginnings: Production Line City

The opposite of Neverland is Gary, Indiana. Planned by the United States Steel Corporation and founded in 1906, Gary was, at first, enormously successful, a single-industry town for one of the heavy industries that built American dominance over the twentieth century, before its pop culture and military hegemony became more important. From the 1960s onwards Gary experienced a particularly severe level of "white flight" and the steel industry started to decline, at around the same time that Joseph Jackson, a crane operator in one of the city's steel mills, began to drill his children into components for the Motown Assembly Line. Neverland, as a theme park city without work and without racial tension, is everything that Gary is not.

The other opposite of Neverland is the Soviet Union, or rather it is the apparent other to the super-capitalist spectacle that Jackson reigned over in the 1980s. In all of those achingly inclusive universalist anthems that he wrote in that and the subsequent decade – "We Are The World", "Heal The World", the final and hubristic messianism of "Earth Song" – you can hear the same sentiment that lay behind The Scorpions' *Wende*-accompanying power ballad "Wind of Change", a dragging of any elements of the world that lay potentially outside of spectacle into it, something that would finally be successful within weeks of the decade's end. The conflation of state "socialism" and the rust belt is not accidental. Gary, when it was still a successful example of American industrial capital rather than one of its waste products, became the model for Magnitogorsk, a steel town planned by the Soviet Union as part of a wave of new towns created in the early 1930s on production line principles (for more on the hidden affinities between the dream-life of the industrial United States of America and the Soviet Union, see Susan Buck-Morss's *Dreamworld and Catastrophe*. Also, Kate Brown's "Why Montana And Kazakhstan Are Nearly The Same Place" in *American Historical Review*: a sharp, bleak account of the similarities of its planned cities.). The composer Hanns Eisler claimed to have heard in the noise of the steelworks as they were being constructed a kind of "blast furnace music", which he tried to put on film in a collaboration with the director Joris Ivens, *Komsomol* (1932). The eventual music that would come out of Jackson's production line would be no less repetitive and industrialized, although you can hear in his finest work that assembly line principle almost escaped through his gasps, and yelps, or embraced and transcended in the machinic, relentless *Off The Wall* – *"put that 9 to 5 back on the shelf"* ...

Despot of Pop

On 14 May 1984 Michael Jackson visited Ronald and Nancy Reagan in the White House. Rather bizarrely, his purpose was to launch a government anti-drunk driving campaign, which would be soundtracked by a version of "Beat It". More than anything else, what the viewer of the news clip of the subsequent White House press conference notices is Jackson's outfit, a blue, glittering military uniform, with a gold sash, worn over the tight, boot-cut black trousers he had been favoring for some time at that point, along with one of the first appearances of the white sequined glove, together with a pair of oversized sunglasses of the sort favored by terrorists from Carlos the Jackal to Andreas Baader. What Jackson actually resembles here is some bizarre, dreamworld refraction of Tito, or Idi Amin, or the appropriately baroque Jean-Bedel Bokassa: an East European or African military dictator come to visit the Reagans in order to negotiate the exchange of hostages or the commencement of *detente.* The effeminate whisper you hear when he opens his mouth, though, is markedly unlike the dictatorial bark one might expect. With his angular cheekbones and his enormous shades, Jackson most resembles Muammar Ghadaffi, then a national hate figure due to Libya's sporadic conflicts with the USA. Why this outfit, so different from the jumpsuits of *Off The Wall,* the red leather of *Thriller*? Perhaps Jackson was inspired by the fact that, at that point, after the unprecedented success of *Thriller,* he was more famous and more powerful than anyone save despots and dictators; perhaps he was embracing the role, mocking it, making it camp, or perhaps the choice was entirely unconscious, but for the next two decades he would regularly return to this outfit. At the same time he was writing horrendous outpourings of messianic sentiment, declaring to the globe his intention to "heal" it, this globe-bestriding colossus was specifically dressing like a totalitarian intent on world domination.

Another video, over ten years later. This time, it's a promotional trailer for a 1995 album. We see an eagle on a plinth, riot police, the Red Army on the march with the red flag aloft, workers in a foundry forging a gigantic steel star. We hear the sound of marching feet, then, leading the people's army, in scintillating silver fatigues and – again – in enormous sunglasses, we see Michael Jackson, an image of whose surgically 'improved' eye hangs alongside the red flags decking a neoclassical edifice, flanked by his adoring fans. The despot removes his glasses, smiles a gleeful ambisexual smile and blows a kiss to the faithful. The Red Army, in formation, does the hand gesture and stamp familiar from the music videos, then panning back we see something resembling Hitler's unbuilt megalopolis, Germania, rows of triumphal columns and one gigantic arch. Then suddenly, fans waving red flags smash the lights and run riot, but are held back by police as masons put the finishing touches to a colossal statue. Unveiled and hit simultaneously by flood-lights, this is of course an edifice to the Despot of Pop himself. Fans scream and faint, helicopters circle overhead, a child cries "Michael, I love you!", then a helicopter flies under the colossal Jackson's legs. This is the trailer, shown in cinemas, for Michael Jackson's 1995 "comeback" album, and if nothing else it suggests that the man still retained a (decidedly warped) sense of humor – here is a vision of pop as totalitarianism that surpasses anything created by Laibach, precisely because here it seems so bizarrely ingenuous – and who else had followers so fanatically loyal, after the fall of the old dictatorships?

In that year, as if in response to the seeming threat to his power signified by the Jordan Chandler case and the (decidedly relative) commercial failure of *Dangerous*, there were many statues of Michael Jackson being erected to promote his porten-tously named *HIStory: Past, Present and Future Part One.* They were intended to inflate a bet-hedging bundling together of a Greatest Hits collection and a disc of new material into an epochal event, something also obvious in the new term being used to describe him at every opportunity and at every event in which he participated – 'King of Pop'. Various fiberglass colossi were placed in strategic locations, including, most tellingly of all, one thirty-five-foot-tall statue placed on the vacant spot in Prague where once, the largest statue in Europe stood – a work by the monumental sculptor Otakar Svec depicting Josef Stalin, with the Czech people loyally behind him. The site had been unused since the '60s and is currently occupied by a giant maniac "They Don't Care About Us", that aggressive, anti-Semitic farrago released around the same time. The lyrics here are seemingly similar to the elliptical mess of tics, paranoia and self-pity of that song, but here a specific story can be drawn out of the threats and gripes. Here, the fallen King, after a *"swift and sudden fall from grace"*, showing only a trace of the nasal snarl that defined so much of his '80s and '90s records, trills an impressionistic, semi-noir, sub-Le Carré tale of surveillance set in a bleak East European city, where Jackson walks, disconsolate across a rain-sodden, lonely landscape of beggars and imposing edifices, chased by the KGB, and most of all, borne down upon by gigantic edifices: not only is the Kremlin *"belittling me"*, attempting to assert its power over this competing despot, but more unnervingly, *"Stalin's tomb won't let me be"*. The metaphorical or imaginary walk through Moscow reveals itself to be a coded gripe against the hounding from the press Jackson had received, in the peculiar couplet *"here abandoned in my fame/Armageddon of the brain"*. Surely, one of the signs of the man's madness was an inability to see any contradiction between his plaints to be left alone and a public persona where he would alternately mimic a dictator or, in "Earth Song", Christ.

The fantasy of "Stranger In Moscow" is necessarily historical, of course – by 1995 the KGB no longer exists, Stalin's system is six years dead. So why does Jackson return to it? A clue is given in the video, shot in a monochrome with similarities to the color-drained Central Europe of Wenders's *Wings of Desire*, here with Jackson in the Angel's role set in a cityscape that is one part Tim Burton, one part Andrei Tarkovsky. The city here is, again, the reverse of Neverland and all it represents, a greying Gotham where ill-looking people mooch around in constant drizzle, all of them in slow motion while Jackson himself moves in real time, relatively corporeal, despite his pallor and emaciation. What is most glaring of all is that none of the other protagonists notice that Michael Jackson is walking among them. He's just another

17

A design for life:

Making Michael Jackson

Charles Holland

The collection of the King of Pop

Back at the beginning of 2009, some seven months before his death, Michael Jackson exhibited the contents of his Neverland mansion at Julien's Auction House in Beverly Hills. The exhibition was intended as a preview to an auction that never took place. Jackson cancelled the sale and mysteriously withdrew its contents in one of the many murky financial deals that characterized his later life. Neverland itself had been sold the previous year, reverting back to its previous incarnation as the Sycamore Valley Ranch after Jackson became a kind of nomadic recluse following his second child abuse trial.

Had it taken place the auction would surely have been the world's most bizarre yard sale. The objects on offer included the Throne of Pop (a "monumental gilded throne with trumpeting putti, cupid heads, horses, lions, sea creatures, and scrolling foliage", according to the auction catalog accompanying the sale), a triptych depicting Jackson as the Holy Trinity, an ermine robe and a number of self-portraits featuring Jackson as a member of the English Royal Family. One of the paintings included various famous figures, including the Mona Lisa, Abraham Lincoln and E.T., all wearing Jackson's iconic white glove and aviator sunglasses.

Jackson's collection of some two thousand household objects exhibited an extraordinary degree of self-obsession: self-portraits, stage costumes, personal awards and projections of himself in all manner of historical and fantastical settings. They were a surreal mix of references: part regal, part childish and entirely narcissistic, a bizarre hybrid of Jeff Koons, Ludwig II of Bavaria and Toys 'R' Us. If the objects didn't literally refer to him then their mirrored and shiny surfaces would have reflected back a thousand tiny Michaels as he stared into their pointless opulence.

Neverland itself was another kind of mirror, an elaborately constructed physical projection of Jackson's public persona. Like a wealthy nineteenth century landowner, Jackson created an idealized landscape around him, one in which his self-image as both man-child and inspiration to the lost children of the world was manifest. Jackson developed Neverland's 2800 acres into a twentieth century picturesque landscape dotted with follies, grottoes and bronze statuary as well as a zoo, funfair and miniature railway.

The most recognizable element of Neverland was not the ranch house in which Jackson lived, but the faux-Victorian station the singer built for his 36" gauge railway. The house itself was sheltered behind a thick clump of trees largely hidden from public view. As the LA Times noted shortly after Jackson's death, the quintessential view of the celebrity home is the tilted three quarter photograph from the air. Neverland acknowledges this in its design and layout. While the house itself lay hidden, the famous sundial created by flower planting in front of the railway station seemed to be designed precisely with the paparazzo's bird's-eye view in mind.

This is an interesting inversion of the principles of picturesque planning which Neverland otherwise seemed to follow, albeit in a late twentieth century Hollywood flavored version. The classic English picturesque garden – such as Stowe or Stourhead – was a three-dimensional artificial landscape based on the allegorical seventeenth century paintings of artists such as Claude Lorraine and Nicolas Poussin. Objects and landscape features including lakes, groves of trees, ruins and follies were lifted from these paintings and grafted into the English landscape.

Although highly artificial in the sense that they were extensive manipulations of existing landscapes, these gardens were intended to be seen as seamless extensions of the "natural" world. The landscape was manipulated and composed for the enjoyment and edification of the landowner, reflecting back through a series of carefully contrived tableaux, a view of the world that placed him at its center.

Neverland though seemed designed to be experienced from afar, via the lens of publicity. It was a three-dimensional reality folded back into a two-dimensional image. Like Jackson's own personality, it combined a flamboyant desire to be in the spotlight with an obsessive need for privacy. Whilst the exotic grounds of Neverland were part of the public image of Jackson, his own house – and of his life within it – was strictly out of bounds.

The layout of this house contained its own secrets. In her extensive articles for Vanity Fair magazine following Jackson's child abuse trials, Maureen Orth described the Neverland Ranch layout in some depth: "Jackson's bedroom," she wrote, "is connected by a secret staircase to a special guest room, the Shirley Temple Room. The floor outside this room is wired so that whenever anyone comes within five feet of the entrance there are ding dong noises".

There were other slightly queasy innovations too, including beds that were orientated like royal boxes in Jackson's private cinema and a rooftop eyrie from which he could survey his magic kingdom. The extreme narcissism of Neverland's objects was also present in the layout of the house and grounds. Jackson is credited with having had a genuine interest in architecture and this extended to an understanding of its complicity in maintaining forms of social control.

Making Michael Jackson

Surgical Procedure: an incision was made in Princess Margaret's temple running downward and backward to the apex of her ear. From here a crease ran toward her lobule in front of the ear, and the incision followed this crease around the lower margin of the lobule to a point slightly above the level of the tragus. From there, at an obtuse angle, it was carried backward and downward within the hairy margin of the scalp.

– From "Princess Margaret's Facelift", J. G. Ballard

Jackson's most staggering design innovations, though, lay in the transformation he achieved of his own body. Starting in the late 1970s Jackson had an enormous amount of surgery on his face including (allegedly) at least ten separate rhinoplasty operations, skin lightening (attributed by the singer to the disease vitiligo and lupus), forehead lifts, cheekbone surgery, lip thinning, permanent make-up, the re-shaping of his chin and the insertion of a cleft that appeared and reappeared over subsequent years. His final operation was rumored to have involved the use of one of his ears to provide skin for a replacement tip to his nose.

In the short story "Princess Margaret's Facelift", J. G. Ballard inserted Princess Margaret's name for that of an anonymous "Patient X" within a genuine medical description of a facelift. Ballard's use of cut and paste makes this story a provocative marriage of form and content. Plastic surgery is a form of collage practiced on the body, a grafting of previously disparate features into a new composition. The disjunctive quality of seeing Princess Margaret's name in the context of a blunt medical description is a graft itself, a violent juxtaposition.

While collage stresses the cuts between displaced objects though, relying precisely on their lack of "fit" to generate meaning, plastic surgery strives to be seamless and invisible. It's often said that rather than making people look beautiful, plastic surgery merely makes them look like they've had plastic surgery.

The truth though is that this is only when things goes wrong, or too far, and the surgery itself becomes the dominant visual characteristic. The ideal is a seamless graft, the sliding-in of one body part for another without anyone actually noticing when it happened.

Michael Jackson's surgery could hardly have been more spectacularly *visible*. The transformation of his face was an ever more extraordinary drama played out in public. The numerous DIY movies available on You Tube morphing photographs of Jackson throughout his life testify to both the extraordinary level of distortion and its compelling fascination.

His clothes were equally fascinating, mutating from the pantomime military dictator look of his post-*Thriller* pomp to the bling and badge encrusted blazers of his later years that made him appear like an ageing millionairess tottering around her Palm Beach condo.

Jackson's face was more like the avant-garde technique of Ballard, a violent clash of objects that no longer belonged together. One's first thought on seeing a picture of Michael Jackson's face towards the end of his life was: can it *really* be like that? Followed by: is it actually him? But if his face became "hideously disfigured" – as an infamous 1999 article in the Daily Mail claimed – what was he striving for? Someone once said that Jackson wasn't using surgery to turn himself white but to turn himself into Elizabeth Taylor. Certainly his shiny black bob, white skin, red lips, penciled eyebrows and heavy make up were undeniably feminine. His tiny triangle of a nose (itself a prosthetic, literally stuck onto the void where his old nose used to be) was a caricature of female desirability.

Stephen Marquardt – a prominent plastic surgeon in California who specializes in rebuilding the faces of crash victims – has attempted to analyze the proportions of the human face in order to help his patients choose their new features. His analysis concluded (somewhat fortuitously) that beauty in human faces was based on the ratio of proportion developed by Pythagoras in the golden section. This proportional system was used as the compositional basis for classical architecture and painting. Marquardt produced overlays of "classically" beautiful faces such as Marilyn Monroe and Elizabeth Taylor to illustrate how the proportions of the features related to the golden ratio.

Such a theory turns out to be not only convenient but also highly suspect. In the early 1930s Matila Ghyka – a mathematician and poet – attempted exactly the same analysis on the face of contemporary tennis star Helen Wills Moody. But as Robin Evans noted in his essay "Translations From Drawing To Building", there is a fundamental problem with the nature of this process: "The analysis is not of the rotund, undulating, folded, punctured surface we call a face, but of quite another surface, onto which the face was flattened by the process of photography".

Both Ghyka and Marquardt's analysis assume a flat surface – such as a drawing or a photograph – on which to mark out the lines of proportion. Both therefore treat the face as a flat screen seen perfectly head on, no different in fact to a picture. The difference is that while Ghyka was trying to establish an academic point, Stephen Marquardt's analysis has a practical application. The starting point for plastic surgery in this case is an *image* of a face that then becomes recreated physically. Plastic surgery is a three dimensional form of collage that relies on choosing replacement features from two-dimensional images.

Once again we are back in the realm of the picturesque, the artificial manipulation of "natural" features according to compositional rules defined from two-dimensional images. The transformation of *Off The Wall*-era Michael Jackson into his later incarnations follows a similar process of distortion and enhancement to the transformation of the earlier Sycamore Valley Ranch into Neverland.

Don't stop 'til you get enough

The most provocative question raised by these transformations is
the distinction between the natural and the artificial. I have
suggested that there is a correlation between plastic surgery and
the picturesque in that both are forms of collage where the
natural is artificially enhanced. In doing so they both throw into
question the usefulness of the terms nature and artifice.
Experiments in re-designing nature occur ever more invisibly, in
a seam that runs from the reshaping of the countryside for
aesthetic pleasure to the development of genetically modified
plants and biological cloning, to the extent that it becomes highly
problematic to distinguish them at all.

Which brings us back to the real horror that Jackson's face
evokes. Jackson was grotesque not simply because his surgery
appeared to have gone wrong, but because he had transformed
his natural features so extensively that he no longer bore any
resemblance to his younger self. In doing so he had become as
much a product of culture as nature, a hybrid form of life created
in the laboratory. He was, in Donna Haraway's terms, a cyborg.

In her influential essay "A Manifesto for Cyborgs", Haraway
defined the cyborg not in the terms popularized by science
fiction – a literal combination of man and machine with wires
and circuits below the skin – but as a more subtle and ambivalent
merging of the two. She argued that we are all already cyborgs,
products of culture as much as nature and part of a network of
machines that we use daily and habitually as extensions of our
bodies and minds.

The term prosthetics relates to physical extensions of the
body such as artificial limbs and replacement body parts. Here
the distinction between real, or natural, and artificial still seems
clear. It is much less so when one considers subtler extensions or
improvements to our physical selves such as contact lenses,
pacemakers or keyhole surgery. Or medicine. In an essay on
virtual technology, Morten Søby described Prozac (for example)

as "a mild form of plastic neurology for tired or sad minds".

Our bodies, like our landscapes, are impossible to imagine as purely natural, except in the most reactionary terms. We resist this process as we give ourselves ever more to it. It is only in the most extreme cases though that this becomes clear. And it is these cases, where nature has given way to a more hybridized form of being, that concern us the most.

A few years ago I visited an exhibition of Playboy magazine covers from the 1950s to the present. What was most striking was not so much the way that the design of the magazine had developed over the years, but how the designs of the bodies within it had. As the settings and scenarios of the shoots became less elaborately staged the bodies had become more so, pumped, primed and almost literally pneumatic. Their disparate body parts had been grafted like a pornographic version of a police identikit image.

Here was a reversal of Dr Marquardt's analysis, faces and bodies designed to be viewed through the flat pages of magazines or television screens. The bodies of porn stars and glamour models are the subject of popular fascination mixed with mild revulsion for a number of reasons. Mostly it is because they represent an extreme notion of the body as culturally determined rather than naturally formed. Like Michael Jackson, they transgress a supposedly clear line that is actually murky and ambiguous. Surgical enhancement of body parts is merely an overt and recognizable version of something that we are all constantly undergoing.

Michael Jackson appeared as an ever-changing series of versions of himself, like new and improved developments of the same original product. That he saw himself in such terms is evident from the fact that in 1988 he patented his own body movement – the ant-gravity lean first used in the "Smooth Criminal" video – much as one might patent a machine or an industrial process.

We transform ourselves every day; change our hair, alter our appearance, take pills that change our behavior. We are seamlessly and invisibly part of technology. We resist this process constantly, countering it with a rhetoric of the real, the authentic and the natural.

18

Don't stop 'til you beat it:

Michael Jackson at the limit of post-race dialectriffs

Suhail Malik

It's a commonplace that Eddie Van Halen's guitar solo on "Beat It" transformed Michael Jackson from a superstar into a megastar, shattering the market-demographic segmentation of American culture that "Billie Jean" had begun to break down some months earlier by landing black music on MTV. A metaphor for what Jackson did to the dominant racial organization of music consumption with *Thriller* is provided by the extended intro of the 1991 promo video for "Black Or White", in which Macaulay Culkin's middle-class white brat launches his couch-potato pop into outer space with an outsize guitar power-chord – literally effecting the propulsive force of music to blast (white) pop from suburban America to black Africa, where Jackson dances with some Masai and the song proper begins. It is a precise image of how Jackson ex-appropriated the guitar-led proto-metal rock idiom of suburban white music consumers to land them in the then alien field of a black pop music dominated at the time by disco. If this division between (white, straight, powerful) rock and (black, deviant, powerless) disco seems now untenable (thanks in no small measure to Jackson himself), the frenzied sell-out public explosion of dance records on "Disco Demolition Night" in Chicago in July 1979 (an event engineered by a rock radio DJ fired from his show because the station moved to disco) signals how the socio-cultural identifications and the antagonism between them – as proxies for not just race conflict but also an incipient version of what has since come to be known as the Culture Wars in America (approximately, the permanent battle over values between conservatives and liberals) – was well understood and quickly mobilized at the time.

It's this socio-musical politics, for which race is the master-category, that "Beat It" at once captured and sought to surpass, and which is commonly ascribed to Van Halen's world-historical solo. In this, if not also in the slightly later trajectory of his own body's transformations, Jackson was already, in 1982, insisting on a post-racial organization of socio-cultural identifications, one that would come to a kind of phantasied fruition with Barack Obama's presidential candidacy in 2008. While it is now a truism that race is a meaningless term in (phylo)genetics and is also at best dubious in intelligibly designating ethnically or culturally homogeneous peoples (if there are such), it does allow the boundedness and distinction of populations organized at the level of bodies, historically given relations and their cultures to be addressed effectively, and this is exactly the typology that Jackson deployed so successfully in pitching "Beat It" as his crossover hit. The question taken up in the following lines is why Michael Jackson the media celebrity failed to overcome racial categorization, his crossover to being white "in appearance" always falling short of the consumer demographic crossover demand and appeal of his production, returning, somewhat abjectly through innuendo, to the question whether race could ever be an irrelevance as to who – more precisely, *what* – he was or might have been. More exactly, the question is whether this "failure" to attain a post-race condition was Jackson's short-coming or, rather, a negation of it.

The rock guitar solo was not itself new in Jackson's music. It had already been deployed in the bridge to Jackson's disco-ecstatic "Don't Stop 'Til You Get Enough" from 1979's *Off The Wall*, though it was there equal in the mix to the horn and string crescendos. Doubtless, Van Halen's cultural capital brought extra attention to the 1982 track as did the promo video's emphasis of it as the soundtrack to the knife fight of gang leaders (one black, one white, though both gangs are multi-racial) that is the narrative engine of its drama, resolved of course by Jackson's violence-ending – or is that violence-absorbing? – dance routine. What was new about "Beat It" – and why it is a disjunction from Jackson's earlier music – was the integration and coherence of emphatic rock guitar solo with the song's sonic texture and genre and as a dance-oriented production. Unlike the earlier disco track, Van Halen's solo in "Beat It" is not subordinated to a disco totality; rather, the song's core is a 4/4 funk-disco synth-drum rhythm and two rhythm guitars playing shredded proto-metal rock riffs, allowing the guitar solo to be accommodated into and resolved by the standard formulas of rock. As much as Van Halen's solo brought a white audience demographic to a black pop music, as the standard account has it, so the rock riffs of the rhythm guitars in "Beat It" structured (black) disco by the phonic world of (white) rock. This duality – that the music is black and white, black or white – is the logic of Jackson's invention from that point on. It was the phonic condition for Jackson's commercial mega-success, providing a code to unlock what up to that time had been American pop music's quasi-formal demographic categorization (a polite, commercially acceptable way of speaking to the historically racial segmentation of its dominant cultures). More than the rock guitar *solo*, the proto-metal guitar *riff* in Jackson's music served not only as a proxy for racial equality in general but also, for that reason, as a commercial innovation in increasing market reach. With regard to race, Jackson's use of the rock riff was a simultaneously political-commercial strategy.

The angular assault of the rock riff as elementary musical structural unit gave Jackson an idiom for the presentation of anguish, persecution and anger that complements/competes with the saccharine soul-gospel schmaltz of his production up to and including *HIStory*. Detached from the standard climactic resolves of rock, the attacking riff (whether played on guitar or synth) gives this dimension of Jackson's music a purposeless pulsing core, a drive without satisfaction. It prohibits the phonic structure arriving to completion, presenting only a pressuring-circulating, foreshortened attack that percolated-transmutated into the clipped syncopated rhythms of the New Jack Swing of *Bad* and *Dangerous*, the discontinuous rock riff there distending to colonize the phonoscape from within, generating one of pop's claustrophobic limits in the epochal "Scream". This logic also came to prevail over Jackson's vocal attack, the exitless, non-climactic release giving his delirious range of staccato tics, breathy reserved sternness, falsetto yelps and quasi-libidinal ecstatic squeaks an intensified if strangulated plosive pressure, as it equally and literally shaped his performing body and dancing into increasingly disjointed hardened structures and movements, again reaching a crescendo of sorts in the proto-statuary of the video to "Scream'" (but perceptible as early as *Thriller*: compare the rigidity and tension of Jackson's limbs in "Beat It" to his languorous curvilinearity in the video to the soul-disco of "Billie Jean" from just a few months prior).

"Black Or White" from 1991's *Dangerous* is perhaps Jackson's most explicit reflection on his politico-phonic logic. The song's sonic formula revises "Beat It" in a number of telling ways, each of which signal an assurance that only nine years after *Thriller* Jackson's audience was already racially desegmented, commercially secured as a *total* market. These indices include: the expulsion of the celebrity proto-metal guitar highlight – by Slash from Guns N' Roses – to the extended intro to the song (which is quite different from the song itself); Slash not performing a guitar break on his guest appearance (as he does on "DS" from the same album) but a recursive rhythm guitar riff distinct from the main body of the song; placing a rap (incongruously lip-synced by Macaulay Culkin in the video) as the added element of the song; and the guitar solo in the bridge equalizing, if not subordinated to, a synth-bass glissando. The superfluity of the proto-metal guitar break confidently asserts that Jackson can marginalize the signifier of a white audience (as he literally does Slash) without undermining the song's market reach. That is, by the early '90s, the becoming-embellishment of the celebrity guitar appearance instantiates the anodyne United Nations/Colors of Benetton liberal universalism that is the song's political-lyrical thematic. For Jackson at that time such a statement of global ambition is not just a pious wish but also a (perhaps unique) fact.

The racial indifference or interchangeability of the song's addressee – *"It don't matter if you're black or white"* – is not only a declaration of liberal universalism it is then also the achievement of Jackson's politico-phonic logic (and so, in a reflexive self-artic-ulation, "Black or White" addresses not only Jackson *himself* - as everyone understands – but also, echoing "Don't Stop 'Til You Get Enough", first of all *itself*). And as the rap interludes tells us in the assertion that *"It's not about races/Just places/faces/ ... I'm not going to spend my life being a color"*, the subject thus interpellated is that of a primary individuality independent of racial defin-ition. If this indeterminacy holds for Jackson himself over the course of his phenotypic transmutation, the extension of the global family indifferently to race – famously imaged by the then relatively new morph sequence at the end of the song part of the promo-video, where busts of a number of races/ethnicities merge sequentially into and out of one another, celebrating difference, asserting equality – certainly speaks more generally to one of the core contentions of a "post-race" condition which commentators have ascribed to American political culture with Barack Obama's successful presidential bid. Here, "post-race" means affirming a condition on the basis of at least four precepts:

i.   There is indeed an indifference to race and racial equality is not only assumed but also effected.

ii. Racism is no longer a powerful socio-political force but at worst a marginal if distracting and worrying issue.

iii. Race is incoherent and without definition according to the very terms by which it is espoused (blood, inheritance, identity, culture) since it is untenable as a genetic identity (itself assumed to be the truth of biology or populations) and is inherently porous and malleable as an ethno-cultural edifice of identifications.

iv. Race is a misleading category to identify the leading cause of inequality in America, which is rather class.

But the ready acceptance of a "post-race" condition, even as a hopeful wish, has worse effects than to prohibit challenging of discrepancies in living standards of discrete populations by ascribing social conditions as race-blind when they are still in fact race-conscious and, in doing so, preventing necessary political recognition and action from being taken. On top of that, it can also serve conservative or reactionary forces since drawing attention to the continued relevance of race-specific concerns in a purportedly post-race condition can be characterized as being either the perpetuation of a victimhood or testimony of individual failures to "achieve" normative levels of attainment (wealth, education, etc.) rather than to structural-historical pressures, thus giving a pass to racist social configurations to continue unaddressed.

Obama's navigation of the politics of race/post-race serves to bring into focus Jackson's own contrasting and contradictory equivocation. In a series of carefully pitched speeches running through the nomination process and into his Presidency, Obama at once acknowledges the necessity of a race-based struggle and its terms – especially the efforts of the Civil Rights movement in undoing State-led segregation and other institutionalized or informal racist practices – while asserting that those terms are not reasons to deny the futurity of a non-racism that they look towards. Obama's name for the dialectical resolution for the mutual negation of race *and* post-race on the basis of the temporal anticipation of anti-racism, for this individual-universalist yet common capacity to exit the sedimented reality of historically circumscribed conditions, of his "own improbable story", is, not unusually, "America". While the politico-phonic logic of the rock riff as a structural element of Jackson's music set a precedent for such a dialectical suspension of race – a praxis whose operation and ends are succinctly captured by the term *dialectriffs* – the horizon of Jackson's praxis was not America but, reflecting the (ambition of the) reach of his own (music's) popularity, the totality of the globe. It was in fact a question of a fully liberal *universalism* whose subject is not even American but an indeterminate individual.

"Black Or White" makes this horizon abundantly clear. LTB's rap captures the two poles of a micro-localized universalism initiated by Jackson's dialectriffs – "*It's turf war/On a global scale*" is congruent to "*it's not about races/just places/faces...*" – as does the video's morph sequence and in its main conceit of Jackson's trans-local gliding across various ethno-cultures of dance (Masai, Indonesian, Native American, etc.) in a "boutique multiculturalism" that marks his own indifference with regard to dance's ethno-history. Yet this affirmation of a global post-race condition is only one aspect of Jackson's dialectriffs and not its final truth. The staccato attack of the rock riff that provides the sonic structure of these songs of Jackson's as it shapes the micro-phrasing of Jackson's voice and the disjunctive movement of his dance is, as we have seen, purposeless, a drive true to its insatiability, caught in a present without exit. As such, the complete dialectical operation of Jackson's racial dialectriffs no less negates its resolution into a post-race condition. Stressing that the present is without purpose, that the temporality of an anti-racism that contends the racially determined present in prospect of a post-race future is not one of continuity and smooth transition but – *pace* Obama – one of disjunction, of the separation of the present from the projective future, the *attack* of Jackson's dialectriffs is not only against the political reality of racism and race but also against the confusion of the present misery-ridden reality of an existence organized through racism with the irreality of post-race.

Though this stress on the disjunctions of Jackson's dialectriffs seems far from the affirmation of racial indifference vocalized in "Black Or White" and the video to the song itself, it is presented in equally clear terms, isolated from the song, in the second part of that video. A black panther (the connotations of which with regard to racial struggle in the US don't need further emphasis) prowling through the studio where the footage for the morph sequence of ethno-diverse individuals is being shot – the final shot accompanying the broadcast version of the video – itself morphs into trademark Jackson who executes a frenzied-anguished-sexualized sequence of dance moves and vocalizations disconnected to anything other than Jackson's isolation (the disjunction of his own singularity...). If these movements and vocalizations are literally incorporated products of Jackson's politico-phonic logic, disjoined in this part of the video even from the song structures in which that logic is established, his condensation of the futureless attack of this dialectriffs through body and voice is nonetheless channeled against the delimitations of race, those oppressive conditions presented now by surfaces carrying various glass surfaces daubed with racist and White Supremacist graffiti. If, then, the lyric *"I ain't scared of no sheets"* in the song's bridge makes metonymically explicit the conditions that race indifference seeks to vanquish, the video's Panther section makes no less clear that that conquest involves acts of destruction and violence against those conditions and histories, be they undertaken in cold strategic calculation or in quasi-impotent frustration and hate (against hate), of anti-racism, as Jackson acts it.

This destruction of the historical conditions and presence of racism and the hatred it demands on all sides is a negation of the futurity of the suspension of race no less instituted by Jackson's dialectriffs. The Panther section of the "Black Or White" promo-video makes explicit that the present(ation) of its attack negates the resolution of its future, the futurity of his dialectriffs literally crashing and shattering into its present. In this, Jackson reverses Obama's suspension of race by returning from the liberal universalism of the song to the historical fact and political constraints of the present – to the fact that America is *in fact* no redemption. While Jackson seeks to act upon those conditions as liberal universalist – globally indeterminate – individual, in the totality of his dialectriffs that individual does not remain attached to the dream or dialectical suspension of history that is an "America" without internal limits or historically present barriers to attainment, but remains ensnared, captivated, by the historical constraints and delimitations of the present. These limitations are tangible, present and forceful. And in this attack, instantiating the disjunction between the present and the future, Michael Jackson is a realist.

19

After pop

Tom Ewing

1

A King of Pop implies a kingdom. Michael Jackson won his in the style of a medieval ruler, carving out a realm piece by piece across a hard year of campaigning. Some of his subjects bent the knee when he performed "Billie Jean" as part of a Motown anniversary special; others when he formed common cause with Eddie Van Halen or Paul McCartney. His fiefdom extended across every school playground with the release of the "Thriller" video and its body-popping zombies. Through it all the album and its spin-offs sold, and sold, and sold. "Billie Jean", its Wikipedia page claims, has now topped 800,000 sales as a digital download, a format invented close to twenty years after its release.

What few mentioned was how strange *Thriller* was, how odd and sincere and childlike in some places, and how nightmarish in others. Half the record is painfully tender, the other half hard-edged and horribly tight-wound. Jackson's stuck in the middle, and the pain is thunder.

"Billie Jean" itself is the album's darkest moment, where the goblin babble pressing in on Jackson during "Wanna Be Startin' Somethin'" goes fully internal and the barely-together bundle of tics that became Jackson's star persona steps into the spotlight. Jackson's one-take vocal is a long shudder – the Gollum-gulp on *"her schemes and plans"*, the betrayed moan of *"his eyes were like mine"* – and the real craziness happens on its fringes. That contradictory *"do think twice!/don't think twice!"* collision; the constant *"ooh"*, *"oh"*, and *"no!"* echoes; the clucks and gasps; and especially the madman's comic book laugh punctuating the track, that eerily deliberate *"hee hee hee"*.

And of course this near-meltdown is the album's most grippingly commercial moment too. Jackson's claustrophobic performance is boxed in by stalking bass and arid drums, underlined by clawing and skittering guitars, counterpointed by those sensuous flushes of strings. A song about the fatal irresistibility of a dancer really does need to be irresistible on the dance floor: at a hundred million weddings and discos since, "Billie Jean" has proved its mettle in that respect. But when you follow Jackson's performance down and in, none of that matters – "Billie Jean" is a disquieting, troubled record. Uneasy lies the head that wears a crown.

Chronologically, it's true, "King of Pop" was a later sobriquet, a title he or his courtiers claimed as a showbiz move. Steeped in the history of black pop performance, Jackson admired James Brown's bombastic montage of titles – "Minister Of The New Super Heavy Funk", et al. He must have liked how they were absurd but always true. "King of Pop" was his "Godfather of Soul", a nice verbal drum roll, a dare to himself to keep proving the title right.

People mocked the idea sometimes, or claimed it was just hype. But where did they think kings came from? Kingship always began with showbiz, a choreography of gestures that concealed and tamed the necessary brutality of a rise to power. Afterwards the storytellers would be sent out to find evidence of bloodlines, ancient charters, she-wolves – all the trappings that might fix the new kingdom as part of a natural order of things.

So it was with the throne Jackson claimed. He could trace his descent from Motown; he owned the Northern Songs catalog – these things, surely, made him the inheritor of a rich pop legacy. But this was an illusion, a way of covering up what he'd actually done. Not musically – he and Quincy Jones had taken inspiration from all over the place but that was no great surprise. But commercially – the conquest of MTV, the deployment of video, the sales, the sales, the endless unifying sales.

Just as rock criticism had come into being in part as an attempt to describe what The Beatles had done, so the all-encompassing "Pop" Michael Jackson became King of existed as an effect of his success. To put it bluntly, pop had changed from a place where a smash album might sell 10 million copies to a place where it might – just might – sell fifty million. For the music business, this was like discovering a new continent.

2

In 1987, Paul Gambaccini published *The Top 100 Rock'N'Roll Albums Of All Time*. It polled fifty "rock critics and DJs", totted up their favorites and turned it into a lavish coffee-table book. This was a pet project: he'd compiled a previous edition in 1977. That book had validated his method, spotlighting, among the '60s untouchables, then-recent albums by The Clash and Springsteen. This new version would achieve something similar, put the confusing '80s into sensible perspective.

Gambaccini's list was a reassuring success. Here's what his critics fingered as the then top ten for their decade to date:

1. BRUCE SPRINGSTEEN - *Born In The USA*
2. MICHAEL JACKSON - *Thriller*
3. ROXY MUSIC - *Avalon*
4. ELVIS COSTELLO - *Get Happy!*
5. THE POLICE - *Synchronicity*
6. U2 - *The Unforgettable Fire*
7. TINA TURNER - *Private Dancer*
8. DON HENLEY - *Building The Perfect Beast*
9. THE PRETENDERS - *The Pretenders*
10. LIONEL RICHIE - *Can't Slow Down*

And naturally the next '80s record on the list was *Sports* by

Huey Lewis And The News.

Some of these albums are good, others simply hard to avoid. Taken seriously – as the voters certainly did – they suggest a first draft of a canon that ended up never really forming. I'm quite sure that people still listen to *Synchronicity, Can't Slow Down* and *Building The Perfect Beast,* but nobody pays these records any cult.

What they do have in common – Elvis Costello aside – is success. These were records with real commercial heft, and the list represents a faith that good work will find an audience, and that high sales are often deserved. In that respect it's a post-*Thriller* list, though *Thriller* itself looks oddly misplaced on it. The particular filter these voters used to view music might not generally have valued pop, but the new records they loved reflected the rush of blood and confidence Jackson's success had given the industry.

What did Jackson gain in return? The day after his death the Village Voice's Rob Harvilla pointed to the "Liberian Girl" video: "just then-A-List celebrities amicably chatting with each other". The clip's music – sweet, flighty - is kept discreetly dipped in the background while Spielberg, Ackroyd, Goldberg and dozens more stand around waiting for Michael to grant them audience. It is the court of pop: he is the man in the Hall of Mirrors. As Harvilla puts it: "Dude had unimaginable power".

That power isn't seen in the fact of the stars' appearance, but in their presence for such a throwaway gesture. Jackson had tapped his rolodex not to launch a comeback but to round one off – "Liberian Girl" was the preposterous ninth single from *Bad.* And yet it feels so casual, this massing of celebrity; its decadence diffused by its offhandedness. This video, like the Gambaccini list, is a glimpse at an entertainment industry at complete ease with itself.

3

If you take music history from the emergence of Elvis to Jackson's death, the release of *Thriller* – the highest selling album there will ever be – sits at the midpoint. This is the kind of coincidence that nags at me, more so when you look at what's claimed for the album – sales of 110 million worldwide when the nearest rival hasn't yet topped fifty. Once Jackson's numbers went stratospheric, of course, there was plenty of room to inflate them further, but even conservative estimates put *Thriller* thirty million or so ahead of everything else.

Put *Thriller* on start-to-end and you'll hear some sublime pop music, but it's hard going – "Baby Be Mine" kills its momentum, and "The Girl Is Mine" treats McCartney with something close to cruelty. Maybe one in every sixty human beings owns this album, and it doesn't even work as one. People expected *Thriller* to succeed, but surely never to this degree. The scale of its sales qualifies it as a Black Swan – economist Nassim Nicholas Taleb's term for a shock, high-impact event which is only explained by rationalizations after the fact.

With Jackson, explanation begins with the combination of astonishing talent and a truly dreadful upbringing. Jackson's brutalization by his father is the kind of horror story we associate with the worst parts of pro sport – the mechanization of ability in a drive for perfection. It's rarer in showbiz, because the structure of success is looser. Michael Jackson's success is actually two achievements, both strikingly unlikely and unmanageable. First that he managed to funnel his talent through his dehumanization, creating music like "Billie Jean", which fused his talent and his terror. And secondly that the public responded in such phenomenal numbers to this bruised, unique perspective.

To organize an ideal of pop, or even a single career, around those two glorious flukes would be insanity. And so his success led to a second dehumanization, which Jackson himself colluded in. When he died, and I sat down to write an obituary-type piece, all I could think about were history and abstractions: the real, dead man was too remote. The Jackson it's easy to empathize with fell into shadow a long time ago. On the night of his death the music I reached for wasn't *Off The Wall*, or *Thriller*, but the strange, sad, overblown records he made in the '90s – overshadowed by headlines and accusations, but home to some of the oddest and darkest pop of any era.

There'll be a reassessment, naturally – songs like "Butterflies" and "Who Is It" are too strong for there not to be. It's true, of course, that in comparison to "Off The Wall" or "PYT" they sound petrified, seized-up. In fact a lot of the '90s material sounds like multiple drafts of one song, a crushed and frightened attempt by a desperate man to get the pain out. Even the much-mocked "Earth Song" sounds like a projection – what if the whole world was as hurt as me?

By "Earth Song", the King Jackson most resembles is Lear, maddened and howling at the storm. Its bombast is all the sadder for still sounding so effectively huge. A better example of late Jackson – the one I ended up listening to most – is 1995's "Stranger In Moscow". Like "Liberian Girl", it's the last single from an album and a showcase for Jackson's delicacy. But now the party is over, the celebrities gone. Jackson is wandering down monochrome streets in a land where nobody knows him. "*I was wandering in the rain/Mask of life, feeling insane*". This Moscow isn't real: for Jackson, being a stranger anywhere was a fantasy. Indeed the city's as trapped in time as he is, a place of persecutors, of Stalin and the KGB. He sings at the faltering top end of his register, free from growls and tics: "*Here abandoned in my fame/Armageddon of the brain.*" He sounds beautiful and broken.

A Black Swan resets its context. In *Thriller's* case, the attempts to understand what had happened, and Jackson's own image-building and mythmaking, led to the creation of pop as a kingdom: something that could – with the right singles, the right videos, the right guest stars – be unified. This went against most of what people had understood about pop music: at the moment of *Thriller*'s release, the best-selling album of all time was the *Saturday Night Fever* soundtrack, a record that was burned by mobs in public for becoming too successful.

It seems to me that fragmentation isn't some horror that can overtake pop and make it meaningless: the music thrives on its flux of different audiences – some reaching out, some protective. It doesn't need a Kingdom, it needs a space where different audiences get to mingle, brawl, eye each other up. But the outrageous success of *Thriller* – the ultimate crossover – created the impression that the fragmentation of pop could be undone, and a generation of new megastars helped Jackson hold back that particular tide. That idea died long before Jackson did, surviving only in his increasingly mocking honorific. The Kingdom of Pop is a failed state.

20

Glove, socks, zombies, puppets:

The unheimlich maneuvers and undead metonyms of Michael Jackson

Sam Davies

Was Michael Jackson still fully alive by the time he came to die in June of 2009?

This is not a question of conspiracy theories, clinical cover-ups, cryogenic tanks, tax evasion or alien abduction. As the months go by and his body remains unburied, his music resurrected in every download chart, it can feel as though he's almost *less* dead now. Or is it rather that his forensic death was a blip or medical detail in a strange continuity? That he had long been living in some unnamable hinterland, flickering uncertainly between a state of life and a state of death, living a kind of half-life, uniquely (FM) radio-active, in which he was as much a collection of things held together in spooky animation, as a single coherent person?

Was this ambiguity – an ambiguity shared with puppets, effigies, waxworks, zombies and other residents of the uncanny valley – what gave Jackson his ability to so utterly compel the attention of his audience? And does it make him a figure of prehistoric, primordial disturbance, or something from our future, an example of the subject under intolerable stress in the post-humanist era?

You feel the cold hand and wonder if you'll ever see the sun

Michael Jackson was the world's first megastar. Grasping the inchoate power of MTV, he was able to fuse the visual and musical in a way that neither The Beatles nor Elvis could, saturating the world with a spectacular image of himself and setting a pop paradigm in which the new, totalized star must sing, dance, act, endorse products and franchise themselves at once. While The Beatles and Elvis could only borrow from black musical culture, Jackson was its demographic representative, and *Thriller's* astronomical sales (as the best-selling album of all time by a factor of two to one) make it pop's Obama moment.

But he was also the world's first Gothic megastar. This Gothic is not the Gothic of the '80s student disco, but one that connects Jackson to a tradition of the uncanny, to the phenomena defined by Ernst Jentsch in 1906 as that state of uncertainty in which one doubts "whether an apparently animate being is really alive; or conversely, whether a lifeless object might be, in fact animate". This disturbing ambiguity was not invented but only identified by Jentsch, and can be found in Hoffman, von Kleist, Dostoevsky, folktales of golems, doppelgangers, homunculi and, practically *passim*, in Dickens. Dickens presents a world of things as people and people as things: with gargoyle surrealism he animates doorknockers, wooden legs, wigs, prosthetic hands, while rendering human characters as dead inanimate objects. Silas Wegg in *Our Mutual Friend*, longing to repurchase his lost leg from a shop full of preserved human limbs; the description of Smallweed in *Dombey & Son*, as a "broken puppet". It is in Dickens's profusion of things that seem to be alive and living beings envisioned as things that John Carey locates his specific genius:

A power of observation that gives distinct and individual attention to each part of a body, and watches it moving as

227

something apart from the mass, is capable of creating a fresh imaginative vision because it contradicts the accepted view of what constitutes a unity.

Is it in this kind of fresh imaginative vision that Jackson's genius resides? Consider those trademarks of his appearance: the single white glove, the brilliant white socks glowing from under inch-short trousers – what do they actually do for a performer? They draw the eye, detaching parts of the dancer from himself, turning them into metonyms – parts that signify the whole. The single white glove, introduced for Jackson's performance at Motown's twenty-fifth birthday extravaganza in 1983, singles out the hand as a phosphorescent white unit of its own, a separate creature, a thing or Thing in itself, reminiscent of the Addams Family's disembodied gofer ("Thing" appeared as a character in the Addams Family series that were broadcast from 1964–1966, when Michael was aged between six and eight). Long before his cosmetic operations began to refashion and rework his face until his nose needed a prosthetic tip, Jackson deliberately dismembered and disassembled himself in order to direct the audience's attention to his dancing.

The glove, the socks; these are not merely canny pop iconography, demonstrations of someone with an astute, intuitive understanding of pop mythopoeia and its profitability. They are part of Jackson's uncontrollable fascination with the undead, un-alive hinterlands of the uncanny. He collected mannequins. He played a scarecrow brought to life but missing a brain in *The Wiz* (1978). The commercial supernova of *Thriller* was illustrated with a video in which he is first a man-becoming-animal (a nod to John Landis's *American Werewolf in London*), then surrounded by a troupe of zombies (dead putrescent flesh brought to impossible motion), then becomes one himself (twice). And Jackson adored the not-quite-human homunculus, claiming to have believed E. T. was real and keeping a chimpanzee, Bubbles, as his companion and familiar.

Even Jackson's voice, with its constant appeal to the unspeakable, its recourse to a spasmodic, tic-like, wordless vocabulary, carries the virus which disperses him into inhuman parts. "The dislocated fragment of language," Carey writes, "has the same sinister potential as the severed limb". Carey is thinking of Dickens characters like Sloppy in *Our Mutual Friend* ("He do the police in different voices"), and perhaps the surreal stenographic speech of *The Pickwick Papers'* Alfred Jingle, but it brings us nevertheless to hear Jackson's vocal style as of a piece with his uncanny separating out of his own body, part of this breakdown into grotesque metonyms for himself. As Barney Hoskyns once wrote of Jackson's a cappella segue on *Jacksons Live*, the enraptured self-involvement of its play between language, laughter and pure sound expresses a narcissism that is "almost not human".

Is that "almost" even necessary? His talent, for singing, dancing, performing, was sublime, and the sublime is as often about all-consuming fear and dread as much as it is about irresistible bliss. Isn't everyone slightly chilled by the level of control which the most superlatively skilled dancers can exert, and the paradox it discloses? The paradox being that such tremendous control is demonstrated by submitting the body to peculiarly inhuman, unnatural, moves in which the dancer's agency, the normative process of control, seems to disappear: the moonwalk, the limbo, the perfect machinic geometry of robot body-popping. In Jackson's case, his command was so perfect that as a subject he seemed almost to evaporate, leaving a body commandeered by the abstract vectors and currents of pure rhythm. He became lost to music as electrifying, colonizing current, a thing possessed like the diabolically reanimated corpses marshaled behind him in "Thriller". His glove, his socks, his dancing, his wordless vocalizations: these are the iconic mannerisms by which he turned himself into an uncanny puppet twitching to the imperatives of rhythm and commerce and audience, not so much a person as a collection of things – limbs, make-up, prosthetics, costume – a collection of things dreaming, like Pinocchio, of being human.

They will possess you unless you change that number on your dial

It's largely the third act in Michael Jackson's career which people consider "grotesque", the period of his life in which, increasingly, he came unmoored from media reality and the validation of massive sales. His chronic resort to cosmetic surgery produced a physical collapse no surgery could fix, because it was an excess of surgery that had caused the collapse in the first place. His obsession with the innocence of childhood ceased to be Peter Pan-endearing and became sinister, libidinal, predatory. The further he moved away in time from the moments that defined his identity – "I Want You Back" aged ten, *Thriller*, aged twenty-three – the greater the psychic pressure internally. As a forty-something, the longing to remain a child, a vessel of prelapsarian potential, the subject of asexual adoration, became a kind of psychosis or pathology.

But the grotesque or uncanny Michael Jackson was there to be seen and heard long before his commercial and personal decline, and long before the body-horror tropes of *Thriller* and its extraordinary vision of the pop-promo as *gesamtkunstwerk*. Before Michael even launched his solo career, Vince Aletti wrote of a 1975 performance at Radio Music City Hall that Michael's dancing was "becoming a little disturbing, at moments even grotesque... he's supreme and so controlled, it's almost frightening".

And his own trajectory aside, Jackson at his peak, at his most potent as a performer, points beyond his death into our uncharted future. Whether this future proves to be dystopian or utopian remains to be determined. Writing in 1987 on the release of *Bad*, Greg Tate argued in the Village Voice that "Jackson's self-remaking can only be understood as a kind of Afrofuturist nightmare, a violent leap into the posthuman." Steven Shaviro calls this leap "a zombified, living-dead simulation of whiteness" – again Jackson is hovering ambiguously between organic life and lifeless thing. Tate credits Jackson as the architect of his own weirdness, but usually the nightmare interprets Jackson's uncanny deconstructions as something done to him as a butterfly on a wheel turned by the culture factory, not something he, consciously or not, was pursuing.

Perhaps. But consider, briefly, the fact that all the true heirs to Jackson's polymorphous pop perversions have been women. The futurist pop militarism articulated by Destiny's Child in "Lose My Breath" – the militant pop futurism of Britney Spears's "Toxic" – and most of all the single Cronenbergian gauntlet worn by Beyoncé as her solo alter ego, Sasha Fierce, in an obvious homage to Jackson. In moments like these, in which women become avatars, destructive and seductive in equal measure, Jackson's androgyny (as a man increasingly faun-like, fragile, elusive, victimized) finds its contemporary echo. It is the lack of this sexual fluidity which confounds other would-be Michaels, whether Usher, Chris Brown or Justin Timberlake, their aggressively hetero posturing leaving them stuck in stale normative positions. It is surely not only that Jackson and the likes of Destiny's Child meet in a zone of androgynous overlap, but that the spectacle of a man dismembering himself into a collection of discrete animated objects, is one that echoes acutely the objectification of women in mass culture.

What both Jackson – terrified of the desiring gaze of the Crowd that had watched him since childhood – and Beyoncé, disclose to their audience, is their condition as buoys in the currents of commerce, the human subject as pure pop commodity. And the commodity, in Marx's famous formulation, contains within itself enormously weird uncanny potential. "The table," he wrote, "continues to be that common, every-day thing, wood. But, so soon as it steps forth as a commodity, it is changed into something transcendent. It not only stands with its feet on the ground, but, in relation to all other commodities, it stands on its head, and evolves out of its wooden brain grotesque ideas, far more wonderful than if it were to dance of its own accord."

Jackson and Beyoncé, in their sublime dancing and uncanny masks and metonyms, disclose the sheer strangeness of their own transmogrification into product. Quick with life themselves, but deadened by commodification, they stage a reversal of this plight, so that in the sublime disappearances-of-the-self in their dancing, the fragmentation of their bodies, they mirror the fantastic transformation of the table into an animated wooden (Pinocchio-like) breakdancer, as products dreaming of becoming human.

Carey continues: "Only habit determines that a man is a unity, rather than his head or his teeth. Only habit determines that when we look at a man we should think of him as wearing clothes instead of the clothes constituting the man". This is a message which runs counter to the discourses of authenticity and integrity that surround soul, and behind it gospel, two of the scenes which nurtured Jackson and Beyoncé. The pop artist is haunted by critics waiting to unleash the accusatory term "soul-less". But Jackson, in leaving his beginnings with Motown's pop-soul sound behind to become the most paradigmatic pop act in history, did so through a series of records and performances which flaunted a negative image of Soul: a "violent leap into the post human", but one that had no need to end the way it did. Jackson's vision saw not a man, but a collection of clothes, a red jacket, socks, a glove; and presented this vision to an audience that loved it. Their adoration surely implies a post-humanism that can be positive, not a dystopian hell.

21

The King of Pop's two bodies, or, *Thriller* as allegory

Reid Kane

On the evening of his death, the nightly news broadcast concluded with a clip of Michael standing before a host of rotting corpses. It felt inappropriate, even disrespectful at the time. Of course the "Thriller" video remains among the most enduring icons of Michael's career, but it nonetheless seemed perverse to announce his untimely death with an image of him standing amongst the living dead.

Yet there is a reason why we want to remember Michael marshaling a crowd of zombified, no-longer-human monsters. That video was and is a sort of prophetic artifact, whose painfully ironic meaning seems so plain in retrospect, almost anachronistic. The whole *Thriller* phenomenon now writhes with unheeded portents. It is as if it was reverse-engineered, imported into the past to mend the radically disjointed timeline lying on either side. Before *Thriller*, Michael was Motown's young messiah, disco's most brilliant voice, an incomparable artistic talent cutting through dance music, R&B, soul, and driving them all toward something greater. Yet *Thriller* marked Michael's break with these roots, his elevation above the music itself into the status of pure celebrity. His art was no longer music or dance, but only the spectacle that was continuously made of him. This break is obliquely thematized within the lyrical, musical, and video content of *Thriller* itself.

There is a methodology tailored to these sorts of anachronistic artifacts, which Eric Santner refers to as the natural history of culture. This method "points toward a fundamental feature of human life, namely that the symbolic forms in and through which this life is structured can be hollowed out, lose their vitality, break up into a series of enigmatic signifiers, "hieroglyphs" that in some way continue to address us – get under our psychic skin – though we no longer possess the key to their meaning."

Santner claims that allegory is the literary form in which this absence of meaning from the natural history of culture is rendered most clearly, as it directly seizes upon this loss of significance in order to use the now hieroglyphic messages improperly, without regard for their former meaningful context.

In its suspension of literal meaning and imposition of an artificial one, allegory is the "symbolic mode proper to the experience of irremediable exposure to the violence of history", Santner argues in his book *On Creaturely Life*. Heard as allegory, *Thriller* seems perfectly suited to serve the figurative role of illustrating Jackson's real downfall and gradual decay. Explicating this allegorical character will be the task of this essay.

You're A Vegetable

"Wanna Be Startin' Somethin'" could almost have a place amongst the workaday disco ethic of *Off The Wall*, but for the almost immediate intrusion of an unhinged vocal inflection, whose warped enunciations contorted Michael's formerly straight-faced style. What had changed to inspire these spasmodic deviations? The lyrical content suggests a sort of tough-guy posturing, a feigned masculinity that will become a dominant theme throughout the album. While the ostensible intention of this posturing is a chivalrous defense of a love interest against scandalous insinuations ("*Someone's always tryin' to start my baby cryin'/talkin', squealin', lyin'*"), it's difficult not to see Michael's "baby" as a stand-in for his own embattled media persona. Michael must have felt his identity was threatened by the rumors that (mis)represented him in the media, as is suggested by the recurring theme of accusation and slander. This theme culminates with the story of "Billie Jean" later in the album, an episode which is foreshadowed in the opening track's third verse: *"Billie Jean is always talkin'/When nobody else is talkin'/Tellin' lies and rubbin' shoulders/So they called her mouth a motor"*.

The character of Billie Jean famously represented the vicious rumors leveled against him by the media – at the time, only the first trickles of an impending nightmarish torrent. Michael regarded masculinity and sexual potency as leaving him susceptible to media attack, as is demonstrated by the latter's equation with Billie Jean's claim to be carrying his child. It is the conflict between, on the one hand, defending himself but playing into the very image imposed upon him, and, on the other hand, fleeing from that image at the cost of losing everything, that gives *Thriller* its unexpected narrative consistency.

Before long the track begins to sound like a chaotic deterioration of his disco-persona, a cacophony of overenthusiastic horns and synths supporting paranoid rambling and a nearly schizophrenic clamor of the whooping chorus now unable to sing together behind Michael's increasingly unstable vocal delivery, culminating in the utterly bizarre refrain:

> You're a vegetable, you're a vegetable
> Still they hate you, you're a vegetable
> You're just a buffet, you're a vegetable
> They eat off of you, you're a vegetable

A vegetable: at once unable to move, and subject to the terrifying whims of ravenous consumers. The almost parodic send up of this fantasized paralysis and cannibalization is cut short by the maddening intrusion of an anxious guitar arpeggio that exemplifies the song's frightening spiral out of control. This delirious descent into madness is barely abated, with Michael finally recovering composure with a pathetically transparent appeal to African authenticity in the unfortunately mispronounced *"ma-ma-coo-sa"* chant, an episode which clearly foreshadows his future forays into feel-good Third-World romanticization, the ideal driving his many anthems for globalization with a human face ("Heal the World", "Black or White", "We are the World", etc.).

This fear-inspiring spectacle, more disturbing than thrilling, is followed by a tamer pair of tracks: "Baby Be Mine", with its slippery, skronky funk and soulful vocal delivery, and "The Girl is Mine", a syrupy, overly-sentimental love ballad. The strange repetition throughout the suite of the word 'mine' suggests a suspiciously emphatic insistence on possession of the woman's love, which is further hinted by the obviously insincere masculine posturing that plays out between Michael and Paul McCartney on the latter track. These suspicions are only confirmed by the unruly melodrama to come.

This Is The End Of Your Life

With its cascading synths and howling wolf samples, creeping bass and twinkling echoes, "Thriller" is, even before the video, more cinematic than musical. Michael is already gasping for breath before he can articulate the first lyric. The paranoia that had infected the opening track now becomes the dominant motif, sending Michael into a desperate narration of his own inevitable demise (*"And no one's gonna save you from the beast about strike.../There's no escaping the jaws of the alien this time/This is the end of your life"*). The irresistible "horror" that pursues him takes many shapes, but is ultimately identified by the paralysis it inspires in its victim, who once again seems to dissimulate Michael behind his "girl".

The terror that at once inspires and is inspired by this

paralysis manifests as claustrophobia (*"You feel the cold hand and wonder if you'll ever see the sun"*), a fear of being sealed away from the world, or equivalently, of the loss of one's life. This struggle – not against the beast itself, but against the paralyzing and de-animating response it provokes – becomes the dominant antagonism of the episode: *"You're fighting for your life inside a killer, thriller tonight"*. Inside the Thriller – which is ultimately nothing more than the monstrous hype-machine of the album itself, the massive media juggernaut that so completely absorbed Michael into the pure celebrity, the pure image of himself – inside this glittering prison, claustrophobia becomes absolute.

The formless beast stalking throughout "Thriller"'s deserted backroads is none other than the protean incarnation of Michael's future hyper-commodified celebrity identity, hunting down the final hold-out of Motown's grounded, working-class idealism, the last remnant of Michael's frail humanity. This dynamic is expertly staged in the song's video, as the bi-polar monstrous transformation that overtakes him. The opening scene stages a paradigmatic display of heteronormative sexual virility, in which the varsity-jacket sporting boy with car "runs out of gas", a idiomatic attempt at seduction. He asks her if she will "be his girl", again repeating the theme of possession. Michael then confesses that he is not like the others, and subsequently undergoes a grotesque metamorphosis, becoming a werewolf. The creature corners the girl, pinning her down, overwhelming her with masculine/animal sexual virility run amok.

At this point, we are pulled back *"from the terror on the screen"*, and see Michael in the audience with a different girl who, being frightened by the image before her (of overwhelming sexual potency), demands to be escorted home, despite Michael's obvious enjoyment of the scene. Yet, once we have been pulled back from the spectacular/mediated horror of sexual excess, a new metamorphosis overtakes the "real world" Michael: no longer the hyper-virile pathos of the werewolf, he is reduced to the cold, crawling flesh of the living dead. The duality is clear – the hypersexual mediated image in which the real Michael revels obscures the impotent plod of his decaying real body. Vincent Price's spoken lines at the end of the song thus seem like the observations of a Greek tragedy's chorus:

> And whosoever shall be found
> Without the soul for getting down
> Must stand and face the hounds of hell
> And rot inside a corpse's shell

Michael, in losing the *"soul for getting down"* that sustained him from Motown to his disco masterpiece, *Off The Wall*, became not unlike Darth Vader – a degenerating husk of pale flesh kept barely alive by a complex mediating machinery. Yet if Michael was more machine than man, his rotting interior was nonetheless exposed for all to see, both literally, in the form of his infamous disintegrating facial tissue, and figuratively, in his perennially compromised public persona.

Funky Strong

The continuity between the videos for "Thriller" and "Beat It" is suggested by, amongst other things, Michael's iconic red jacket being prominently displayed in both, and in the opening hoots and howls of the gang members, which recall Michael's own lycanthropic masculine misadventure. They also share Michael's alienation from masculine norms: his mortification in the face of the sexual relationship in the former, and his distance in the latter, as he dances in locations recently vacated by authentically masculine gang members.

"Beat It" also revives the album's central theme of paranoia (*"They're out to get you, better leave while you can"*), which again inspires masculine posturing: a desire to be *"bad"*, to *"be a macho man"*. The threat is, again repeating "Thriller", one of life and death (*"You wanna stay alive, better do what you can"*). Yet for the majority of the video, this lyrical content is abjured in favor of a withdrawal from the masculine spectacle, as recommended by the song's title. That is, until the video's strange resolution, in which Michael, who for most of the duration was in a world apart from the escalating suspense of the anticipated gang fight, intrudes as a *deus ex machina*, resolving the conflict regardless of who's *"wrong or right"*, by showing how *"funky strong"* a disco-istic ethic of collective expression through dance can be, disarming and unifying a once throbbingly antagonistic scene.

Unfortunately, this one glimpse of nearly utopian discipline is assimilated into the "peace on earth" ethics of humanistic capitalism that Michael would later champion. He was ultimately incapable of intervening in the mediated spectacle of masculine posturing, and instead obsessively fixated on changing *"the man in the mirror"*, the real person behind the image. Rather than attempting to change the image itself, he was convinced that it reflected real defects that had to be corrected (*"If you wanna make the world a better place/You better look at yourself and make a change"*); he was, in turn, incapable of recognizing the manner in which the image retroacted on the real thing, or how the mirror itself created the man it reflected. His frustration with the media, evidenced in a paranoid manner throughout *Thriller*, was displaced onto frustration with himself, an obsession with changing himself, through plastic surgery, drugs, masks, madness, and whatever else. Guy Debord perfectly formulates this displacement in *Comments on the Society of the Spectacle*:

> The erasure of the personality is the fatal accompaniment to the conditions of existence that is concretely submissive to spectacular norms... Paradoxically, the individual must permanently repudiate [it] if he wants to be respected a little in such a society. This existence postulates a fluid fidelity, a succession of continually disappointing commitments to false

products. It is a matter of running quickly behind the inflation of devalued signs of life. Drugs help one to conform to this organization of things; madness allows one to flee it.

Debord might as well be talking about Michael. We can very tangibly see this succession of false products unfold in the series of increasingly poor sequels to the "Beat It" video: "Bad", "Smooth Criminal", and of course, the anamorphic tantrum that concludes "Black Or White".

Spark My Nature

"Billie Jean" stages the showdown, evaded in "Beat It", between the paranoia-inducing media (and the hypermasculine reaction it stimulates), and the disciplined disco-workerism that would undermine this posturing. Yet the haunted atmosphere of the song, as much as the post-apocalyptic melancholy of the video, signal that this confrontation does not end well. It is followed by "Human Nature", an affected paean to the authentic immediacy of life on the street, comparing the latter to romantic caresses and sighs, to seduction and passionate longing (*"Reaching out/I touch her shoulder/I'm dreaming of the street"*) – a longing, in short, to reclaim the virility he so confidently denounces in "Billie Jean".

The remainder of the album only continues to pine for full sexual potency, for the legitimacy to claim Billie Jean's child, as a symbol that "the girl is really his". "PYT", with its smooth mutant funk, is hung up on proving Michael's manhood, thereby resolving the painful divide between wolf and zombie, mediated image and real body. This fantasized resolution is represented in a longing to return to the city streets (*"Hit the city lights/Then tonight ease the lovin' pain"*), ultimately dependent on the woman's direction (*"Where did you come from?"* and *"Won't you take me there?"*; *"Honey, come set me free"*). Michael needs someone to rescue him from hermetic isolation within his *"corpse's shell"*, his sterile image which only poses as potent. In the closing track,

"Lady In My Life", Michael finally associates this redeeming return to the real world, which for him is *"paradise"*, with immortality: *"And meet me in paradise, girl/You're every wonder in this world to me/A treasure time won't steal away"*. Trapped behind his image on the screen, Michael's real physical body degrades ever more rapidly, forcing him to figure his struggle against his own image as a resistance to death and obsession with youth, ultimately exemplified in his notorious "Peter Pan Complex".

A Corpse's Shell

Thriller's melodramatic struggle with the gap between mediated spectacle or posture, with which Michael never ceased to associate sexuality and masculinity, and the frail childlike life that it imprisoned, already prefigured the gradual decline that so famously followed it. Here, we are reminded of Kantorowicz's famous study, *The King's Two Bodies*, which analyzed the strange tradition of mourning a king's death. The work of mourning was divided into separate rituals, one for the body's biological death, and another to cope with the loss of the "political body" or symbolic status ascribed to his person.

Kantorowicz describes the way that the influence or charisma of the sovereign, his *dignitas*, outlives his physical death, and requires its own ceremonial execution to "reset" the circuits of power for his successor. It was not only the king as a living human being that had to be mourned, but the very symbol that he embodied, his status as that which holds the nation together. As the spectacular body of royal *dignitas* had a relative autonomy from its physical bearer, it was not enough for the kingdom to see the corpse of the king. Rather, his death had to be staged by way of an effigy, which served as a surrogate for public mourning. The king could not simply die without warning; his death had to be incorporated into his dignified image, whose integrity secured the power and stability of his kingdom.

This autonomous, extra-natural image has today attained a

new efficacy in the phenomenon of celebrity. While earlier celebrities, such as Elvis and John Lennon, were effectively mourned and laid to rest in the public imaginary (although Elvis did haunt us in so many mysterious sightings and impersonators), Michael is in many ways immortal and unmournable. It is as if, from *Thriller* onward, Michael's natural body was already dead, animated only by the life-support system of his massive media apparatus. The unmistakable signs of necrosis were written all over his face. He remained alive only as his own effigy and impersonator. Michael's career from *Thriller* onward was already an elaborate mourning ritual, an image mourning the loss of its original, a mirror coping with the loss of what it once had reflected.

One photograph accompanying the story showed Alberto, also known as "Little Death", hooded and masked as the Grim Reaper, posing in a Mexican graveyard with a scythe, while another revealed Alejandro's tiny coffin, adorned with flowers and the full-face cowl he wore in public. Their untimely demise was the result of unfeasibly large quantities of prescription drugs administered to public performers by professionals who should really have known better: a state of affairs not without precedent at that particular time.

Scandals are secretly welcome. They serve to distract the rebellious masses by offering them the best of both worlds: the one that ends in disgrace and the other that goes on to pass judgment. What else can a nation in mourning do? Contemplating the end has become a significantly smaller affair since the start of our own third millennium. There was a time, however, when Michael Jackson was unable to sign his own name without adding "1998" to it, convinced that this was the year when either he or the entire world would die. There was also a time when Elvis Presley elected to start his Las Vegas shows striding onto the stage to the opening climax from Richard Strauss's tone poem "Also Sprach Zarathustra", popularized by the film *2001: A Space Odyssey*. Both of these incidents hint at the cultural enthusiasms of the period between 1998 and 2001: the millennial fold that separated the twentieth century from the twenty-first. The future, as always, is whatever you can get away with. By the time of his death, Elvis had wreaked total havoc with the cosmic evolutionary agenda set by Kubrick's movie. Reborn in Las Vegas, he proceeded to refashion himself into a bloated white fetus with the internal organs of a man twice his age. In fact, the autopsy carried out on Elvis's body revealed that his entire digestive system had already ceased functioning prior to his actual death. Glowing in the light of a million instamatic flashbulbs that glittered about him like stars, his mind and body ravaged beyond redemption, Elvis had become the trash *übermensch* of our age. Behind the extensive reconstructive surgery, the bleached skin and the heavy stage makeup, Michael Jackson was also shut down chemically, thanks to a regimen of powerful painkillers, synthetic opiates and anesthetics. With the assurance of a moonwalker, the apocalypse continues to close in upon us.

2

Now that Michael Jackson and Elvis Presley each has a story that starts at the end, their deaths can undo the scandals of their lives but only by rendering them both as trash. The masked hero is ultimately considered unworthy, even though the wearing of the personalized cowl in public is a point of honor among the *lucadores* of the Mexican wrestling scene. An identity that remains secret is somehow beneath contempt: a fall from grace just waiting to happen. Part industrial by-product, part refuge from the very values that have created it, trash is the consumerist ethic torn inside out. Prominent among the crazes that emerged from the millennium fold, this passion for trash continues to exert its influence. In an age when beauty and truth, belief and desire, poetry and music have all become so compromised and debased by the culture of the mainstream that we can barely stand to look directly at them anymore, we prize trash not for what it is but for what it tells us about the forces that have created it.

Genuine beasts of the apocalypse like Elvis Presley and Michael Jackson show a complete disregard for the things that helped define them. "Let it burn, Daddy. It's only money," Elvis said to his father one night having just fired enough machine-gun bullets into an outbuilding on his Graceland estate that it had burst into flames. "Oh, Mark. It's only money," Michael Jackson exclaimed to a former Neverland estate manager while tearing up a stack of $100 bills. "Isn't it pretty? Money makes the best confetti."

During the summer of 2000 a voodoo ritual was conducted in Switzerland to rid Michael Jackson of his enemies, including former friends such as David Geffen and Stephen Spielberg; forty-two cows were ritually sacrificed in order to seal the deal at a reputed cost of $150,000, wired by Jackson's business adviser to a bank in Mali. The King of Pop was also said to have paid a further $1,000,000 for a ritual cleansing in sheep's blood so that he might be showered with "free money" in return.

"I wake up every day and think I'm in hell." Michael Jackson had said at the height of the Jordie Chandler scandal in 1993. "I don't even want to be alive." By then he had grown accustomed to going on tour with a frozen supply of his own blood for fear of catching a fatal disease from some tainted human stock. It cost over $300,000 a year to replace each flower in Neverland Valley the moment it showed signs of withering. "You know I hate to see pretty things dying," he tearfully explained. "I wished they lived forever, like in the movies." After crazed gunman Patrick Purdy attacked Cleveland Elementary School in Stockton, California, killing five children and wounding a further twenty-nine plus a teacher, Michael Jackson turned up wearing a blue military uniform and flanked by armed guards to hand out gifts. Purdy had the misspelled mission statement "Death to the Great Satin" on his flak jacket and the words "victory" and "earthman" carved into his assault rifle.

Near the end of his life, Elvis had been interested in financing and starring in a violent martial arts movie whose plot would involve drug dealers and hit men. Presley wanted to play the villain, and he had very definite ideas on how he should be presented: "I want to be the baddest motherfucker there is."

But it was left to Michael Jackson to ask: "Who's *bad*?"

Among the "sexually offensive contacts" listed in Jordie Chandler's complaint filed against him on 14 September 1993 was mention of "Defendant Michael Jackson eating the semen of plaintiff": an act which has the arcane ring of blasphemy about it.

"Go home, Michael Jackson!" a yeshiva student shouted when the Jackson entourage attempted to visit the Wailing Wall in Jerusalem that same year. "You are an abomination." Another student, this time from Tel Aviv University, saw things differently. "Michael's so electrifying," he exclaimed, "we think he may be the Messiah." Later, when Michael Jackson took his own children out shopping for toys, he would ensure that they were masked like comic-book superheroes.

3

"You kids be good," Elvis once told Michael Jackson and his brothers after they'd come to see him perform at the Sahara Hotel and Casino in Lake Tahoe. That was in 1974 when the Jacksons were playing the MGM Grand in Las Vegas. Sweating and bloated, drugged to the eyeballs, having already entered his final steady decline, the King grabbed hold of Michael's hand as the young entertainer turned to leave. It's not hard to imagine the decision Michael Jackson must have made at that moment.

Every pleasure that a king can gratify through his body can also be inverted or denied to more or less the same effect. Elvis took pills, getting so whacked on prescription opiates that he could barely move; Michael Jackson, however, started out swallowing vitamins by the handful. Elvis gorged; Michael starved himself. Elvis abused his vital organs, his liver smashed to a pulp by the time of his death; Michael Jackson gulped down oxygen and followed a macrobiotic diet. Both of them, like true kings, chose, after their respective fashions, to have their myths reside completely within their flesh. And the end result has turned out to be absolutely the same.

The official verdict on Elvis's death was "cardiac arrhythmia" while others claimed it was a drug overdose. There is a fifty-year suppression order on the post-mortem findings, although with the right connections it is possible to buy a video of the King's autopsy. For lesser mortals, copies of his death certificate have also been made available. The true nature of Michael Jackson's end has yet to be determined. Everything has to be laid out once again. The entrails are to be inspected for fresh portents. The power no longer resides in the body but in the separate organs. To prepare him for immortality, the pharaoh is opened up and his organs placed in individual canopic jars. The brain is extracted from the skull through the nose, although in Michael Jackson's case this might not be such a practical proposition.

As well as sharing Elvis's fondness for prescription painkillers, even to the point of stopping his own heart with them, Michael Jackson also managed to do extensive damage to the outside of his body as well the inner organs; the heavy make-up, wigs and sunglasses had become a way of preserving the royal head as a holy reliquary. While the Jackson family continued their argument with the LA coroner's office over whether Michael's brain would be buried along with the rest of his body, the media carried stories that the prosthetic attachment used to cover up what was left of his original nose had been stolen from the mortuary table. A hole fringed with gristle was all that now remained of this flimsy anatomical mystery that had once been the fascination of so many.

4

True kings are obliged to work much harder once they're dead: deprived of rest, the corpse is destabilized by the demands of the rebellious masses, and the organs become separated from it. Following an attempt to steal his body from its mausoleum in Forest Hill Midtown Cemetery, walled-in behind heavy slabs of concrete and marble, Elvis Presley was moved back home to Graceland and buried in its grounds. Fears that Michael Jackson's tomb might be robbed or desecrated mean that his remains have yet to find a final resting place: one heavy gold coffin and an equally ponderous memorial service are all the public have been allowed so far.

Just as Elvis has his Graceland, Michael will always have his Neverland. Like Charles Foster Kane's Xanadu, or Hearst's castle in San Simeon upon which it was based, these trash palaces were destined to become national monuments to collapsing values. As yellowing lawns fade and die outside suburban mansions, built on cheap credit and then abandoned during the recent economic downturn, the prospect of Michael Jackson's inevitable entombment at Neverland seems entirely appropriate. The rented fairground equipment has long since been repossessed, and the private zoo closed down, leading to speculation while he was still alive that Jackson would have to sell up his former fantasy home. Since his death and uncertain burial, however, there has been talk of reconstructing Neverland in Las Vegas to stand alongside Caesar's Palace, the Venetian, the Paris and the Luxor: the only thing missing would be the pillar of black smoke rising from the chimney as another childhood leftover is carelessly fed into the furnace.

It would take the body of a king safely buried beneath it to hold this much specially-commissioned trash together. Graceland can still boast its stained-glass peacocks and ceramic animals, the Tiki furniture and indoor waterfall in its "Jungle Room" and a main dining room whose "1974 look was red crushed velvet, thick blood-red shag carpet, red satin drapes and wild appointments", according to the tour guide. Neverland's entire contents were withdrawn from sale by auction mere days before the bidding was scheduled to start and barely three months before Michael Jackson died. "Monumental gilded throne with trumpeting putti, cupid heads, horses, lions, sea creatures, and scrolling foliage", ran one entry in the lavish catalog, published by Julien's of Beverly Hills to accompany the sale. Other items included no less than six separate portraits of Michael Jackson tricked out as a king, pharaoh or nobleman. If Elvis scandalized the public by seeming cheap and vulgar in his tastes, Michael achieved the same effect by appearing expensive and vulgar in his own royal choice of setting. The landscape that shapes itself around him at Neverland, in death as in life, represents a twenty first-century version of the picturesque in which William-Adolphe Bouguereau and Roche Bobois meet as equals.

"It's all magic," Michael Jackson said of his life at Neverland. He wanted to make a film of himself waking up in his room and saying "hello to the most gorgeous day ever". Such an ideal existence comes at a tremendous cost, however. "The film must be too good to be true," Michael specified, "like a fairy tale." The most ruthless exercise of power is required to keep everything so beautiful and perfect, even from someone accustomed to wearing full stage makeup in his own home. To live at Neverland was to exist within "a radiating circle of fear", according to one former employee.

5

Then there was the elaborate reconstruction of Maxfield Parrish's *Daybreak* in the 1995 promotional video for the song "You Are Not Alone". The source for one of the most commonly reproduced prints in the twentieth century, the original painting shows two girls bathed in the golden light of dawn. The scene itself is a Hellenic blending of classical columns with a rugged landscape of overhanging branches, distant peaks and tranquil green waters: the overall effect is of a natural proscenium arch framing the start of a new day. To see the two young females at the center of Parrish's painting played by Michael Jackson and his then wife Lisa Marie Presley is to encounter a form of innocence that could only ever be staged in such a contradictory and paradoxical fashion. The gaze exchanged between two female presences suddenly takes on new meaning, particularly when we recall that Parrish had left space in his initial design to include a third. Who could possibly be the missing figure watching Michael and Lisa Marie from the right-hand column? Elvis Presley? Jordie Chandler? Joe Jackson? The song is called "You Are Not Alone", after all.

Genuine beasts of the Apocalypse are incapable of irony, preferring paradox and contradiction, confusion and lies. Don't even think of looking for double meanings – only hidden ones will be found here. The prospect of two figures reflected in each other's eyes by a body of water suggests another possible inter-pretation: one that would also include the missing third. Gazing intently into the reflection of his own eyes, Narcissus fails to recognize himself but thinks he has fallen in love with another. He is not alone either. *"I'm starting with the man in the mirror,"* Michael Jackson declared on one of the songs from *Bad*; and the literal truth of this statement is that he ended with him as well. "He loves childhood because he was a child star," one close friend remarked of the Jordie Chandler scandal. "He loves to remember it. Michael is narcissistic in the extreme." Having amputated his own face, thanks to repeated bouts of plastic surgery and intensive skin bleaching, Narcissus was forever able to remain innocently in love with someone else. He took to frequenting maternity wards in hospitals to stare into the eyes of newborn babies. "He feels then that he can really see their souls." A nurse explained to one startled parent who had just been handed a release form on Michael Jackson's behalf. "I am the seeker, the seeking, the sought" runs a line from the poem he wrote for the central panel of a particularly regal triptych of portraits. In his eyes, *Daybreak* has become a recreation of the primal scene in which Michael gets to play all three parts: mother, father and child.

As his face continued its transformation, Michael Jackson learned to dread the actual break of day. "I can't go out in the sun," he admitted to one close friend. "My face would fall off." He looked at the world through dark glasses or hid away watching cartoons on TV. Michael Jackson was fascinated by them. "Cartoons are unlimited," he once said. "And when you're unlimited, it's the ultimate." Accounts of his life at Neverland are filled with references to secret chambers, darkened anterooms and hideouts with permanently drawn curtains and a color television in every one of them. "It's like everything's all right," he remarked from deep within his shadowy labyrinth. "It's like the world is happening now in a faraway city. Everything's fine."

6

The labyrinth is a place where a monster can live in safety. The son of a queen, the Minotaur was treated as royalty so long as he resided there. Hiding his disfigurement from the light of day, he fed upon the sons and daughters of the privileged few and feared no one except perhaps Ariadne and the youth she would be bringing with her. "Only a woman can destroy me," Michael Jackson confided to a business partner. The birth of a child means the death of the father: a course of events that might have led Vernon Presley and Joe Jackson to share an interesting perspective on life. Michael's marriage to Lisa Marie may have been hailed as suitably dynastic, even though it appeared to be taking place inside a snowstorm paperweight. The happy couple spent their honeymoon residing at separate villas, located five miles apart in a Santo Domingo resort complex owned by fashion designer Oscar de la Renta. The marriage held together for less than two years and produced no offspring to establish a possible Jackson-Presley bloodline.

But what precisely would this inheritance have entailed? "King of Pop" is a real taco platter of a title to select for yourself, while allowing yourself to be called "the King of Rock 'n' Roll" during the 1950s was to revel in the transitory nature of national fads to the point of sarcasm. Here on the rotting outer edge of postmodern "affirmation", where trash and consumerism are busy making history together, what elevates Michael Jackson and Elvis Presley as true royalty is their heroic intake of painkillers and opiates. Their capacity for blocking out the external world was truly prodigious. Michael Jackson kept a full medical library at home, while Elvis's favorite reading matter was *The Physician's*

Desk Reference, containing details of every drug on the market and their various effects. Medical records reveal that the day before he died the King of Rock 'n' Roll' took delivery of 150 Percodan, 20cc of Dilaudid, 262 Amytal and Quaalude and 278 hits of Dexadrine and Biphetamine in preparation for another grueling concert tour. The King of Pop's own consumption ran to Percodan, Demerol, codeine, Valium, Xanax, Ativan and Dolacet; and there were also rumors that he was also being treated for morphine addiction brought on by a chronic sleep disorder. "I've tried them all, and nothing beats Dilaudid," Elvis once remarked to a girlfriend, referring to the particularly potent form of "drugstore heroin" used in the treatment of terminal cancer patients. What would he have made of today's pharmacopeia? A police search of Michael Jackson's room has revealed that the cause of death may well have been Propofol: a hospital anesthetic so powerful that it is administered intravenously under strictly controlled circumstances, including heart monitoring.

"To be honest, I guess you could say that it hurts to be me." Michael once publicly admitted. "Sometimes it hurts so fucking much," Elvis was overheard mumbling to himself during one of his last-ever live performances. A trained physician was always close at hand, however, ready to stay with both kings until the very end. Dr Conrad Murray attended Michael Jackson on his last night on earth, while 'Dr Nick' Nichopolous served as one of the pallbearers at Elvis's funeral.

7

It wasn't the death of Elvis Presley that first permitted the public to read about his physical deterioration, the weight problem or the erratic behavior: during the last three months he spent in the seclusion of his Graceland bunker, copies of *Elvis: What Happened?* were already on sale in bookstores and supermarkets. Written by three former bodyguards whom Elvis had summarily dismissed, it told the "shocking and bizarre story" of assault rifles in Las Vegas hotel rooms, pills, midnight visits to funeral parlors and a sleazy, distorted version of masculinity. The capacity for pain is not the same as the capacity to no longer feel it. Just as Elvis rarely took a drug that none of his fans could have purchased legally, so he also surrounded himself with guns because he needed their protection; and no American citizen who believed in the right to keep and bear arms could have disputed that. What made fan and citizen alike recoil was the way in which Elvis took the consumption of such items to what was, for him, its absolute conclusion: popping pills as casually as sticks of gum and stockpiling weapons as if they were packs of cigars. With more chemicals pounding through his system than Roche could produce in a month, an M-16 cradled in his lap and surrounded by a small group of trained guards, each one tough and loyal unto death, Elvis Presley was simply defending himself.

Surveillance and security were equally tight inside Neverland: confidentiality clauses written into employment contracts ensured that none of the staff were free to reveal what they saw there. For years Michael Jackson repeatedly had himself photographed posing amid phalanxes of armed and uniformed men: in fact, he was so open about it that the obsession barely drew public comment. Is it the pain or only its medication being protected behind this hardened masculine wall? "When Michael Jackson grabs a gun, he turns into a tough-talking terror," ran the caption to a 1992 newspaper photograph showing the King of Pop at Neverland firing a TEC-9 automatic handgun. The following year Jordie Chandler's complaint against Jackson was met with more armed guards, death threats and a suspected attempt on the plaintiff's life. Michael's defense team also included Hollywood private investigator Anthony Pellicano, who had already proved himself back in 1977 when he helped to recover the mortal remains of Mike Todd, Elizabeth Taylor's third husband, which had been stolen from his vandalized grave in a

Chicago cemetery. Pellicano had just begun serving time in a federal prison for possession of illegal explosives, including a quantity of C-4 and some modified US Army grenades, when police raided Neverland for a second time in 2003. Hired by the Jackson family to prove that this fresh round of child-abuse allegations was all part of an elaborate plot by Sony Records to gain control of Michael's music publishing rights was security consultant and "soldier of fortune" Gordon Novel. "He kept asking me what prison was like." Novel recalled of his conversations with Michael Jackson about the trial. "Can he watch TV and movies there? He wanted me to stop the show."

8

That which has become hardened often turns out to be hollow as well: consider the plaster cast Michael Jackson took to wearing on his right arm the year he first met Jordie Chandler. Lacking solidity, such a body rearranges itself around the possibility of injury. "I am just like a hemophiliac who can't afford to be scratched in any way." The King of Pop once admitted. In a Tokyo hotel room during the *Bad* world tour, he also sat down and composed a handwritten note to the world that ended "HAVE Mercy, for I've been Bleeding a LONG TIME NOW". The Living Dead lurch and stagger through a dance routine on MTV. Parts of their bodies fall off, and they keep losing their balance, but Michael Jackson really used to like them a lot. He obtained a human brain, pickled in a jar, which was kept on the shelf next to his favorite dolls and games; and he observed several brain operations, enjoying every detail. "Even doctors can get a little grim-faced with all the blood involved," a surgeon revealed of one visit to the theatre, "but not him. I mean he was *smiling* through the whole thing." Elvis was also fascinated by what lay beneath the body's protective outer shell, going on carefully organized nocturnal tours of local mortuaries and funeral parlors, where he would often linger for hours among the sheeted dead, examining the corpses and admiring the embalmer's skill.

Transformed into Zombie Jackson, Michael comes out at night and dances down empty city streets with the Living Dead. His limbs twitch under his costume, a decomposing second skin of red leather. The real horror of the human body is that it continually changes. To expose the mechanics of this change is to render the constituent parts unstable, detaching organs from each other and rendering the flesh itself insubstantial. By his appearance alone Michael Jackson made bodily change acceptable to an almost unacceptable degree. A true immortal, he managed to create *himself* in his own image, thanks to at least six rhinoplasties, several face lifts, a "forehead lift", a cleft inserted into his chin, cheek liposuction, bone grafts, implants and tattooed eyeliner. Once begun, however, the process could never be halted. Michael Jackson turned himself into animals, cars, robots and space machines. "He arches like a wild cat," TV Guide reported from the set of the *Black Or White* video, "crawls forward, unfurling as if he is about to take off. Then it's over. The energy is gone, and the near invisible man is back again. Jackson disappears into his trailer, locking the door behind him".

The only creations powerful enough to rival Michael Jackson in his rise to world domination were the Transformers. Able to turn themselves at will into cars, trucks or any other automobiles, they had no fixed form or center of gravity. Michael Jackson beat them all, however, establishing himself as the changing face of change. The image he now presented to the rest of the planet had nothing to do with differences being reconciled: male or female, black or white, human or nonhuman. The question of what he might be changing into was nowhere near as interesting as the actual process of change itself. Such a controlled transformation suggested an intense amount of activity concentrated into one place. It had a dynamic that was totally internal and yet produced nothing at all. Meanwhile the Transformers came and went, then returned again – some people called it progress. For Zombie Jackson, death was not an end. When his heart finally stopped beating the latest Transformers movie was still playing the multiplexes. Part of the recently revived franchise, it was subtitled "Revenge of the Fallen".

9

Body dysmorphic disorder is the term for a common psychological condition in which an obsession with some minor or imaginary defect distorts the way in which people see themselves. What did Michael Jackson glimpse in the mirror that made him want to change so radically? Perhaps a creature that Narcissus would never be able to recognize: the "huge pudgy, bloated boy working one of his little desiring machines" revealed in the frontispiece to Deleuze and Guattari's *Anti-Oedipus*, for example. Painted by Richard Lindner in 1954, *Boy with Machine* refers to a longstanding tradition in his native Nuremberg: the *wunderkinder*. "Gifted with preternatural intellectual powers at an early age," according to The New York Times, "they brought many mathematical and mechanical marvels into the world, only to die very soon after. Himself reared and educated in Nuremberg, Lindner pictured them as potato-pale indoor children. Walled up with their unlikely apparatus, they stare us down."

Elvis Presley and Michael Jackson, the two greatest "potato-pale indoor children" of our age, appear to have merged together in Lindner's *wunderkind*. Examine the uniformed men and corseted women, the eroticized jukeboxes and pinball machines that populate the adult world as depicted by Lindner, and the connection becomes clearer still. Michael Jackson's housekeeper often gave the Nazi salute as she drove through the front gate at Neverland and would nod with satisfaction whenever the guards responded with shouts of "Heil Hitler!" Worse things can happen than dying before your time.

Accompanied by synthesizer versions of his greatest hits in the *Moonwalker* videogame, Michael Jackson overpowers opponents by dancing them to death and causes fire hydrants to gush spontaneously before finally transforming himself into a heavily armed robot. "Lindner's painting again asserts it presence," *Anti-Oedipus* observes, "where the turgid little boy has already plugged a desiring-machine into a social machine, short circuiting the parents". One eye-witness account has Michael Jackson playing with a toy train on the floor of his Dorchester hotel room and weeping over newspaper allegations that his face was collapsing. Another describes him dosed up on painkillers watching a videotape of Disney's *Fantasia* over and over again.

The same machine kept assembling itself out of disparate parts.

His contractual arrangement to produce children with Debbie Rowe, who had previously worked as a nurse for Jackson's dermatologist, was a means of bringing semen and a uterus into contact with the least possible intimacy. The agreement did not even allow for visitation rights on Mother's Day. "The request for Mother's Day is a concern because Debbie now appears to be viewing herself as a mother," Michael Jackson's lawyer asserted. "This is different from the image and position that she accepted in the past."

Sperm and eggs form a masturbatory relationship as if they were mechanical parts. "I don't have to bring my own into the world," proclaimed the King of Pop.

How else could you connect up a mouth with a Pepsi can to form such a perfect mechanism? *"You're a whole new generation, you're loving what you do,"* Michael Jackson sang in a highly successful television campaign for Pepsi; although Jackson refused to be seen drinking the stuff in public because he didn't "believe" in it. Even so, the can and the mouth kept on coming together. "Jesus drank it so it must be good," He reasoned, offering wine in Diet Coke cans to his special young friends.

Defects can still distort the way the machine functions, however. "I'm trying to get him to remember what Michael Jackson's penis looks like," Jordie Chandler's lawyer complained, "while his therapist is trying to get him to forget it." At one point the King of Pop had considered marketing his own soft drink under the brand name "Mystery".

10

Misanthropy and a love of machines often go together. Elvis Presley and Michael Jackson both spent huge amounts of money on cars for people, buying four or five Cadillacs at a time "like a fairy tale out of the movies", as one witness remarked. All around them new versions of the same machine jerk into life. "Grab your crotch, it's Michael Jackson," comments one impersonator. "Put on a white glove, it's Michael Jackson". Similarly, no representation of Elvis is complete without the white jumpsuit emblazoned with Sun God imagery and bursting at the seams. According to CNN, Jackson's body had track marks on the arms and his veins were collapsed, suggesting repeated intravenous drug use; the network also claimed that the remains were emaciated and "lily white" from head to toe and that the King of Pop "had no hair". Isolated from the world since his early childhood, Michael Jackson learned everything he knew from watching TV, according to one close friend, and "everything he saw on television that represented class and glamour was white". No wonder he wanted a blond, blue-eyed white boy to play him as a child in *The Jacksons: An American Dream* and in one of his other Pepsi commercials. "Men like this live to die of old age," declared Louis Farrakhan in a personal attack on Michael Jackson when at the height of his fame, "because they threaten nothing." Dr Arnold Klein, Michael Jackson's dermatologist, described how the entertainer had appeared in great shape just three days before his death. "He danced in my office," he told *Good Morning America*. "He danced for my patients."

"Everything is tape recorders and photographers," Jean Genet remarked to William Burroughs before returning to France in the autumn of 1968. "Reality in America is dead, absolutely finished." He had come to the US to cover the antiwar demonstrations taking place outside the Democratic National Convention in Chicago at the end of August. In an attempt to get time away from the tear gas and confusion, Genet had tried to take a trip into the rural outskirts of the city but ended up wandering around Gary, Indiana, Michael Jackson's old hometown instead. The Jackson Five would have just signed up with Motown Records that summer; and it is worth imagining what might have passed between them, had the French writer and the young pop star met each other at a time when the dance was still an innocent one and the world seemed at its brightest.

23

Michael's labyrinth:

A tabloid sublime

Alex Williams

The point of excess, for the imagination, is like an abyss in which it fears to lose itself.
 – Immanuel Kant, *Critique Of Judgment*

The labyrinth is a flint desert exposed to the Near-Eastern sun, without wall, door, or window, a chalk surface... the beast learns nothing, hence it multiplies incomparable labyrinths.
 – Jean-François Lyotard, *Libidinal Economy*

The body of Michael Jackson lies cold now, mere meat packed slab flat in the Los Angeles morgue: skin scalpel-incised, scar-infested, hypodermic needle pin-prick cushioned. Alien flesh. "Bald peach fuzz scalp" – the leaked autopsy report bristles with porn-vivid detail throughout. A new Roswell. The man who fell to Earth.

Shocked but not surprised.

Greeted with such glee and hunger by the cannibalistic masses, as if the zombie throng of the "Thriller" video returned to unlife, with John Landis exchanged for George Romero, now rending the flesh apart and gorging on raw organs and blood. Xenoprotein.

Michael lost to an eternal reverie, swallowed up by the anesthetic milkbliss of the great white-out. A hermaphroditic James Brown in indelible black metal corpse paint.

The brain of Michael Jackson – what passions ripped through it, what inhibitions, pains, euphorias, reflexes, personae – now the great god Pan, now Peter, transducer of dreams and night-mares. The line that traces out a series of grotesquely looming hybrid creatures:

- Disney Allan Poe
- Pedophile Bambi
- Lovecraftian Dumbo

His unique neural architecture, hard-wired into the great accumulative machines of the commericum, but now bereft of electro-chemical impulse, ceased, terminated, silent, a grey neural steak, jarred. Further tests to follow. Tomorrow's headlines lie in wait inside.

At 10:47p.m. on 25 June 2009, I first learnt of the death of Michael Jackson. Almost immediately I was held in a digitally mediated trance, captivated in a hypnotic state of fascinated and withdrawn horror, a peculiarly negative yet undeniably *gratifying* pleasure. Jackson's death presents a personal quandary: given that I had never been a particular admirer of his music and nor had I followed especially closely the contortions of his living after-life which played out over the last twenty or so years in the tabloid media, what was it which was so grimly fascinating about this current event? Certainly Jackson's reach was both memory-deep and planet-wide, a reach which probably exceeds that of any prior or subsequent pop figure. But no one, surely, could have been especially surprised by Jackson's death, and indeed sadness seems a strangely inappropriate response. Rather than thinking along the lines of a mourning (either for Jackson's actual life, or as a remembrance of the potentials he had squandered), this mode of enjoyable displeasure must instead be considered as a strange example of the sublime. Or perhaps not quite the sublime, but the *tabloid* sublime.

The tabloid sublime is exceptionally close to the weird cinematic register of David Lynch's films, a disturbing splicing of the hyper-normal and the dismally dark. The Lynchian thrives upon the extreme tension between these two zones, between the artificially reconstituted American post-war pastoral and the Freudian hellscape beneath. Though seemingly incompatible, these two domains are actually always imbricated with one another, and the plasticized 1950s normalcy and nightmarish stygian underworld are ultimately equally strange and disturbing. With neither zone conforming to a conventional realism, above all it is the diabolical passage *between* these two realms which marks the fundamental horror of Lynch's works. The consensual sentimentality which Jackson trafficked in such songs as "We Are The World" and "Earth Song" (all pumped-up on pious moral capital), or through his charitable foundations, or in the Neverland ranch in its role as cancer-stricken boy-refuge, must always be confronted by its raw underbelly, the child abuse court cases and allegations, the senselessly (weak) nihilistic drug abuse and surgery scalpel-fetish, and each is revealed to be conspiratorially linked to the other, to be interconnected in a manner which sets the mind *reeling*.

As Lynch's career progresses the layering of his cinematic territories becomes ever more intricate, leading in films such as *Lost Highway* and *Inland Empire* to a terrifying cosmology in which reality is revealed as little more than a series of membranes, subterranean tunnels, and holes leading infinitely down into ever-receding depths. This extrapolation reveals every stratum of reality to be utterly unstable, and always liable to collapse into a further plane beneath. An endless warren of (plot) holes, a puncture-ridden space akin to the Menger Sponge, where characters switch identity, space and time bend and flex, and an array of black (Pandora's) boxes are opened, leading ever further down. This place is both limitless and without hierarchy, without the anchor of a given dimension with predominance over any other, indeed without any "normal" to return to, and hence radically "weird". This weirdness corresponds to Jackson's own, for it is this cinematic (an)architecture which acts as the best guide to Michael's tabloidic maze, a place without limits and where every plot must necessarily be qualified by another. Just as Nick Land writes of George Bataille's labyrinth, Jackson marks a point of "infestation or irresolvably complex collapse, replacing being with an illimitable corrosion. [This] is precisely the positive impossibility of privileged scales, and the recurrence of irreducible diversity in the transitions between scales [here] life is infested by death; terminally infiltrated by the unsuspendable reality of its loss…"

Alice in Wonderland/Jackson in Neverland: and down the rabbit hole we go. In every direction lies another interpretation, another storyline, the plots tied up in Borromean knots, or unspooled into a messy pile of loose ends and lost threads. The twofold domain is blown apart in death as every rumor and possible theory explodes out, each tiling on top of the other in a lurid tabloid topology. In a life so richly encoded, so encircled, no master narrative can ever emerge, or at least, any single one can operate its convincing mastery over the others from the correct perspective, like an M. C. Escher edit of The Sun newspaper. Indeed, the sublime moment with Michael Jackson arrives, as in Lynch's finest films, when you obtain the vantage point from which it is possible to see that the black boxes go on forever without halting point… A limitless, shapeless space from which our senses can only withdraw in revulsion, but which our ratio-nality enables us to endure and moreover, to *enjoy*.

What makes this experience uniquely *tabloid* in nature is the lurid nature of our enjoyment. With Jackson it is difficult to separate out the inflicted from the self-inflicted, the torments wrought upon him by his father, from those of the media apparatus, his diseases and misfortunes, from his own hand. It is this which leaves him as such a figure of undecidability: did he bleach his skin to alter his superficial racial appearance or did he suffer from vitiligo, did he abuse children or protect them (on the walls of the room in which he died was apparently pinned a piece of paper with the words "Children are sweet and innocent" – pederast's self-help memo or... what precisely?), was he a closeted gay man with a string of hidden lovers/heterosexual squirer of Elvis's progeny/loving father to his children/predatory pedophile/auto-castrated asexual, etc... This is in part due to the myriad of media forms circulating around the empty core of the individual himself, but it is more than simply this, his radically undecidable nature in part due to his own machinations, his will to self-transform, to evade, leading paradoxically always further into enmeshment within the tabloid net. This undecidability leaves Michael Jackson as a kind of hideous hybrid creature, a doe-eyed yet rapaciously pedophilic Bambi, or Mickey Mouse-as-Frank Booth sucking on an anonymous narcotic gas, high-pitched helium-effeminate voice exclaiming, absurdly, sickly, unbelievably: "It's Daddy, you fuck." That *both* realities exist within the same space, beneath the same name, leads to that addictive quality familiar to any consumer of tabloid media – that even though your tastes are jaded, the placing of ever more incompatible storylines on top of one another delivers a powerful libidinal punch. These incompossible chimeras lurch out from the gloom to confront us, conducting immensely powerful emotional and affective currents in their wake.

Jackson is distinct from other such tabloid-fodder because of the sheer richness of potential narratives collected under the sign of his name, and the highly developed conspiracy between corruption and innocence. This corruption evidently had a distinctly physical correlation with Jackson's own bodily health. Though Jackson's later album titles *Dangerous* and *Invincible* speak of his seeming desire to establish an indefatigable and pitiless pop-Reich, his own physical status became markedly ever weaker. Jackson affected (or perhaps was affected by) a confrontational and unsettling frailty, "dangerous" only in the sense of a perilous porcelain fragility, a slow and asymptotic fade-out to silence, from frenetic hyper-kineticism to an eerie stillness. This was a kind of living and perhaps even willed afterlife, a heavily tranquilized and opiated drawing-in of the night. In most conventional explanations Jackson's quest towards this self-erasure is thought in strictly Freudian terms: the project to erase the image of his father, a lifelong mission to wipe clean every trace of Joseph Jackson which presented itself to him – race, gender, sexuality and all. A line of flight, of escape, through an absolute white out and subtraction perhaps? Or simply the physical traces of Jackson's edging ever closer to the unsettling zone of incompossibility, of indiscernibility, a fade out and perversely anti-libidinal corporeal reaction to the great coursing surges of libidinal energy conducted through his tabloid-body?

Beneath the name "Michael Jackson" lies a limitless media architecture, an infestation and corrosion of a most peculiar form of space. We enter the maze of Jackson's body, his corporeal body leading out onto his incorporeal body, his scars and his neuroses, feeding into the network of story-line/lies stretching all around him in a spider's web, and we are lost in an enchanted revulsion at the possibilities of contemporary capitalism itself. This form of space, produced by capitalism's ability to relentlessly abstract whilst simultaneously investing such structures with intense libidinal force is not just restricted to the tabloid media. For the same form of hyper-libidinized, yet abjectly abstract, architecture underpins the configurations of international finance, whose recent catastrophic collapse and aftermath ironically coincided with the death of Jackson. The error, after all, was to believe that it was simply he who was trapped within the mirror maze, rather than ourselves.

24

Notes towards a ritual exorcism
of the dead king

Ian Penman

This is the end of your life.
– Michael Jackson, 'Thriller'

MALIBU

On the weekend after Michael died I went to a party.

It was a good party: a genuine celebration.

There were little kids there, and teenagers, and us older sophisticates, still throwing lumpy shapes to Chic and Madonna. I sat down with a bunch of sixteen to eighteen-year-old girls: professional duty. They passed around the bright white Malibu. I said: I'm writing about Michael Jackson. Not much stirs. "Yeah?" Nothing. I persist, ask: what did they think? They don't seem too ruffled, or much bothered. "Quite liked some of his music..." That's it: that's the limit of what I get from them. Fair enough – on one level, it's pretty much all I felt too at that moment. Not that you'd know it from the deluge of press and media comment in the week after his death; we were all supposed to be – that pervasive, insidious, irritating "we" – heartbroken, devastated, in mourning.

This is the problem, here: the huge disjunction between how people are, what they feel, or don't, what they talk about, worry about, what they actually watch and listen to and are affected by, in their day-to-day lives; and then what the media – under the legend of that too convenient "we" – tell us we are all feeling and thinking.

In the immediate aftermath of his death, no sensible middle ground: the choice lies between hagiography and character assassination. Some of us stand on the sidelines, perplexed. What is all this? I wail at the TV wall each day. OK, I can buy that once upon a time he was a kind of cross-cultural role model, strange and new and difficult to read, but... come ON! People! This wasn't Martin Luther King; this wasn't even Marvin Gaye. I mean, just no one I know is at all bothered by this. It's not as if he even really "died young". Even on the level of OK-entertainer (OK-kid's-entertainer, which is what he mostly was) he hadn't really mattered for 20-odd years. A washed-up drugged-up blocked entertainer (whose palette was never that wide or deep), a maybe/maybe-not pedophile (in private 99% say: I think he was, don't you?), who so maddeningly and confoundingly went from billionaire power broker to payday-snuffling failure and recluse. So why this storm of pious, keening, sentimentalized, hysterical, pseudo-worshipful media overkill?

Was he always waiting, up ahead of us, programming every next/last response, like a bony fright-wigged Wizard of Oz for the digital epoch?

Did he pull off one final improbable coup?

Colonizing our unconscious: like a riff, a headline, a drug, a ghost.

Staging death as his last great re-appearance, return, media apotheosis, far more effective than any putative stage-bound comeback. (They surely would only have disappointed, those fifty shows. One show, a weekend at most, I can understand. But fifty?)

The only way to top yourself, is to top yourself.

NATURE VS NURTURE

He defied the former, was damaged by the latter.

He would make himself over, a singularity without lineage, without predecessors.

Michael, born of Media, postmodernist archangel.

POP ESCHATOLOGY

As we know from previous experience, certain figures transcend the usual human script: John Lennon, Bill Clinton, Princess Diana, and now Jackson. They radiate some analysis-defying "x" factor, crowd magick, mass appeal. This ability to be consistently forgiven. Failings and fallings and flaws overlooked.

Look at Lennon – heroin addiction, support for the IRA, weird foreign missus, dabbling in avant-garde conceptual art, breaks up The Beatles... what more could he do to lose the love of his popular audience? But he remains the Lads' favorite pop star, bar none: the love never goes. He preaches anti-materialism and mass togetherness but holes up inside therapy-occluded privation with only stock market deals and a freezer full of furs to keep him warm: they love him more. Puts out god-awful AOR sludge. Still the adoration increases.

Do we really need to adumbrate Michael's own perplexing choices? The myriad ways in which he would seem to be the exact opposite of anything like contemporary black pride? His almost luminous propensity for bad faith and bare-faced lies? His progressively less urgent or pleasing or interesting music?

The jacked-up psychopathology of Hubris: I AM THE KING. I AM THE KING.

SCREAM (FAUST MIX)

There's always a price to pay. Those dream-maker scenarios are haunted by specters of will-theft and blood. *"There's demons closing in/On every side/They will possess you."* You don't welsh on deals like this! You can't proclaim yourself messiah, re-incarnation, King of Pop, imagist revolutionary, you can't claim popularity on this global scale... and then shrug your shoulders and say, sorry guys, I'm like *through* with this shit, I want a bit of privacy, I'm retiring. There's no "retiring" on contracts like these!

You're taking the lift to the penthouse floor, alone, when suddenly you feel the temperature drop... something re-arranging its carious folds in the empty air. What's that? It feels like a bony finger between your ribs...

I knew it would be you.

Matter forming out of thin air.

I knew it would be you.

It's never the gun or knife or hypodermic you see first but the feral and liquid eyes: black, blank, accusing. And this pulse-quickening smell redolent of absences beyond mere absence...

> *"You hear the creature creeping up close behind.*
> *You're out of time..."*

You can't make deals with the daemon world and then expect to play by the same old Wendy House rules. You can't assume a kind of platinum sainthood, in this mucky secular world, and expect things to go purely to plan. In breaking traditional ties one sets free unknown forces, the consequences of which might not be immediately obvious; even the supposedly "good" guys, like

Lennon and Marley, discovered that sainthood comes at a stiff price.

ALREADY DEAD

How many gods did Michael defy? Starting with his own Jehovah's Witness faith? This is a very murky area. In the week after his death I logged on to a few JW chat-rooms and sites. (It started with just wanting to know a bit about the faith, and discovering for instance that in their theology MICHAEL is the archangel, the true boy king.) From what I could gather from the chat in the air (even zealots gossip in the ether) the JW "community" has an enormous respect for Mrs J, his mom. She is well known and admired and respected and loved in the JW world. She is down there at grass roots level, doing the work, sowing the seeds of righteousness proper. As far as anyone else knew, that was the current extent of Jackson family involvement. The rest were lost souls, given their worldly track records. No one knew for sure, but given some of the things that had been said and some of the things that had been done... well there is a thing called "disfellowshipping" which is just as it sounds. Excommunication, de-Witnessing.

Which, when you think about it, what else was Jarvis Cocker's 1996 gestural interruption, his symbolic objection but a kind of pop world disfellowshipping? Embarrassing, for Jackson, not so much for the moment itself (which none of his devoted fan-base would take any notice of anyway) but for what it said about him being finally beyond the pale, hipness wise, being terminally un-cool. If he had died at that moment it's hard to imagine he would have received the same wash of cleansing hagiography as he did that week in June 2009.

There were late rumors that he had maybe "converted" to Islam. (African-American comedian Katt Williams: "You can't be no

Muslim, Michael! You got a white woman pork face!") Although would Islam really have taken him? The other rumor in the air at the time was that in Saudi Arabia Jackson had been seen going into *women's* public lavatories (in, where else, a mall) dressed in a burka. If these burka-in-a-rest-room rumors were true... what *was* that? A last way of testing out if he was still beyond human law? "I'm Michael: I can do what I want"? Or childish drugged-up prank? Or evidence of a man toppled over into serious pathology? Or was there even any sure way, at the end, of differentiating between such things?

And a lot of stuff at the end invites such speculation. On the Bashir program [2003], his image in tatters, what does he do? (If nothing else, he did used to be *king* of media manipulation, after all.) He preaches brotherhood and love, should be stressing charity and human frailty and so forth. Instead we get shots of him zipping round empty hotel corridors on his own little *old people* cart; and splurging millions of dollars on this real horror show of Las Vegas style home furnishing... "I'll have this, and this, and this..." It felt grotesque, sad, almost like he was buying the nearest sparkly thing. (It wasn't even the sort of art or décor that would be a long-term good investment, if that's your thing.) The buying spree, this spasm of excess, ends with his purchase of a life-size replica of an Egyptian sarcophagus. The dying king, his golden shell.

(Plus that whole baby-on-the-balcony episode. Which wasn't even the most disturbing moment: rather, that was the next day's footage of a Jackson who was visibly *shaking* with rage, or drugs, or anxiety, or delirium, or all of the above, trying to bottle feed the same poor little kid on this jackhammer speed freak leg going 100 mph.)

He is wholly oblivious.

(It's probably worth remembering that the reason he miscalculated so badly and got trapped in that Bashir apocalypse was Bashir's connection to Princess Di – Bashir as medium in the world of media gods. Did they ever meet, the King of Pop and the People's Princess?)

Then again he still seemed able to ride such bad conflagrations out: things like this didn't seem to register as much resentment among his public as one might have expected. He exists in another dimension already, like the latter years of Howard Hughes. A dimension of rumor-mist and electronic static. The myth-self sustaining a kind of deranged heat, while the real life withered and atrophied.

A DRY SEASON
"They drag around at the end, stuporous, drained, shivering in near autistic spheres of solitude." (Avital Ronell)

>King of painkillers. Intravenous anesthetic. Oblivion.
>The end of the rainbow in Room 101.
>"This used to be Mr. Hughes' room when he stayed here..."

Just like H. H.... the last few years Michael slipped beyond the bonds of everyday anything. Specter drifting round the globe. Pure air element: no earth, no fire. Flown from obscure spot to obscure spot. Rumors, sightings, photos of him where OMG you have to look but really don't want to see, bald, a pin cushion, narcotized beyond addiction, rich but emaciated, popular but alone, loved but adrift and untouched... spiritless.

Like Hughes, there is (in Iain Sinclair's words) "a time price to pay".

Like Elvis, like Hughes, Michael – as essence, myth, imago – slips into a kind of symbolic death-in-life long before his own mortal death.

With Hughes it was the Mormons, with Jackson the Nation of Islam: this isolated figure who buys further isolation to hide inside. Someone to administer the deals and the drugs. Cocoon vigilance. Insects in shiny gangster suits. Praying/preying mantises.

No point in asking: "protection" from what, from who?
From all the gathering shades.

Like Hughes, this Vegas life of mirage and morphine, become a threnody of rumor and dispossession. Hughes supposedly rides out alone in the desert twilight on his souped-up rally bike. (Or maybe it was one of the Manson dune buggies?) Michael supposedly dresses as a woman and goes downtown to procure sex with young corn-fed hustlers in shabby Vegas motel rooms.

Maybe. Who knows. It's another rumor. Another hallucinatory stitch in the Myth. Another ragged whisper in the turbid spirit air. And he can't complain because way back when he started half of the rumors. Fatal. You signed away your *soul*, boy.

And there will be no "Rosebud" whisper: he's already dead. Posthumous post-human.

At first you might think this figurative license; but then as the first reports became public this one odd, unnerving, insistent detail: Everyone around him said that by the time they arrived... he was already dead.
Ahead of everyone one last time.

Let's face it: he had looked living-dead for years.

Remember that police photo from 2003 when he was arrested and booked. It was not merely that he no longer looked black. He no longer looked human. Like the cover of an alien abduction paperback, he is ALL EYE.

Look upon this graven image, media kids and shudder: this is your future. All you would be E4-presenters and would be IT Girls and would be VJs, look into the future of your race: atrophied hands and blown-away nose and under-nourished soul. ALL EYE. Live by the image, die by the image.

XANAX AND NEON

I've read postmodern theory that posits Michael as kind of avant-garde paradigm, remarkable post-Human, a kind of postmodern Gnostic liberated from mere flesh, destiny, fixed roles of race and sex. But no one ever wants to PAUSE the trendy verbiage and wonder... what was it like to BE Michael Jackson? To be inside that NONtology. To be, or to not-really-be.

Because after a certain point, being Michael Jackson seemed to involve an abyss of fathomless pain. The irony being that his life had become all too fatally a thing of FLESH. Erased and enervated and shoddily reconstructed face flesh. Child's flesh. Crimes of the flesh, scarred flesh, scared flesh. Cauterized, castrated, cut up... Pain. Legs. Head. Nose. Hip. Demerol. Morphine. Dilaudid. Sex. Masturbation. Public hair made public. Circumcision. Test tube. Bald. Starting with the man in mirror. The first, the last. The end of HIStory.

Hit the road Jackson.
Don't you come back.
DON'T COME BACK.
No more no more no more.

Or maybe the only choice left is the no-choice of return in penitent "comeback" form: maybe that's the sum of your stunted destiny now. All you'll ever be is a return, a ghost of your former glory. To be measured accordingly. As a "return" – in the cruel double meaning that term has. You're not acting/performing, as you once did, to measure up to your own high standards now: only to fulfill someone else's investment, someone's backing. And they do want their return.

Privately he dreams of no comeback: ever again. He wants to arrest time, all the time. Starting with the man in the mirror. Diving down into the pool of narcosis. Disappearance as headline. Absence as mnemonic. Destined to live many lives, all at once. The sum of people's projections. So many difficult re-births. All these flows bigger than any individual subject.

If you're a black entertainer, it's not enough just to entertain. On one hand – why can't he just be great, period? On the other – all this stuff about being a role model. "He was ours, we only lent him to you." (In a certain light have you any idea how CRUEL that sounds?) In a sense it's like, you're BLACK – you're not allowed any neurosis! You can be excessive, flamboyant... but not... *this*. You are always an example. Inside this skin forever. The shadow for other people's Peter Pan fantasies and socio-cultural agendas.

Entertainment? Tain – doesn't that mean skin in some old language or other?
Skein. Tainted. Taint. Color.
Entre-tain-ment then, which might mean: *between skins*.

I have no self-presence any more. None.
Only occasionally when the drugs hit right.
And then just for a moment or two.

And you want me to perform?
To be that old me?
How on earth, this close to midnight?

Late in the night, a palatial but empty and borrowed room. Vegas with all its Howard Hughes echoes. Vegas city of permanent night. Makes no difference if it's black or white. Neon and Xanax. I will do away with all clocks and all mirrors.

I will do away with all clocks and all mirrors...

Easy as one two three.

Off the wall Michael is crouched at the feet of the final curtain.

Michael? What went wrong? Michael? Who are you? I don't recognize a thing about you.

When the myth takes over and people want the myth every time they see or meet you. They want you to *explode like fireworks* every time. Your blood has stopped, gone sluggish. You can't find a peaceful place anywhere inside your mind. You just want a hushful lake or a clean log cabin in your mind you can go to, sit a while, listen to the song of the air.

Now there is pressure on all sides.

Fifty dates.

Waking and waning. Dancing and cursing. Hurting and fading.

This is the mask of torture: fifty dates.

AND SO IT BEGINS
The night he died and the morning after, all the quotes from

other entertainers tended to... "Let's forget all the awful stuff and just remember the music. Remember the great entertainer he was." Remember. Bring back. Honor the ghost he had become even while still alive. This was why the idea of these "comeback" concerts was so unthinkable. Maybe one concert would have been just about do-able, thinkable. Even if it flopped a little bit... the fans would have been pleased, the "deal" in a sense honored. The fabric kept. But to have to get up the next morning and face doing it again. And again. And again.

For a while that first night I toyed with the idea that his for-the-time-being unverifiable "death" would turn out to be the ultimate showman's bait and switch. That he would resurrect himself onstage: the ultimate zombie/Christ comeback. Unbeatable. Obscene. Shameless. Macabre. Wouldn't that be something? Life imitating *Thriller*!

(Until his brother Jermaine stepped up to make that announcement. Was I the only one to find something, I don't know, just a little bit off, somehow wrong, in that one-last-time mode of address? "My brother, the legendary King of Pop Michael Jackson"? As if it had become – literally – a matter of life and death, that ludicrous out-dated honorific?)

If Jackson had played his comeback concerts it's hard to imagine anything but a kind of generalized disappointment (Those rumors that he was only contracted to a – probably lip synching – thirteen minutes a night.) In the event, in the end, why not just employ a (younger, fitter, more reliable) look-alike? Could anyone really have told the difference by this point? Wasn't it rather the audience's fantasy of his mere re-appearance? (Like Christ. Or Elvis.) Wasn't that the whole ticket price right there for his more demented fans? Rather than the relative merits of specific songs or dance routines or whatever? It being more a question of his BEING. Of his electric-flash return. Prophecy and resurrection.

ANGER IS MY FATHER

When (and why) exactly did Michael begin to change, curdle – when did anger take the place of joy? He went from playful to portentous, to pissed off, to poisonous. At some point in the mid-to-late '80s his face seemed to settle into a near permanent sneer of – what? Rage? Contempt? Disgust? Watch all those videos again. It's horrible. It's far more scary than the faked transmogrification in *Thriller*. OK, in therapy speak you're supposed to "own your anger", I know – but he seems *possessed* by it, or by something that expresses itself as anger. Watch as it ossifies into a kind of demented self-pity, in which the world's ills only exist as an index of his own current mood.

He may well have begun with a proper and delicate sense of injustice, not just the macro, global kind – the kind that comes accompanied with video collages of matchstick thin African children, and washes over you, like a negative ion field – but the Alice Miller kind, sympathy for the diabolically careless cruelty that is routinely doled out to children everywhere.

Beatings and humiliations great and small certainly seem to have been routine in the Jackson home in the '60s. Even so the details can still surprise. This, from Wikipedia: "One night while Michael was asleep, Joseph climbed into his room through the bedroom window. Wearing a fright mask, he entered the room screaming and shouting. (Joseph said he wanted to teach his children not to leave the window open when they went to sleep.) For years afterward, Michael suffered nightmares about being kidnapped from his bedroom." Not by Peter Pan, presumably.

The word that rings with an extra awful tone, here, surely, is: MASK.

In the process of trying to eradicate any/all resemblance to his father, Michael's face becomes a form of mask. Or just maybe that's the point. Not to look plainly human: which is to say REproduced. But rather a one-off. Halloween night become an entire life. Because he so doesn't want to be in the loop of sexed reproduction. The loop of abuse. The loop of family and race. It's a contagion he must cut out. He is his own cubist re-presentation: dancing an eternal present. And so his face comes to resemble THAT moment – the white scare face at the window. It scares, it scars, but you still have to look. (And score your videos to its looming memory.)

If you'd seen him in 1979 – and then submerged into a Rumpelstiltskin-like dreamless sleep for two or three decades, and not seen him again until a late shot, you'd surely then react with real horror and concern: you'd presume there'd been some kind of horrific accident or incident or disaster. Fire and/or crash. Reconstructive surgery for an accident that only happened in his head.

Cutting himself out of the loop of history.

HIStory: he is become statue – monumental, without precedent.

If he ever got his childhood wish and visited the Wizard of Oz he would want to lose, not gain something. LOSE his brain, face, body: all the things that fix him in the loop of precedence, lineage, familial temporality.

(Looking at his dance moves after a certain point, they aren't fluid, funky, sensual; rather, in their mime-derived angularity, he looks like a man trying to fight his way *out* of something,

something no one else can see. Some loop of repeating sameness. Some endlessly repeating night.)

He's trying to pretend he is without ancestors; that he has to answer to no one. Starting with father. No more going back/forward. He rewrites the word itself: HIStory. Doesn't split it into two, but capitalizes HIS. How history dances inside our lives, cells, veins, thoughts. You can un-knot your face, skin, voice, sex; but you can't un-tie or de-time the real. It is waiting like an unpaid debt.

As if color were only that – color.
    As if sex were only that – act, itch, duration, climax.
    As if he – and he alone, at the end of history and the beginning of HIStory – could RE-encrypt the corrupted dyads of male-+-female, mother-+-father, black-and-white, us-and-them.

Let's not forget that even on the level of symbol – and Michael was nothing if not attentive to the regalia of symbol – even if all the messy business of reproduction was literally farmed out to laboratories, he still chose to have white kids. Twice. And then again, a third one. Michael so set against being a father, a father like his father, that he detoured reproduction, the most intimate act, over to anonymous science and selection. Sonless sons. Named two of his children Michael. Doubles, models. Birth-less, therefore deathless. Not part of the disease of time and nations, races and families.

Of course, with raw material like this as fact and foundation, it also allows press and populace alike to take off into realms of nasty fantastic rumor (e.g., from early on in his career: that his father actually had Michael EMASCULATED, castrated, eunuch'd, to save that cash-wow of a voice.) Depending on one's post-Freudian whim one might still wonder about the symbolism of what Michael did to his most prominent feature, that formerly big, formerly black, nose. Pinocchio reversed. The nose eating into the face. Absence becomes the focal point, the one thing you can't take your eyes off.

So Michael is maybe haunted, in his own skin, by being black. History come back to haunt. To claim its UN-buried. To catch and (b)eat its young. We'll never know for sure how much his own skin revolted (on) him, but Michael definitely gave the impression of really wanting *not* to be any kind of black. So he takes the knife to himself. Bleach knife. Makes himself a freak. Neuter.

It is not that he is becoming-woman or even drag... just erased male. He is not becoming white – he is just erased black. He is not Woman because there is no seduction in his arsenal. He even puts it in one of his videos, an easy-to-miss voiceover: "You don't know about women. You don't have that kind of knowledge."

If you have no God knowledge, and no Woman knowledge (and if, even though you are gay, you have no gay social life, so no self-other in-out) what do you push against, culturally speaking, what bends you, what might you allow to speak thru you? Is this maybe one of the reasons the music became so arid? He has left no other/ness in his life to rub up against?

What happens to the Mirror Stage when your reflection is a different color from all those looking at you? Did he want to be white. Or did he want to be *not*-black? He becomes hyper white, more than white. Given that most white people aren't, strictly speaking, "white". But see Michael in photos and on film and he is whiter than the white people around him. He SHINES, a malignant singularity, polarity, negative.

But to be the father of literally motherless children: that really is some kind of postmodern achievement. Maybe not so good for the kids, in the long run. An apparent heaven, an actual hell. No other kids, no real play. No teachers, no authority figures. So no otherness in their little lives, either. Is this psychologically healthy? What reflection? What kind of being? (You hate to even think it, but maybe his dying was the best thing that... no?)

What heaven, what hell.

How does he relate to them, these children? A serious question: *can* you relate to children, at all, without any Oedipus in the house, without a sexual relationship somewhere in the equation?

What fresh hell... In one of the Sunday tabloids the weekend after his death, excerpts from this handwritten story he wrote for his kids. Terrifying murder tale. Dark forests with no end. Blades, blood, exsanguination. Eyeless creatures. Toiling in fields like slaves. Still slaves. Still eyeless. Not allowed to look, not allowed to see.

Look at the white lady he's become.
He is the slave master's wife.

It's one way out of the loop of history.

Mostly, what we are avoiding speaking of here is race, and fathers.

IS NOT, AM NOT, WILL
The kid is not my son. The kid is not father to this man. The kid is not. I am not his son. I am HIStory.

Billie Jean is not my other. No one is my other – that's my

problem. I am the boy without others. That is the eternal pain of being Peter Pan. You are everyone's dream object, everyone's escape.

I can have anything I want: I can have children without having to have sexual intercourse. Sexual relations. I have no sexual relations. I have no sexual relationship. There are only ghosts. Ghosts of the boy I never was. Ghosts of the boy I dreamed of being, when I was a boy. When what I was seemed to be a boy. From the outside you all might have thought I was a boy. That age. But at the time I hardly knew what to think. I had no private life. I had no privacy. I had no time. Poked and prodded from all directions – my father, my brothers, others. I was an "o", the "o" I recapitulated into song, hiccupping and hiccupping like a pain or an orgasm or the pleasure pain of an orgasm that can't seem to start or stop. Adolescent orgasm – before you've learned to control or truly enjoy it, get lost in it. I dreamed of being a boy on his own. Out in fields. Behind fairgrounds. Trousers round my ankles, skin against skin. Skin as yellow white as Kansas wheat fields. Skin like the sun. Not the dark skin of sallow hotel rooms and my ever angry Pa. Not that skin of sweat and toil and punishment and supposed reward. Rewind > rewind > rewind. Skin like daylight, like daylight and Christmas.

The light is dying now.

Painkillers are the last pulse... painkillers at least are... well, they're the last loop I have control over. An endlessly renewable little slice of time. I can't believe no one noticed when I sang a love song to Demerol.

These little sparkles of dying light.

I can sustain stardom even though I am now a black hole. I can remain a star through starlight alone: all my manifestations and permutations.

I don't need to *be* a star ever again... but then that dream collapsed. Light bent back on itself. Oh two. Zero squared. I have to *be* on stage again – an O to the power of two. O diminished, or O doubled. All those eyes, probing me, stealing my light. I have this terrible dream – this nightmare, that this nightmare that, once on stage, I will not be able to breathe.

And the real trouble is I love this idea of not breathing, of not having – ...

I used to look at Bubbles and think, how lucky you are, you don't have to think about this or that or any of it. I wanted to be Mowgli but I became the snake. The snake slithers its prick its poison into my blood. A snake up and down my arm.

The drugs are the nearest I get to being animatronic, robot, dummy.

Animatronic: that's a funny word for inanimate things. And didn't it sometimes look like there was something bigger than me –

Who is going to stop me? I have no others. I am become destroyer of men, starting with myself.

I am far more suited to death than life.

RES IN MEDIA
Michael is better this way, a ghost. In the end wasn't that what he was for us anyway? Far more media trace than living breathing subject? Better suited to ghostly dissemination in rumor and headline...

If he has a legacy it is certainly not music. After *Thriller* he followed rather than led. His music was a confection, sticky and glittery and turgid, utterly soul-void. Light as helium, heavy as metal. He wasn't, let us remind ourselves, the King of soul or funk or R&B. pop, rather. Good ol' Pop. King of Pop. King of Pa. King of Pain.

Surely if he has a legacy it's not music at all, but all these kids today who know MEDIA as life, breath, second nature.

In his glory years Michael knew and anticipated and maneuvered and manipulated the media like a canny ruler. Lennon & McCartney reborn as Little Stevie Wonder reborn as Max Clifford. A modern prince. Machiavelli, Kane, Hughes. He was intelligent about media, and awful at life. That's the trade-off. He had a good teen-prank giggle when he started all those rumors about oxygen tents and elephant man bones and so on; it was less funny when they all came back to haunt (and imprison) him, like Scrooge's ghosts at midnight. How to grow in such soil? It was a media swamp. Matter without matter. *"We are growing used to... soul-less souls."* Life continued to perplex and defeat him. Media became second nature – as long as he was pulling the Oz like levers. When he actually had to deal, face to face, with ordinary adults, with the sort of questions adults pose (Oprah, Bashir, attorneys) he was utterly out of his element and depth. He could not finesse or seduce other adults: he spoke to them as if they were children. (Children who will believe the sincerity in your voice rather than the fact of your face.) He'd had as little as possible to do with adults on that level since he scoured the hated Joseph from his life.

His only other obvious mistakes were when he confused media for life – like that "marriage" to Lisa Marie Presley. Everyone groaned: it looked like merger, not marriage. Corporate account, not metaphysical love. (One of the most gruesome things in a gruesome field = the moment in the video for "You Are Not Alone" in which they kiss for the camera, or should I say "kiss". It really is hard to watch. The only thing it recalls is the "alien sex" scenes in Roeg's *Man Who Fell To Earth*.) Like Howard Hughes, his notions of love/sex were fatally tied up with contract, merger, signature, dotted line, pay off, brown bags. Why not – it was the way he did everything else.

New generations of kids now operate thus.
Sex = media, friendship = media, music = media. Life = media.

And this is what maybe accounts for the sheer sugar-O.D. hagiography attendant upon Michael's death, the unconvincing tributes, the utterly white-washed version we were given... because all the participants – from the lowliest E4 presenter to the biggest superstar – did what they were supposed to do, obeyed the protocol, the media law. React immediately and react sincerely. Don't say anything negative, and stress the pitch, the BRAND, repeat the Good Points. It's so ingrained they don't even notice any more how like an ad campaign it has all become. At any given moment you may have a microphone shoved in your face and asked... anything. 24/7. The smallest incident becomes a febrile drama and disaster and talking point. You have to react like a White House press officer to almost unbearably trivial matters. Reporters use Cold War methods to gain the most personal, meaningless, demeaning details. Or trail you round the city as if you were a foreign assassin, when you're only a nineteen-year-old pop singer. The whole world of entertainment has become a strange Nixonian nightmare.

They all behave like they are members of the same *corporate* team. Some kind of team "re-birthing" weekend in the Catskills. All this reflexively bland, unctuous "sincerity" – where a tiny little bit of honesty, to balance things out might... well, certainly while he was alive, it might have saved his life. Think about that. If he had so many dear dear friends, then how come –

Why is there this desperate need to deny the less sparkly/more human aspects of someone's life, and install them as this sheerly unbelievable figure of untainted worship?

I think of *The X Files*, Mulder, his ambivalent legend, his poster, his ambiguous catchphrase: I WANT TO BELIEVE. Not: I DO believe. But the want, rather, indigestible, like a ball of anxiety under your ribs. I want to believe BUT.

    I want to believe in ANYTHING SOMETHING ANYTHING.

(At which point you have to wonder, as a sidebar, if this is why those egregious some might say bogus words "icon" and "iconic" have run amuck at just this moment in time: the free-market isn't enough, and religion has vacated the space of worship for so many in the West, leaving... what? I WANT TO BELIEVE.)

And not for nothing do certain images, scenes, image-knots seem to blurrily echo one another. i.e., I now find it hard to think of THE WALL COMING DOWN, without the next image to flash up being that huge Jackson sculpture for HIStory floating unsteadily down the Thames; and then on, making an absurd fetishistic pilgrimage across mid-'90s Europe. As if to say: this, THIS is your future. Life dominated by the whims of media and market. The new theocracy of Capital.

Worship, little people, worship.

All that Hosanna and hardly a word of it felt truthful.
We know everything about him and nothing.
At the end of it all no more than surface.

Already dead. Or: fixed at one point forever – which amounts to the same.

This postmodern media twenty-first century paradox: We know everything about him and nothing.

FREEZE on eyes.
And fade.

ABC
A black Cupid, with immortal puff in his cheeks. On the edge of uncanny, off-putting, as some said. Abject black child, like a midget size adult playing a child playing an adult. (Who is it I see when the mirror of the audience reflects me?)

People reminiscing in the days after his death, especially black singers and celebrities, what they all seemed to recall, was the history of his IMAGE most of all... Remembering their *own* childhood watching him move and dance and smile. Remembering 'ABC' go POP!, then his bashful *Off The Wall* smile, then white jackets and tigers and red leather and zombies from the *Thriller* moment. In the same way as they remember: *Star Wars, E. T. Halloween*, the local video store. The VHS generation.

A mirror stage at a time when there was virtually NO images of black people, kids, families on TV, in the media, this little black boy made of joy was a hot signifier.

You have to wonder how much of Michael's early success (and how much of today's fond remembering of his Jackson Five years, or rather, of the commentators remembering of their experience of them) was down to his being the ONLY ONE. People forget, but at that time, especially in large parts of Britain, it was comparatively rare to find black or Asian or other "different" kids. As much as there was racism there was also occasionally of course, an attraction to their difference. People reacted to Michael, on TV, because he was cute, without being kitsch, he was male, and datable, without being too threatening, he was – paradoxically given what was to come – *normal*. It was nice to have a black family there, as if it was just the normal given thing.

(There are certain things you *really* can't fake – and bad taste is one of them. This is not a small or flip point. The matter of taste being something that is very personal and very relative, after all. But I would hazard the speculation that one of the reasons so many ordinary people responded (so fondly) to Michael would be the matter of his relative lack of taste. The way he bought, and the things he bought, after he became monstrously wealthy, very much followed a kind of prole dream arc. Lottery winner splurge. Gold on everything (including, yes, his casket.) He had manifestly un-cool taste in clothes, furnishings, dreams. Bad taste on the borderline of camp. In which respect he's something like the non-hep non-self-conscious version of someone like, say, John Waters: someone from a working class background who unapologetically pursues their own "bad" aesthetic. Clown art. "Life-like" dolls. Kitschy kiddy portraits. (Hustler sex in bad motel decor.) The outré and outlandish. The line separating one person's "ironic" appreciation of this sort of stuff, and another person's genuine love for it... how thick, how thin? In the Bashir program, Michael seems genuinely enthused by the prospect of his awful gold tat – seems incredulous at the thought that anyone might not appreciate it, its craft, its sheer awesome THERE-ness, the fact that you could just buy glorious things like this! All in all, the kind of non-arty non-trendy "art" that poor people might imagine owning if they ever hit it big. And that's Michael's background: working class, poorly educated, steel town, big family. You can imagine an inner psychological/aesthetic war between that background, and his, let's say, camper proclivities.

(If asked to nominate the latest exemplar of this tradition, I might have to answer: Eminem?)

As though in some strange trans-dimensional way, Michael sacrificed himself so Obama could triumph. (The dimension couldn't stand both of them at the same time.)

You have to wonder if M had to die now that O was in the White-house. Some kind of po-mo-Poe like torsion... WHITE NEGATIVE, BLACK SHADOW... white glove, white eyes, white as ashes, morphine, brain matter... turning IN, IN, IN, eating into self, more, further, thin air, thin heir, thin hair, abstraction, absolute privacy privation, which this *just couldn't be broken* to perform "live" again... not once The Deal was struck... to serve DEMOCRACY, public life...

My favorite image is that photo of Michael with the Reagans. I fall asleep dreaming of a kind of history or HIStory as sitcom, with Ronnie and Nancy installed as Michael's parents. From Prince of Bel Air to... King of Washington. And don't you think he could have done it then? Done pretty much anything he put his sparkly hand to? There was a moment when he could surely have done anything. He could have been a proto-Obama before his time. If he could just have been "born", out of colorless air, beginning from nothing, in that Reagan photo, or with Liz Taylor as Make-Believe Mom, he would have been happy beyond the dreams of Kane-like avarice.

And I wake up thinking: maybe the one thing Michael really wanted he could never get: to erase his memory, completely.

I DANCED WITH A ZOMBIE
This is the thriller time: this is the opposite of "punctum". Ubiquity. Omnipresence.

It's hard now to remember clearly just how different 1983 is, media-wise: no satellite TV, no mobile phones, no computers, infancy of remix culture, infancy of magazine culture. Michael's *Thriller* video was an EVENT in a way that's hard to imagine now. Long form. Mini movie. The binary of recorded music/live performance is elided. Michael in *Thriller* becomes the black imp in the marketing machine.

(The *Thriller* video – if there's a notable oddity, watching it now, I would say it's how *serious* it feels – if that makes any sense.)

In some way, it might be argued, the *Thriller* video inaugurates the Reagan years. "It's morning in America!" Rebirth. Re-awakening. A kind of coup.

Elvis meeting Nixon out of his head on prescription drugs is one thing. Maybe Michael goes it one better – a black, gay, entertainer out of his head on pills... jheri curls in the White House! Chocolate City in the house!

But this "new morning" is also, paradoxically, the end of history. No such thing as society. The triumph of the market, the dawn of Reaganomics. (Which were critiqued as? "Voodoo economics".) Zombie logic: Reagan declares a "War On Drugs" whilst the CIA is busy importing tons of crack and cocaine into black US ghettoes in order to fund the Contras. And produce a generation of de-politicized crack zombies. Is it too easy to see the dancing living dead of the *Thriller* video as the dispossessed, crack-addled of the years to come? The "under society", those cut off by white market voodoo?

The triumph of death over life. Living on unstable border lines. Living on: past your time. One "eureka!" moment – and then decades of "left over time". The paradox being that in the end it was his *Thriller* success that ultimately cut Michael off – its huge and overwhelming breakthrough seems to have begun the process of warp which ended in drugs bitterness debt, etc.

Reagan and Jackson both symbolize attempts to stop or arrest or reverse the flow and the floes of cultural time. "New Morning in America" ... and in Neverland. The irony, the dreadful irony, is that both Reagan and Jackson found out what it was to be alone, really fatally alone, in their ends.

This flesh is inescapable.

MEDS
Morphing. Morphine.

Terminal addicts don't notice how alienated they have become from old life, old friends, old ways, old interests. One day you realize you'd rather stay *right here* in this warm and comfortable drug chair, here, in the cool un-cruel shade, this the only place my mind don't ache, this the only place my soul feels ripe, this the one place my body don't itch and yelp and hurry, I like it here, what's the problem, here I don't need to DO anything, don't need to meet anyone else's demands, don't need to stress or argue or bargain or barter or seduce or shine... I can just be me. And dream. Endlessly dream.

For most addicts the daily oscillation between high and low gets to be too much – usually when their money runs out, or their scuzzy dealers become too unreliable, or the discrepancy between how much time and effort and cash you're putting in, and how little relief you're getting out, becomes impossible to ignore. But at the level Michael operated there is essentially never any need, ever, to come down. A man who can procure *children* to his own specifications from the medical profession isn't going to have much trouble getting his daily meds now is he?

This maybe kind of makes sense of Michael's "mania" phases, the inane shopping sprees, the baby-dangling... because at that level of drug intake you can feel totally *possessed* by the energies at work inside you. (As he used to feel possessed by dancing.) You take a fistful of uppers and crash. You take an armful of downers and become pure speed.

I'm sure most of Michael's audience would prefer to think that the "medicines" were something he took to indeed "kill the pain". That it was something he took, and then he gets up and goes about his biz – song-writing, rehearsals, public appearances – and is "Michael" all over again. Except it doesn't work like that.

Painkillers on such a scale are not used to take away the pain – they are to make sure it doesn't go away. They are used to in/stall your fabled "pain" – so that you always have a reason to take these lovely pain meds! As any good junkie will tell you – you don't take painkillers to eradicate pain; you cultivate pain in order to get painkillers. The last thing you want is a cure or resolution to those aches and pains. You take more and more time dwelling on the pain, holding it close, cultivating it, quizzing it, stroking it... and less and less time doing whatever it was you used to do, all that annoying stuff take you away from you and your dear dear sweet singular pain, and pain relief.

This would also explain why his music got less and less song-like, structured, harmonic – because it was less crafted, because he spent less and less background time on it. Just went in the studio and made a vaguely Michael Jackson like noise. Subsequently his music becomes less and less meaningful or soulful. It is hermetic, a tantrum wrapped inside a snub wrapped inside a pout. It is masturbatory. It references only itself.
Jackson's dancing likewise never changed, modulated, became

more "adult". It seems stalled at some pubescent stage of the invasion of erotic energy & drive. But not quite knowing whose the drive was or where it came from. From the father? From the audience? From space? From hell?

The drugs are there as walls to stop time, to stall growth, to insulate his inner I WANT I WILL, to listen down, down into his precious self. Self-zombification. Loup garoo. *"Rot inside a corpse's shell."* Lifedeath.

The zombie, like the vampire, and the junkie, is a way of transcending the immutable life-death binary. (If the vampire = the eroticization of this transcendence/stalling, then the zombie/werewolf = what? The zombie is proletariat to the vampire's aristocracy. Blood = vintage wine. A supply. The count has control over the supply. The proles just eat one another – brains like a bucket of chicken. Fast food.)

Not fully alive, not fully dead, rather UNdead.
(Which is just how Michael looks in some of those later photos.)

While alive, he messed up all these dead binaries: black-white, Avant-garde or conservative, authentic vs. entertainment, twenty-first century hi tech vs. plain old freak tent.
"Remember to always think twice/'Don't think twice!'"

It-don't-matter-if-you're: black-or-white.
It don't MATTER
It isn't matter
I am not matter
I am neither black nor white, I am black and white, black AS white, sometimes black sometimes white, sometimes beyond white –

Michael = de-railing of coding and decoding.
Neither alive nor dead, neither living nor not-living.

Normally pop stars hire image-makers and PR gurus and guerrillas and stylists to construct an image and maintain it. Michael goes another way, deconstructs his image: You think I'm black then? Lets see. You think I'm hetero... you think I'm *sexual* at all? Let's see. You think I'm HUMAN? Michael goes subcutaneous. Sub cute. Beyond kitsch, into a kind of tinsel horror. The *Village Of The Damned* remade by Cronenberg as blaxploitation sci-fi.

You think I'm telling you nothing, hiding everything?

He had already confessed to everything long before the putative end.

Viz. the quite extraordinary forgotten/overlooked song "Morphine". "Morphine", musically, is just another "Scream", till we get near the end and then it all stops... and recommences as a kind of castrato Clayderman-ish Vegas lite opera. *"De-mer-ol: O my god he's taking Demerol!"*

The seductive jouissance of total anxiety.

Less like entertainment than cathexis of terror, the zombie within – zombie, prole, son, historical subject, debtor...

Zombie: neither alive nor dead. His own profane worship, which does away with the wisdom of ancestors. Father sacrifice. Air possession. Dance as painful exorcism. Possession and non-possession. The zombie is dispossessed – of volition, identity, future. Dance of death. Needlepoint ceremonies. The zombie is a loop. A stalling, a suspension.

I conjure a different kind of terror: a body without a soul.

And isn't that a perfect descryption of so much of Jackson's later music? He went from soul music without body ("Human Nature") to body music without soul ("Scream").

Another erasure of another binary... Jackson became both master and servant in one body. White master black performer/worker. White poison black zombie. A reversal of the alchemist's nigredo: white outside, black within. (*I Danced With A Zombie*: allegory of slavery on Haiti.)

In that sense *"– it don't matter if you're black or white –"*, you can imagine the phrase, with a different inflection, coming out of the zombies feared overseer, BOSS MOUF: fuck it, nigga kid, you gonna be worked to deaf either way, don't matter if you're black or white...

This is your life.
You're a zombie either way.
Prole, zombie, corpse.
This is the end of your life.

Or is it?
Or is it just one more beginning?
Or is it just one more starting over again?

How many times must I do this?

How many lives, how many deaths – till I can no longer tell the difference?

THE PLEASURE PRINCIPLE
Michael's idea of dance, of seduction, of acting smooth, is so preposterous, outlandish, you'd like to think it was a joke. But it

doesn't feel that way. Replay the video for "The Way You Make Me Feel": the look on his face, faced with this gorgeous young (black) woman is not far short of actually (and unintentionally) really rather scary. Genuinely nasty. The way he looks at this gorgeous young woman – the mask-like contortion of his face... disgust? aggression? contempt? Any/all of these. Like slave master, or wife beater. A desire that can only admit it is desire within the prophylaxis of negation and contempt. He will acknowledge no debt, relinquish no command. But never, at any instant, is there the slightest signal flash of desire or pleasure or ache. His eyes don't know what to do with her, this breath-intimate but galaxy-distant object. He does these awful jack-knife hip thrusts, which come off more Benny Hill than Mick Jagger or Tina Turner somehow, and are the least sexy thing you can imagine. It's embarrassing and distressing and perplexing all at the same time.

Michael's only comfortable in his own shaded nimbus. Completely alone, no one to see. When the street empties out of all social buzz, all flow, chatter, all possibility of contradiction, adult commerce or congress, women... and he can do his dance, his scary little dance. To safely touch himself. (The truly odd thing is, if you freeze the frame at one point, you could swear this particular girl was chosen for her passing resemblance to... well, let's say, to someone Michael thinks he might look like one day.)

Ah, his dance, yes: the one thing left him, surely?

But more and more the dancing became something he did on his own – utterly on his own. No sensual connection. No hook ups. Full of all this RAGE and jerk and spasm and SMASH and destruction. He touches things they explode and disappear. Gone in microseconds. (It kept bothering me, this dance like a form of personal algebra – all sharp angles and severe Xs and Zs violently drawn in the video air. And then it came to me in a phrase: PRESEEEEENT ... ARMS!)

He keeps touching himself: the only communion.

In order to cum he has to smash up the set. (The set of all desiring others who are not Michael Jackson.) His rage swings to the dialectic beat of two poles: why are you looking at me!; to: why are you NOT looking at me?

The dance is the only way of touching himself without embracing himself or being embraced. No losing of self in the Other. He always remains the King. King of all he surveys. Always *in charge*. King of the board AND player, of black and white. Makes no difference. Touches no difference. King of his own plot. Even, whisper it who dare, finally, the son's revenge, king of his ... Pop?

The question at such times of course – if I were an analyst and you were my study, you'd want to ask: "Michael? Who exactly is it you think is watching?" And then maybe: "Who do you *want* to be watching? Who do you *fear* is watching? Who do you presume is watching...? When you do all these "bad", "dangerous" things? Do you want saving or punishing (again)?"

MAKES YOU WANNA SCREEN

I imagine Michael at night, watching certain films (*Imitation of Life*, *E. T.*, *Blade Runner*, *Donnie Darko*) through a perma-haze of drugs. So drugged he mostly sees only glint, sparkle, shade; only hears snatches; only views in short loops, forever rewinding back to zero. (Howard Hughes's favorite flat-line viewing was the film of Alistair MacLean's cold war fantasy *Ice Station Zebra* – I almost typed *Ice Station Zero* there, transposing Hughes's own metabolic state. He watched it over and over again, hundreds of times, always in little ten minute bursts.) All these films he's seen the first ten, fifteen minutes, nothing more, except maybe the last five or ten minutes too.

Great beginnings, and a baffling end.

Glint and sparkle: that's how that film begins, isn't it, I remember right. Paste and diamonds, diamonds and paste. Everyone has to pay. A time price. Pearls a waterfall of sweet little painkilling pills. Pearls, pills, ills. This sweet sound of all sounds the same, gold and black sun of the inner moment, roar and momentum of the world stilled to this tomb like *sssshh*. Inner gold, balance, black become white, all my malevolence turning to soft frothy creamy liquid like android tears and white made black with sad knowledge, black made white with royal benevolence. Something like that cohering now before the sun – before the sun –

Alchemy and dredged up thisness and drugged down nasty dadness. Dread: this is a light that I dread. 'Til I die. Into the blood, into the blood. Signs turn to sludge in my nodding head. Into the blood, into the coming sun. Burn the petals off, turn the fur inside out. Tear the petals off a rose is it still a rose? What remains? All shit. Black mud, bleak earth.

Sirk? Was that it? The one about the little girl didn't know who she is or how or black or white. Church versus entertainment: Mama's church versus the devil's nightclubs where all the fathers hang, hypocrite lechers their snakes eyes follow the young girls. Thou shalt not da-da-da your neighbor's something. Daughter? Dollar? Ass? The film resplendent with all these icky lil' oppositions and examples, like, *no – way – out* rats maze, if you're born black you're always going to be an *example* of some kind, no way out, no freeway exit except death and tears... when uh the real solution is staring everyone right back in they face: stop *being* the fucked up little black girl and be the shining right white girl instead. What could be better than that? Honestly! What could be better than that: up on the altar of desirability and light, the whole world wanting to fuck you... your white white sun-comin'-up skin...

Then the funeral procession at the end, Mahalia (gosh, I never noticed this before) Jackson, and the little girl fall upon her mother's hearse, tears in the desert of her soul.

I am that little girl.

THE REAL PINOCCHIO.

Michael to Bashir: "I *am* Peter Pan."

A block of unformed matter. This is where we begin: unformed matter. Carve something out of it. A face? Features? Junior golem, child of the abyss.

King of pine. Puer boy, long way from homme.

Search out the original Italian fable, the real, original *Pinocchio*, and you will find (as with most of these old tales for children) it contains scarcely credible levels of cruelty and pain. A tale improvised by a sadist sipping ketamine. Accusations of abuse. Thrown hammers. Burned off feet. Children used as firewood: innocence kindling. Curiosity rewarded with concussion and kidnap. Hanging, amputation, suffocation. A snake laughs so hard at Pinocchio's fear he bursts an artery and dies. On his way to school Pinocchio sells his schoolbooks to join a Street Theater: forget education, become a marionette. A dancing fool. Apprentice Golem. Malignant clown. Neuter, castrato.

These original pre-Disneyized tales show boundless ambivalence and ambiguity about childhood and what people who know nothing about children like to think of as its "innocence". The shadows on the lawn are not gambol and play. The idea of some "eternal child" (the so-called "puer aeternus", in academic parlance), and their unending childhood is ultimately viewed as far nearer punishment than paradise. Against nature: anything which does not grow, grows stagnant, airless.

Pinocchio: pino meaning "pine" and occhio meaning "eye". Pine eye not pop eye. PAIN EYES.

As with Pinocchio, read a bit further into Jackson's beloved and fetishized Peter Pan figure and you find all kinds of ambiguity. A bad-tempered boy "clad in skeleton leaves", PP's outfit is made of cobwebs and autumn shades. Time congealed. Time fallen. Suspended, lifeless. And played, traditionally, by a woman, not a man: under the web and shadow, another anatomy, not your own, riper, ready to reproduce. Adult woman playing a boy-child: disguise, ambiguity, shape shift, something undecided, in-between. Uncanny. Panic. With his blissful unawareness of tragedy of death he says "to die will be an awfully big adventure".

This PP is "boastful and cocky", verging on nasty and selfish. As how could he not? If he doesn't grow, he doesn't learn – either from books or life. He must forget anything he does learn about the world in order to stay "child-like". Author Kevin Orlon Johnson argues that the Pan stories are in the German-English tradition of the *Totenkindergeschichtei* (roughly, "tales of dead children") and the idea that Peter and all of the lost boys are dead in a Neverland afterlife is consistent with that genre. PP's everlasting/stunted youth is attributed to an unearthly substance called "starstuff".

Stardust, music (he plays the flute) and misogyny (he "is afraid of nothing except adult women"). Adulthood is a shadow, hanging on the wall. A scary mask, come to life in the darkness.

More shadows – always more shadows.

And another ambiguous PP up ahead, too – the Pied Piper.
O, I foresee trouble down that road, I really do.

SONGS OF DEAD CHILDREN

And it seems to me Jackson's music waned, became progressively less urgent, human, appealing, because he himself stopped becoming: he didn't alter himself so much as arrest himself, trying to freeze time.

To begin with it may have been no more than a whim, this notion of being able to revisit/remodel a lost childhood; but then, post-*Thriller*, he suddenly became rich beyond the dreams of avarice, and regaining the lost time was suddenly do-able. The worst thing in the world for certain fantasies: you try and make them breathe. You take your own body and designate it the site where this fantasy comes alive, becomes some kind of touchable reality.

Michael: was he really this postmodern dream of becoming something new, becoming sleekly sneakily un-raced or beyond race or new-race? Or wasn't he, rather, a going backward, a scrubbing out. He didn't want to become something new or be that different; no, he wanted to not BE this someone old, someone previous. Most of all he didn't want to be his father, to be black like pops. He wanted to be timeless not time-lacking –, and the time he wanted back, the missing time, the lesser time, was his own kid-into-teen time, spoiled by the rude and cruel interruptions of his family.

He didn't want to be beyond gender, either, really – he just didn't want to be the man his father was. He wanted to erase the old, not improvise something new. Unfortunately, what this gives us is not some fantastic new hybrid – like a black version of Eno from 1972 or a character out of Samuel Delaney – but a vacuum. A no-place. You might say: a never-land. For a never-man.

He wants to stop time. Time is too much of a lesson: always insisting on limits, plucking examples from the past. He wants time to stop-start to his beat. Michael, he dreamily supposes that the Law and all its bi-laws why-laws don't apply to him: he can even escape from the bonds of sexed reproduction via test tube and surrogacy. (He can by-pass those laws; he can buy new laws.) But what happens to paternity once you take the father figure out of it? It doesn't just disappear, that's for sure. It's still there, symbolically: Name of the Father. Maybe it even matters (it haunts) more when it's absent or uncertain. How can something important-but-absent *not* haunt?

"Billie Jean": is this the last time he even glancingly admitted to sexuality, to being gendered, and all that entails? Even if it was sung in denial: *"Billie Jean is/not-my-lover."* What he wants is a reproduction-without-organs.

"– that I am the one./But the kid is not my son."
Which lyric snip foretells the future, pretty well, paternity wise. He is the one – father – but the kid is still not his son. He is father to a child who is not strictly speaking his son.

It's written all over your face: he castrates his phallic nose, and makes huge his vaginal eyes. There is no sexual relationship feeding into his music. Along with tenderness – or are they one and the same thing? If there were any sexual relationships in his life they were ones he felt he had to hide. (All those strange showbiz beards: in his Neverland castle the King upholds a strange Cult of The Virgin.)

Given this degree of disavowed sex, and of disappeared sexuality, you could easily think that the ridiculously high levels of prescription narcotics he was taking had little or nothing to do with supposed physical ailments and everything to do with tamping down all manner of internal discomfit and derangement, and anger and pulsion and drive. (That degree of narcotic intake insures that whatever sexuality you have left remains terminally bottled up, anyway.) Maybe this is the reason the rest of his career produces music that feels so brittle and sterile and un-tender, music in/out-of a vacuum.

The singer of these scream-songs is fighting a losing battle to be nothing but in the present: he doesn't grow so his music doesn't grow. No tenderness or, at best, fake tenderness (although by and large his music has a pornographic feeling, all those mid-to-late period videos full of grimace and jerk and in-our-face smash and kick). Which is where I have a problem with all those circumspect post-mortem profiles in the broadsheets, all these writers saying this was some of the greatest post war American music, bar none, when we know fine well they sit at home listening to Gram Parsons and Miles Davis and Bon Iver, and do they really think we're going to believe they have at *any* time in the last fifteen to twenty years sat down at home, on their own, and put a contemporary Michael Jackson CD on (unless it was for a weary dismissive job of work)? Sorry, but no. Not even *Thriller*, because it just isn't the sort of thing a grown-up sits down to listen to for forty minutes, I'm sorry, it just isn't. There isn't the range or depth of emotion to reward such listening – because nice as the *idea* of "puer aeternus" is – as strange and misty myth – in reality it's not a very pretty sight. Or sound.

(Sidebar: the reality of being an emotionally retarded, "childlike" boy in a man's world, replete with repressed sexuality and suppressed rage, until it can't be repressed and suppressed any more, is made delirious black comedy in Paul Thomas Anderson's wicked *Punch Drunk Love*. Adam Sandler gamely essays something like an echo of the "return of the repressed" for all the glazed-eyed whiny boy-man characters he usually plays.)

So very hard to enjoy any of this music past a certain point, also, because it seems to have been designed with only his most bonkers fans in mind: it's all infused with this strain of adolescent US AGAINST THE WORLD-ism. Could any adult pop fan really take on board something like "They Don't Care About Us"? (Answer: only if it had been *heartbreakingly* sincere, and it wasn't.) Look at the video: as with so many of his other late period videos, it feels like a WHITE view of BLACK life. If black people aren't street scum and gangsters, in these videos, they are hopeless victims. (Make-believe gangsters, or CNN-footage problems: poor, hungry, beaten.) But then again maybe these were the two psychological positions Michael swung between – feeling himself "bad", "dangerous", an unpunished criminal; or literally hopeless, a skinny black Pinocchio without any Geppettos or Good Fairies on the horizon.

As even his much trumpeted version of "childhood" seems, finally, to be insidiously Reaganite, a Saturday night fairground ride with your smiley pony-tailed gal, Hitchcock with the anxiety taken out, white horses, gleaming rides, Saturday night candy floss and an un-crooked midway where everyone always goes home with the toy they wanted. Very un-ghetto. Not just un-ghetto but ALL darkness and detail erased: childhood here is merely a Platonic Ideal, a hygienic abstraction. Nothing real. And for a long time it was a vision of childhood dreamed by someone who was not himself a parent. And didn't he then just slot "his" children into that pre-existing mould? Like they were something he bought off eBay?

Dolls, with their uncanny little features veiled.

NATALIE WOOD (AFTERLIFE)

And he is dreaming like a prophet of robots who will serve your every secret need, even go so far as to stand in for your every comeback (which, you *know* this isn't any one-off: this will be your LIFE till you *die* now), yes, dreaming of steel and wire, but looking himself like some forgotten scarecrow. What did the scarecrow want? Is that the same film? I see crows – crows yapping, crying, gathering. A still black cloud. They got hats on: cotton picking crows. Is that the same film? What film are we in now, Michael?

Michael?
Do the crows want my heart?
Does the scarecrow need a new hand?

He's a scarecrow right enough but the function is reversed: Michael is a scarecrow who attracts, who seduces children (sickly and unwanted children) into the whorl of his fairground circumference.

Strange ambivalent attraction he exerts on the world: in an era when the ultimate villain was the pedophile, Michael for a while occupied a supremely ambiguous position in the public eye, what, something like the "good pedophile". For whatever reason, people just seem disposed to give him another chance. And another. Like he was just another child himself; like he was still that little ABC boy, cheeks full of summertime wind.

The writers write as if we had only love or hate to choose between.

But to say you feel more than anything a huge and tensile *indifference* is not nothing. It seems to me, if anything, a far more interesting reflection.

Nearer to something like trance. "Strange ambivalent attraction..." And that if we dig down for the reasons why we might want and need and enjoy such states... just as if Michael, himself, if he could only have found out why he craved oblivion so...

An awfully big adventure.

A bigger capacity, therefore, to go badly off course.

There's a line... "*Where the danger is/Grows the saving power, also.*" (Heine) Which maybe you could also translate: when you're at your sickest, apparently beyond help, that's when the possibility of redemption flares up, unexpected, unannounced, and irresistible.

Remember that day when the land was still as waxwork, and the skies were like a wristwatch around your heart? The war inside you stopped for a beat or two?

John Wayne: John Wayne going out that door for the very last time.

Looking for another little girl who was neither black nor white.

She is, rather, the light inside his masculine darkness; and so he just can't bring himself to slaughter her, rub her out, take her out of this world, because she lives inside of him. As the sun going down and the moon coming up.

Her face the nickel the coin that holds every memory in place.

Smell of warm copper in your pudgy ABC fingers.

Green like Robin Hood, like Peter Pan, like –

(What did HE used to say? "*Green* the only color *I'm* interested in – ")

Your first check. Daddy's mask. A Peter Pan shadow, under the bed, off the wall, out in the world now, homeless.

Mama, I still love you.

It's like I was born of some other wish, not mine, not ours, something altogether bigger. An awfully big adventure.

Mama, I love you.

I just can't remember your face any more.

In the Dust of This Planet
Horror of Philosophy vol. 1
Eugene Thacker
In the first of a series of three books on the Horror of Philosophy, *In the Dust of This Planet* offers the genre of horror as a way of thinking about the unthinkable.
Paperback: 978-1-84694-676-9 ebook: 978-1-78099-010-1

Capitalist Realism
Is there no alternative?
Mark Fisher
An analysis of the ways in which capitalism has presented itself as the only realistic political-economic system.
Paperback: 978-1-84694-317-1 ebook: 978-1-78099-734-6

Rebel Rebel
Chris O'Leary
David Bowie: every single song. Everything you want to know, everything you didn't know.
Paperback: 978-1-78099-244-0 ebook: 978-1-78099-713-1

Cartographies of the Absolute
Alberto Toscano, Jeff Kinkle
An aesthetics of the economy for the twenty-first century.
Paperback: 978-1-78099-275-4 ebook: 978-1-78279-973-3

Malign Velocities
Accelerationism and Capitalism
Benjamin Noys
Long listed for the Bread and Roses Prize 2015, *Malign Velocities* argues against the need for speed, tracking acceleration as the symptom of the on-going crises of capitalism.
Paperback: 978-1-78279-300-7 ebook: 978-1-78279-299-4

Meat Market
Female flesh under Capitalism
Laurie Penny
A feminist dissection of women's bodies as the fleshy fulcrum of capitalist cannibalism, whereby women are both consumers and consumed.
Paperback: 978-1-84694-521-2 ebook: 978-1-84694-782-7

Poor but Sexy
Culture Clashes in Europe East and West
Agata Pyzik
How the East stayed East and the West stayed West.
Paperback: 978-1-78099-394-2 ebook: 978-1-78099-395-9

Romeo and Juliet in Palestine
Teaching Under Occupation
Tom Sperlinger
Life in the West Bank, the nature of pedagogy and the role of a
university under occupation.
Paperback: 978-1-78279-637-4 ebook: 978-1-78279-636-7

Sweetening the Pill
or How we Got Hooked on Hormonal Birth Control
Holly Grigg-Spall
Has contraception liberated or oppressed women? *Sweetening
the Pill* breaks the silence on the dark side of hormonal
contraception.
Paperback: 978-1-78099-607-3 ebook: 978-1-78099-608-0

Why Are We The Good Guys?
Reclaiming your Mind from the Delusions of Propaganda
David Cromwell
A provocative challenge to the standard ideology that Western
power is a benevolent force in the world.
Paperback: 978-1-78099-365-2 ebook: 978-1-78099-366-9

Readers of ebooks can buy or view any of these bestsellers by
clicking on the live link in the title. Most titles are published in
paperback and as an ebook. Paperbacks are available in
traditional bookshops. Both print and ebook formats are
available online.

Find more titles and sign up to our readers' newsletter at
http://www.johnhuntpublishing.com/culture-and-politics
Follow us on Facebook at https://www.facebook.com/ZeroBooks
and Twitter at https://twitter.com/Zer0Books